THE CAUSES OF THE
ENGLISH CIVIL WAR

British History in Perspective
General Editor: Jeremy Black

PUBLISHED TITLES

FORTHCOMING TITLES

THE CAUSES OF THE ENGLISH CIVIL WAR

ANN HUGHES

St. Martin's Press   New York

© Ann Hughes 1991

All rights reserved. For information, write:
Scholarly and Reference Division,
St. Martin's Press, Inc., 175 Fifth Avenue,
New York, N.Y. 10010

First published in the United States of America in 1991

Printed in Hong Kong

Library of Congress Cataloging-in-Publication Data
Hughes, Ann, 1951–
    The causes of the English Civil War / Ann Hughes.
    p. cm.
    Includes bibliographical references and index.
    ISBN 0–312–05226–X
    1. Great Britain—History—Civil War,
    1642–1649—Causes. 2. Great Britain—
    Politics and government—1603–1649. I. Title.
    DA415.H83 1991
    942.06′2—dc20   90–47353
                                                  CIP

CONTENTS

Contents

ACKNOWLEDGEMENTS

I would like to thank Tom Cogswell for valuable help and advice with chapter 1, and Richard Cust for reading and commenting on the whole work, besides all his other support. As the parent of a young child, my professional work is made possible through the help of friends and members of my family. Amongst many others I would like to thank Arthur, Caroline and Margaret Cust, Gwladys Hughes, Joan Wilson, Colin Divall, Karen Hunt, and, most especially, Jane Thompson. Finally, I am grateful to the History Department at Manchester University for a teaching programme which has helped me put seventeenth century English history into a broader context.

Manchester
April 1990

ANN HUGHES

INTRODUCTION

The seventeenth century is probably the most studied period in English history and the period that arouses most passion and controversy. The civil war, in particular, still matters to us. Historians quite rightly try to avoid the distortion of their interpretations of the past by their current attitudes and involvements. Yet we often accuse our intellectual opponents of bias while failing to acknowledge our own prejudices. We do take sides and the views we take of the nature and origins of the civil war are often connected to our stances in the modern world. One recent analysis of the historiography of the seventeenth and eighteenth century argues that the dominant historical interpretations of the 1960s and 1970s were produced by a 'politically explicit' 'class of '68', historians whose own commitments were 'closer, more strident and more central to their purposes than that of any other cohort of historians since the 1830s'. Yet it is by no means difficult for a reader to discover the contemporary political opinions of the author of this apparently objective analysis. The text is full of references to Trotskyite Liverpool Councillors, the SDP's interest in the 'harmless virtues of localism', and the allegedly outmoded views of ageing historians: 'It is understandable, however, that socialist or liberal doctrine should seem vital and important to men who are themselves contemporaries of the Russian Revolution or of Mr Asquith.'[1]

The English are often supposed to take their history for granted in a way not found amongst the inhabitants of continental

Europe or of other parts of the British Isles. While this book was being written, the French celebrations of the bicentenary of the Revolution of 1789 were marked by passionate debate on the nature and significance of that Revolution and included such incidents as a physical attack on the soloist at a musical commemoration by right wing critics of 1789. In the Federal Republic of Germany a bitter controversy about the legacy of Nazism has occupied the press as well as academic circles. The English do have muted versions of such debates. In July 1988, the House of Commons discussed the presentation of a humble address to the queen to celebrate the tercentenary of the 'Glorious Revolution' of 1688, which, it was claimed, 'established those constitutional freedoms under the law, which Your Majesty's Parliament and people have continued to enjoy for three hundred years'. The debate was not the expected formality, and two hours were taken up with mainly hostile speeches. The prime minister was not one of the doubters: the 'Glorious Revolution' was 'the first step on the road [to] ... full parliamentary democracy ... the events of 1688 were important in establishing Britain's nationhood ... to that renewal of energy and resourcefulness which built Britain's industrial and financial strength and gave her a world role'. But other MPs felt that the 'wrong' revolution was being commemorated: radical Labour members argued that we should instead, 'celebrate the Levellers'; 'or the triumph of the armies of Parliament over the armies of the King during the civil war'. The 'real revolution had already taken place', long before 1688, 'when, the day after the king's head was cut off in 1649, the House of Lords was abolished'. One Labour member remarked sardonically: 'I was puzzled that the Prime Minister – a Tory with the instincts of an eighteenth century liberal – should invite the House to celebrate a seventeenth century Whig theory of history.'[2]

Disagreement amongst historians about seventeenth century English history, and specifically about the civil war, has not focused simply on debate over the causes of the war, but also ranges over the whole nature of the events of the 1640s and 1650s. When historians use terms such as 'Great Rebellion', 'English Revolution', or 'Civil War' these are not random choices but indicate the significance being attached to developments. Laurence Stone took pains to demonstrate why he considered the civil war a revolution 'more than a mere rebellion against a particular king', in his book, *The Causes of the English Revolution, 1529–1642*; in contrast Conrad Russell's edited collection of essays sought to explain the origins of civil war, not revolution. Russell's later work has emphasised the role of Charles himself in provoking a conflict which did have parallels in earlier rebellions. Christopher Hill has consistently made a case for the mid seventeenth century as a crucial turning point in British history, in economic and social developments, politics, and culture in its widest possible sense. Mark Kishlansky, who is not usually to be found in this company, sees the same period as vital to the emergence of adversarial, 'majoritarian' politics, where division and the taking of sides is regarded as normal. On the other hand, Russell again can be seen as representative of a countervailing interpretation, arguing that the civil war changed nothing because neither the financial weaknesses of government nor the religious divisions between Protestants were settled. Yet both these problems could have been settled without war.[3]

It is logically possible to hold that great events do not necessarily have great causes, but in general those historians who consider the English civil war to be a 'revolution', a significant turning point, also tend to see its causes as long-term trends – social tensions, or profound and increasing cleavages over religion and politics. Stone went back to 1529, the year of the 'Reformation parliament'. He wrote that the 'outbreak of war itself is relatively easy to explain; what is hard is to puzzle out why most of the established institutions of State and Church ... collapsed so ignominiously two years before'. Those who argue that the civil war was a more limited rebellion, concentrate on short-term accidental factors, especially the failings of Charles I as a monarch. They hold that all political systems are subject to strains and tensions and there was nothing in the society or politics of early Stuart England that can be seen as leading inexorably to civil war. Here it is war, specifically, that has to be explained, usually through a detailed narrative of the political history of the late 1630s and early 1640s focusing on the presuppositions, negotiations and mistakes of the king and leading political figures.[4]

As many commentators have demonstrated, the debate on the causes of the civil war was begun by the participants in the events themselves.[5] The royalist Edward Hyde, Earl of Clarendon, Charles II's Lord Chancellor, began his *History of the Rebellion* with the reign of Charles I and presented an analysis of political mistakes and confusion which turned an England of peace and prosperity in 1625 into the arena for a bitter civil war. The republican political philosopher James Harrington described the collapse of a whole political structure as a result of social changes going back to the reign of Henry VII. In his 1680s account the royalist historian Sir William Dugdale blamed Anabaptist plotting for the war: 'our late troubles in England, and other his Majesty's realms', came 'from the principles of those persons, who, about one hundred and fifty years before, under the same hypocritical pretences, did grievously infest Germany'. They embroiled the king in foreign war and planted, 'schismatical lectures in most corporate towns and populous places throughout the realm, so to poison the people with anti-monarchical principles'. In contrast the moderate parliamentarian Benjamin Rudyerd claimed in the Short Parliament that: 'The main causes of this infelicity and distraction of these times have been the frequent breaking of Parliaments.'

Because the civil war is so important to us historians are continually re-evaluating it, maintaining the process of debate which began in the 1640s. It is not possible to write a definitive, generally acceptable account of the causes of the civil war in a long book, still less in a brief analysis such as this. Too many passions are involved, and any general overview runs the risk of rapidly becoming out of date. This second point can be illustrated by considering one of the most important works published on the civil war in the last decade, Anthony Fletcher's *The Outbreak of the English Civil War* (1981). This carefully researched work remains crucial for an understanding of local politics, and their interrelationships with national developments, but two of its presuppositions have been called into question by more recent work. The first is that it is possible to discuss developments in England with only brief references to Ireland and Scotland. The other British kingdoms are discussed only for their impact on England, an approach challenged by historians' broader current interest in the 'British problem', as will be shown in chapter 1. Secondly, Fletcher sees the House of Commons playing the most crucial role in politics. John Pym is described as the 'chief spokesman of a distinct group of peers', but the Lords are seen as Pym's allies, or 'intimate friends', rather than vice versa and Fletcher's introduction states: 'It is proper to start an account of the outbreak of the civil war with Pym, since he was the acknowledged leader of the Long Parliament'. Chapters 2 and 3 of this book will show that much recent work is seeking to emphasise the dominant role of the peerage and the House of Lords in the politics of the early 1640s.[6]

Current historical debate is focused on 'revisionist' challenges to what they perceive as erroneous 'Whig' and 'Marxist' interpretations of the civil war.[7] Both these frameworks saw the civil war as a major landmark in England's history with long-term causes and a significant impact on later developments. The 'Whig' version, dominant in the nineteenth and early twentieth centuries but with roots in seventeenth century views, stressed intensifying divisions over religion and politics, with Parliament defending the rule of law, property rights and individual liberties against an autocratic monarchy. Parliament's victory in the civil war, confirmed in 1688–9, laid the foundations of constitutional government and, in a more complicated fashion, of religious liberty. The Marxist version takes a less straightforwardly favourable view of the ideological stances of parliamentarians and sees political division developing on a foundation of long-term social and economic change. The major impact of the events of the 1640s and 1650s is that they comprised a 'bougeois revolution' which paved the way for the further development of a capitalist economy in Britain. Mrs Thatcher's view of 1688 could indeed be seen as both Whig and Marxist.

It will be seen in chapter 1 that some 'revisionist' analysis centres on the long-term structural problems in the English state, especially stressing the financial weaknesses of the crown.

Such practical difficulties are not, however, seen as posing insuperable dilemmas which could be resolved only through war. Neither were there profound and deep-seated cleavages over religious and political principles, although there were serious conflicts provoked by the ideas and political practices of Charles I and his closest associates. Recent work has also denied that it is possible to link political conflict or particular allegiances to social change. Finally revisionists have rejected the implicit notions of inevitable and progressive development found in both Whig and Marxist accounts. On the contrary, it is monarchy which is seen as the aggressive promoter of change; resistance involved a stubborn, conservative defence of tradition. Political tension is derived from specific problems in the conduct of high politics: the breakdown of trust and cooperation between the king and the great men who expected to be his closest advisers provoked by the mistakes of Charles I. Armed conflict was not inevitable or even likely before the late 1630s or even the early 1640s; in G. R. Elton's memorable phrase, there was no 'high road' to civil war.[8]

Most recently however, there has been in turn a reaction to revisionist accounts, sometimes pretentiously described as 'post-revisionism'! It is in this spirit that this book has been written. It is important to take revisionist insights seriously as a basis for further discussion. Their work has brought a creative questioning of some simplistic elements in earlier analyses. We are, for example, moving towards a more complex understanding of the interrelationships between events in England and those in the other British kingdoms. The role of court politics and of elite political relationships more generally has been given fresh emphasis. We cannot assume that division in the political process was seen as normal and widely accepted, that there was any clear split between 'government' and 'opposition', or that there was a 'rising tide' of conflict that led inexorably to civil war. Nonetheless significant current work does not accept that revisionists have found an acceptable new analysis of the roots of civil war. The arguments put forward in this book are based on a conviction that the civil war did have long-term origins; and will suggest that there are connections between social changes and relationships and conflicting views of religion, politics and 'culture'. Furthermore, it will be shown that it is impossible to view practical problems in isolation from the frameworks of ideas within which people understand their problems. This book is not intended as a bland and neutral rehearsal of different explanations. Like almost all accounts of the causes of the civil war, it is a partisan attempt to construct a coherent interpretation while showing respect for the arguments and research of other scholars. The arguments in the individual chapters are closely connected and the overall interpretation emerges in a cumulative fashion. The book should be read critically, with an independent spirit, and it is hoped that it will arouse further disagreement and debate.

The book is made up of three analytical chapters, the first two of which take 'revisionist' frameworks as their starting point. Chapter 1 examines the 'functional breakdown', the notion that the most fundamental problems of English politics centred on the financial and administrative weaknesses of the monarchy and on attempts to rectify these problems. This notion of a 'functional breakdown' has now been broadened to include the 'British problem', the complex difficulties James I and Charles I faced after 1603 in ruling over diverse multiple kingdoms. Throughout chapter 1 we will explore the benefits gained in analysing English conflicts in a European context. The second chapter examines recent work that stresses hierarchy and consensus as the basic characteristics of early Stuart politics and religion. It challenges revisionist beliefs that there were few profound cleavages over religious and political principles before the later 1630s.

Chapter 3 returns to the deeply unfashionable topic of the 'social origins' of the civil war, which has now become a live issue again with David Underdown's stimulating book.[9] As suggested above, important 'revisionist' work has concentrated on high politics – on the activities of elites in London, Westminster, or Whitehall; it has often produced a more complex, but more convincing account than earlier, simpler versions. Since the Second World War there has also been pioneering work done on the social and economic history of early modern England, such as that of Joan Thirsk, or the studies at Cambridge stimulated by Peter Laslett. There have been, however, fewer and fewer links made between political and social history, and the third chapter tries to suggest ways in which some connections can be made. The book will conclude with a chapter which focuses on the reign of Charles I and particularly on the years 1640–2. Unlike some revisionists, this author does not believe that the outbreak of civil war can be explained simply through detailed narrative. Rather the intention is to show how the deep-seated tensions and divisions in early Stuart politics and society erupted in the form of civil war, and here it is to Charles I's reign that we must look.

1

A BRITISH PROBLEM?
A EUROPEAN CRISIS?

The European Crisis

The English, and those Americans who regard themselves as the heirs to the traditions of seventeenth century England, have often been inordinately proud of 'their' civil war:

> By common consent the rebellion against Charles I belongs to the handful of the 'great revolutions' of Europe and the West – cataclysms which appear to mark the turning of times and to signify some fundamental change in the condition of humanity.[1]

Fifteen years after this passage was written it is no longer possible to speak of 'common consent'. A major trend of 'revisionist' scholarship has been to cut the English civil war down to size; to see it as a much more commonplace struggle than the term 'great revolution' suggests. Throughout much of the British education system, courses described as 'British history' in fact consist of English history, considered in isolation from developments in continental Europe and in ignorance of events in Scotland and Ireland. Yet the 'English civil war' was only one of many struggles between European rulers and their peoples in the mid seventeenth century: the French monarchy collapsed in the late 1640s under resistance from many sections of the population in the complex risings known as the *Frondes*;

9

the Spanish monarchy faced revolt in Catalonia, Portugal, Naples and Sicily; there were severe, if less dramatic, tensions between rulers and ruled in Sweden, the United Provinces, and several German states. Like the king of Spain, Charles I of England ruled over multiple kingdoms and he faced revolt in all of them: England was the last to rebel against him. Indeed it has now been argued that there could have been no English civil war without the risings in Scotland in 1638, and in Ireland in 1641; the troubles of the 1640s are better understood as the 'War of the Three Kingdoms'. The English civil war can thus be regarded as part of a 'British problem' which in turn was a manifestation of a 'General European Crisis'; with this approach revisionists challenge the Whig or Marxist stress on the particularly advanced nature of the English. This chapter examines the insights to be gained through interpreting the English civil war in these wider contexts, and the problems with such an approach.

The nature of the 'general crisis' in Europe, and the prior question of whether any such crisis occurred are topics which have occasioned much debate amongst historians. Some of this has involved sterile, nit-picking wrangling over terms, and luckily only a brief discussion is necessary for our purposes. R. B. Merriman wrote of the 'six contemporaneous revolutions' of the 1640s before the Second World War but recent interest was stimulated by Eric Hobsbawm and H. R. Trevor-Roper in the 1950s.[2] Hobsbawm saw the crisis largely in economic terms: the depression of the 1620s following the expansionist sixteenth century revealed the problems of the long European transition from feudalism to capitalism. In this framework, the English civil war was a bourgeois revolution which ultimately was crucial to the resolution of the crisis. This Marxist synthesis has not been much developed or even debated, and it was Trevor-Roper's alternative, more directly political interpretation which prompted most response. For Trevor-Roper the European crisis was a crisis between 'court' and 'country'; the revolts were challenges to the overblown, parasitic and exploitative courts which laid such heavy burdens on their populations. Only states which engaged in administrative retrenchment and reform avoided such violent challenges. The most widely accepted views of the European crisis have developed from an engagement, and usually a disagreement, with this argument. It has been noted that reform was not an alternative to revolt; in Spain at least the attempts by Philip IV's minister, Olivares, to equalise the financial burdens on the Spanish kingdoms so that Catalonia paid a share proportionate to Castile's were the stimulus to revolt. In France, as Mousnier outlined in reply to Trevor-Roper, the most serious challenges to the court came from within the government itself – from the office-holders whose salaries and jurisdictions were being undermined. But the most fundamental dissent from Trevor-Roper, and a crucial element in the most widely accepted accounts of the European crisis, is over his designation of courts or governments as parasitic. Instead governments are regarded as dynamic and creative while the opposition to them is conservative and traditional. The revolts of the mid seventeenth century can only be considered as a general phenomenon if they are taken as 'contemporaneous reactions' rather than revolutions, attempts by nobles, provincial institutions, peasants and townspeople to obstruct the advances of ambitious, absolutist rulers.[3]

Crucial in turn to the advancing power of centralised, absolute monarchy was the 'Military Revolution', the massive expansion in the scale and cost of warfare in the sixteenth and seventeenth centuries. There is some disagreement on the precise chronology and the detailed tactical foundations of military change, but all agree that armies became much larger, and that permanent 'standing' armies became a feature of many states. In the 1470s, France's army amounted to some 40,000 men; by the 1660s it was 100,000 strong, with 400,000 men in arms by the end of the seventeenth century. Sweden's army grew from 15,000 men in the 1590s to 100,000 by 1700. The rising importance of infantry, and the stress on siege warfare meant that larger forces were needed, while the necessity for more training and the basic fact of almost permanent warfare in sixteenth and early seventeenth century Europe underlay the trend towards standing armies. Prices in general rose dramatically in sixteenth century Europe, exacerbating the escalation in the costs of war. In France grain prices rose sevenfold while prices of industrial goods trebled, and trends were similar in Spain. The new armies required ever higher taxes, and a larger and more efficient administration to collect taxation, and organise the conscription and provision of the soldiers. The demands of war merged with monarchs' own ambitions for greater control over their dominions and led rulers into struggles with independent-minded nobilities and particularistic provinces as local rights and traditional liberties were overridden and the central power of the state had more and more impact on the population.

Changes in warfare both promoted and obstructed an increase in centralised authority: only with strong finances and reliable officials could monarchs be effective in foreign affairs and ultimately a standing army could become a vital prop of monarchical power at home; whereas in the short term the burdens of war were an important cause of difficulties between kings and their subjects. In 1618, the Thirty Years War began with the rebellion of the Protestants of Bohemia against the Austrian Habsburg ruler; in 1621 this conflict merged with another heroic struggle of Protestants against Catholics when the truce between Spain and the Netherlands expired and a new round in what was to become the Eighty Years War for Dutch independence began. Finally in 1635 France entered the war against Spain in a renewal of the long-standing attempts to prevent Habsburg encirclement. Most of northern, western and central Europe was embroiled in these vast and complex wars, in which religious ideology was inextricably mixed with power politics.[4]

The role of France clearly indicates the complex relationship between principle and practicality, for Catholic France's anti-Habsburg policy involved it in extensive Protestant alliances abroad, even while Protestants were suppressed at home. The impact of war on the development of the state is also well illustrated from France. The French monarchy was granted a vital tax, the *taille*, for one year in 1439 during a crisis in the Hundred Years War, and thereafter it was levied without the consent of a representative body. By 1575 half the royal income came from the *taille*. These years of war against Spain from 1635 until 1659 saw decisive steps towards absolutist monarchy:

reduction in the influence of local estates and of the political power of the nobility; the introduction of *intendants*, officials responsible to central authority, to supervise the hereditary office-holders. Behind these developments were massive rises in the costs of war and thus in the taxes needed to pay for it: French war expenses were 5m *livres* at the beginning of the century, 33m in 1635 and 38m in 1640; major taxes brought in 10m *livres* in 1610; 36m in 1635 and 72.6m by 1643. But the strains of war brought both the French and the Spanish monarchies to the verge of collapse. Government bankruptcy in France triggered off the revolt of the office-holders, whose salaries were not paid, and permitted the eruption of all the resentment from those who had lost out under the wartime administration. In Spain Olivares, Philip IV's chief minister, wanted his master to become 'King of Spain' rather than 'King of Portugal, Aragon and Valencia, and Count of Barcelona'. He believed that the war against France could only be successful through a 'Union of Arms' whereby each unit of the Spanish monarchy provided a fixed number of men if any part was attacked. There were rumours that Olivares planned to impose 'one king, one law, one coinage'. In the spring of 1640 the Catalan peasantry rose to expel the Castillian troops billeted on their villages. The Catalan nobility, alienated by the threats to their autonomy and traditions, put themselves at the head of this popular anger. At the end of the same year the Portuguese elite followed suit and led a secession from Castile. The 'military revolution' thus played a major role in producing the widespread tensions between rulers and ruled in mid seventeenth century Europe which several historians have summed up as the 'general crisis'.[5]

The English Crown and the 'Functional Breakdown'

Conrad Russell has described England during the Thirty Years War as a country that could not fight; it was in a condition of 'functional breakdown', a term coined by Professor Aylmer, but best known through Professor Russell's work.[6] The functional breakdown refers to the structural weaknesses of the English crown in a period of inflation and faced with a military revolution. The civil war was in many ways a reaction to the attempts of Charles I to rectify these weaknesses, one of the 'contemporaneous reactions' of the European-wide crisis; the parliamentarians were not fired by a progressive, revolutionary ideology. The problems which Russell, in particular, identifies as creating the functional breakdown were in many cases the same as those which afflicted other European rulers, but some were particular to the English monarchy. In practice the problems were inextricably interrelated and mutually reinforcing, but it is useful to separate them out for the purposes of discussion. The comparative external security of sixteenth century England as an island kingdom, and its comparative internal stability with the Tudor taming of the over-mighty nobility, ironically meant that the English monarchy was worse off in financial, administrative and military terms than some continental rulers. Its financial base was extremely weak; English monarchs had never been granted permanent direct national taxation such as the French monarchy had in the *taille* but were dependent on ordinary income from crown lands, feudal dues such as wardship and customs, and on grants authorised by Parliament from time to time. It lacked an extensive and reliable bureaucracy and had no standing army; for many functions from the enforcement of law and order to the collection of taxation the monarchy was dependent on the unpaid cooperation of local elites. Further structural weaknesses arose from the fact that Stuart kings after 1603 were rulers of the multiple kingdoms of England, Scotland and Ireland; these problems will be addressed later in this chapter.

Financial problems were of course multiplied by inflation and the rising demands of war. In the sixteenth century royal income doubled but grain prices rose sixfold, and the prices of industrial products more than doubled; general expenses of government must have risen at least fivefold and the costs of war more still. In the decade of the Armada Elizabeth's wars had cost some £165,000 per annum, but when Charles I prepared for war against Spain in 1625, his government estimated £1 million would be required. No doubt they exaggerated, but the true figure of around £500,000 is startling enough. Only half the cost of Elizabeth's wars against Spain and in Ireland had been met by parliamentary grants and so she had sold crown lands worth £650,000, thus squandering the crown's resources for the future. The expenses of the wars of the 1620s prompted another bout of land selling to clear royal debts: between 1628 and 1640 over £350,000 was raised through sales or mortgages to pay debts owed to the city of London. By 1642 there were no significant parcels of land left to pawn or sell. The government found it hard to exploit crown revenue efficiently in an age of inflation: crown lands were let at long leases for low rents; in the absence of efficient surveys there was little notion of their true potential value. When James I came to the throne in 1603 there had been no revision of the Book of Rates, the schedule of customs duties, since 1558. Early Stuart governments were able to exploit customs revenue more effectively, however. In 1608, Robert Cecil Earl of Salisbury became Lord Treasurer, and at last a new Book of Rates was introduced. More significantly Salisbury also levied systematic additional customs duties or impositions. These impositions had been declared legal in 'Bate's Case' (1606) but unlike the traditional customs they had received no parliamentary sanction and aroused great opposition in parliaments, particularly in 1610 and 1614. By this latter date impositions were bringing the crown some £70,000 and it was not likely the House of Commons would offer anything to make giving them up worthwhile. Further increases in impositions in the 1630s meant that customs brought almost half of Charles I's annual income of £900,000 at the end of that decade.[7]

In the early seventeenth century the practice of customs 'farming' was introduced whereby a syndicate of merchants and courtiers collected the duties in return for a rent paid to the crown. The benefit to the government was the fixed and guaranteed income, but the drawback was equally obvious – private individuals rather than the 'state' benefited from any additional profit. Farming was more efficient than relying on the crown's traditional customs officials who nonetheless kept their posts and their salaries. Attempts to improve the revenue from crown lands were sabotaged by grants of favourable leases to leading courtiers and officials, and by the fact that local officials pocketed a cut of revenue collected. The connections between inadequate finances and administrative weakness are here suggested. The government was in a vicious circle because it lacked the money to pay its servants adequate salaries and so was forced to reward them with pensions and concessions of various kinds and to turn a blind eye to miscellaneous corrupt practices. In the process the crown's financial basis was further weakened, and resentment was fostered amongst those excluded from the spoils of office, whether members of parliament, or the population at large.

'Corruption' is perhaps a misnomer for many of the practices of early modern government which would not be sanctioned today. In the sixteenth and seventeenth centuries there was not the same clear distinction between public and private concerns: monarchy was a personal form of rule, and office-holding and governing in general was regarded partly as a product of private social position or a form of personal property. Thus it could be legitimate to buy and sell government office, to hold positions for life and to make profits out of them. Consequently it was accepted that litigants, for example, should pay fees to all the officials of the court they had business in, or that revenue officials had the right to a proportion of the sums they collected. Given the low level of official salaries, fees and tips were the only way of obtaining an adequate reward. But there were strongly felt if ill-defined notions of what was unacceptable; some of these were to do with the scale of the sums exacted, others with a conviction that officials should not actually pervert the course of justice or disrupt the king's government. On several counts it was outrageous that one of James's most rapacious Lord Treasurers, the Earl of Suffolk, would only send the money for the army in Ireland after a backhander from the Vice-Treasurer of Ireland. Lionel Cranfield, Earl of Middlesex, and Salisbury, to a lesser extent, both have reputations as reforming Lord Treasurers, yet both seem to have obtained excessive personal profits from office. In 1612 Salisbury was getting £12,000 per annum through subletting the farm of duties on silks and satins; as Master of the Court of Wards Salisbury virtually doubled the crown's profits during 1603 to 1612, but he also presided over a situation where only a quarter of the revenue raised through wardship actually reached the crown, the rest being creamed off by officials. Cranfield was Lord Treasurer for some two and a half years before his fall in 1624; in that period his landed income trebled.

The crown was doubly weakened when unpopular exactions brought little profit to the kings themselves. Monopolies were amongst the most controversial of the government's revenue-raising devices. These patents granting sole rights to produce particular commodities such as salt, vinegar, starch, or soap worked through the patentees levying a fine on growers or manufacturers. Monopolies were causing scandal by the end of the sixteenth century because it was clear that revenue raising took priority over their ostensible purpose of protecting new techniques or industries, and several were abolished in the early 1600s. In 1624 Parliament passed an Act confining grants to genuine inventions and to corporations, but these restrictions could be circumvented and the monopolies on tobacco, salt and soap remained profitable in the 1630s. It was not the monarch who profited, however; a modern estimate is that the crown's share of the profits was a mere 13 per cent. In general in England, private individuals and royal officials benefited from procedures which on the continent were exploited directly by the crown. Sale of office is the obvious example. Henry IV of France institutionalised the sale and inheritance of government office and ensured the royal finances were strengthened by the *paulette*, an annual tax on venal officers. The French system had its own drawbacks and vested interests, but it was perhaps preferable to the English set-up where senior officers rather than the king sold subordinate offices and pocketed the proceeds.

The most serious by-products of the interconnecting financial and administrative weaknesses were the obstacles in the way of any attempts to break out of the vicious circle. Attempts to reduce the costs of government through cutting back on fees and corruption were predictably unpopular with courtiers and officials. Attempts to increase royal revenue through limiting grants of land or of profits of wardship to favourites and servants met with a similar response. In 1609, Salisbury introduced a

'Book of Bounty' which listed acceptable grants to courtiers to try to stop James I granting away permanent revenues from land; but in 1610 the generous monarch was still spending £80,000 on pensions and fees of various kinds, whereas Elizabeth's annual expenditure on comparable grants had been £30,000. Between 1617 and 1624 when Lionel Cranfield held high office he cut household costs by a fifth and marginally increased revenue; but he alienated the courtiers whose perks and frauds were lost. George Villiers, Duke of Buckingham, James's favourite, had originally supported his rise to high office as part of his struggle against the dominant Howard faction who were only too obviously vulnerable to an attack on corruption. But the Villiers clan proved no less grasping and Cranfield was increasingly seen as a liability. When he opposed their war with Spain in 1624 – war was a calamity to a frugal, reforming Treasurer – Buckingham and Prince Charles supported impeachment proceedings against him in Parliament and he was disgraced. In any case, both Salisbury and Cranfield were compromised by their own share in the spoils. Another potential way out of the financial impasse was to obtain a regular, adequate revenue from Parliament, the method typified by the 'Great Contract' of 1610. The reasons for the failure of this, and similar attempts before 1642 are complex and debated, but opposition in the House of Commons to increased and permanent taxation was clearly encouraged by perceptions of waste and corruption within the king's administration. Finally, any thoughts of reforming profiteering in the customs farms were blocked by the increasing reliance on customs farmers as sources of credit.

Patronage was fundamental to the workings of all early modern governments, and it was not necessarily detrimental to efficiency or to royal control: 'for a king not to be bountiful were a fault', as Salisbury told Parliament in 1610.[8] A reasonable degree of competition could balance different interests and factions, thus facilitating political stability, and for much of James's reign such a balance seems to have prevailed. Increasingly, though, it seemed that patronage was degenerating from a system in which prestige, honour and protection dominated, and patrons brought practical benefits to their clients in the shape of office or favours, to a system where cash was dominant and clients paid their patrons for any favours they received. The crucial development which poisoned the political atmosphere from the mid 1620s was the domination of the Duke of Buckingham, his unprecedented monopolisation of patronage and his increasing vindictiveness towards opponents. Jealous rivals promoted attacks on the duke in the House of Commons, while Charles's determination to protect his favourite exacerbated the already dire problems involved in the war effort. Tensions surrounding favourites and patronage of course make up another European-wide pattern with Olivares and Mazarin only the most obvious parallels. Where the English crown was significantly disadvantaged in comparison with sophisticated continental regimes like the French and the Spanish was in the lack of an elaborate and efficient conciliar system. The English Privy Council was not capable of the consistent effort necessary to fight a war. In quiescent times its flexible even ramshackle procedures could aid political harmony through openness to a wide range of pressures from influential elites, but these characteristics were weaknesses when the government wanted to enforce its orders or extract revenue. In 1627, for example, the Privy Council's responsibility for the latest court masque prevented it from carrying out threatened punishments on obstructors of the forced loan in Hampshire.[9]

Parliament and Finance: 1. Localism

Most historians would agree that the English monarchy had serious financial and administrative problems in the early seventeenth century, although emphases and details vary. There is significant disagreement, however, on what was most to blame for these problems and how they could best be solved. These disagreements are in turn vital to differences in explaining the causes of the English civil war. Conrad Russell has laid most stress on these problems as a long-term cause of the political crises of the 1620s and the breakdown of 1640–2; he has also drawn fruitfully on European parallels. We must now follow the development of his argument into more controversial topics: the nature of central-local relationships in the English polity, and the attitude of members of parliament towards the crown's financial problems which Russell sees as deriving from their local preoccupations. Fundamental to his arguments, and to much important 'revisionist' analysis is the work of historians who have emphasised the importance of the 'county community' to the gentry of seventeenth century England.[10] Alan Everitt, who pioneered such an approach, argued that national and local awareness were both increasing in sixteenth and early seventeenth century England, but that there was an inevitable tension between local and national concerns in which local interests almost always took priority. The landed gentry of provincial England naturally focused on their county as the arena for most of the important aspects of their lives. Their economic activities were based in their county, revolving often around estates which had been in their families for generations; their wives were chosen from among their neighbours' daughters so that the gentry of a county like Kent formed 'one great cousinage'. Friendships and rivalries were carried on within county boundaries; while a major intellectual interest of the gentry, antiquarianism, resulted in a series of county histories and surveys such as William Dugdale's *Antiquities of Warwickshire* (1656). The leading gentry of each county were proud members of the commission of the peace, holding the crucial local office of Justice of the Peace. As such they presided over the court of Quarter Sessions, a sort of county parliament, where administrative disputes were adjudicated, poor relief and road repairs supervised, criminals tried and the gentry and yeomanry gathered as jurors, constables or petitioners debated matters of general concern. Local governors perceived their main duties to be the maintenance of local stability and social bonds, and to spare their neighbours as much expense and trouble as possible.

In this view of the county community, which as we shall see is open to challenge, there is little room for gentry interest or involvement in national or international affairs, or for provincial enthusiasm for doing the king's business. Yet because the crown lacked an extensive bureaucracy it was greatly dependent on the cooperation of local elites in such crucial matters as the assessment and collection of taxation, and the raising of troops for foreign war. These functions were overseen by subsidy commissioners and deputy lieutenants respectively, who were the same senior gentry as made up the commission of the peace, while much of the donkey work was performed by village constables and divisional High Constables. These too were amateurs, serving for a limited period (a year only for constables) and their zeal for the king's business was severely qualified by their realisation that they would still have to live at peace with their neighbours when their service was over.

Russell's account of the parliaments of the 1620s is based on a view of members of the House of Commons as first and foremost local gentlemen with local priorities. Perhaps their service in Parliament suggested and promoted some concern for wider issues but Russell believes their attitudes to domestic affairs or foreign war were structured particularly by a desire to spare their neighbours and constituents disruptive or heavy exactions. Thus the parliaments were incapable of redressing the 'functional breakdown'.[11] In contrast to older historians who saw the House of Commons increasing in confidence and ambition in the early seventeenth century, Russell argues that MPs were seeking to evade the initiative in foreign affairs in a period of extensive conflict in Europe. England was concerned with the Thirty Years War almost from the start for the Protestants of Bohemia had invited James I's son-in-law, Frederick the Elector Palatine, to be their ruler. In little more than a year Frederick had been forced from Bohemia by imperial troops; in 1620 the Palatinate itself was invaded and Catholic control was complete by 1623. Frederick and his popular wife, Elizabeth, were sad exiles dependent on the charity of the Dutch. English and Stuart honour, as well as Protestant hopes were sullied by these developments. James at first hoped to recover the Palatinate through negotiations with the Spanish, but when these hopes failed with the breakdown of the proposals for a 'Spanish match' between Charles and a Spanish princess, Charles and Buckingham roused Parliament to a war against the Spaniards. Charles felt that in 1624 the Commons had enthusiastically endorsed a war to recover the Palatinate but had thereafter refused to pay for it, and Russell endorses much of this view. Most members of parliament, he suggests, had little concern for, or understanding of, the costs of central government or foreign policy. They believed the government had enough money and were aghast at the sums requested for the wars of the 1620s. Such 'backwoods' attitudes were not confined to obscure members: Sir John Eliot, Sir Francis Seymour, Sir Edward Coke and Sir Robert Phelips, amongst the prominent parliament-men, took this approach. The exceptions were usually men who owed their seats in the Commons to the patronage of a peer, rather than to the wider approbation of their neighbours, so they could take a more detached view of the impact of taxation on the 'county community'. Sir Benjamin Rudyerd, a protégé of the earls of Pembroke, was one such man, who argued consistently for a permanent, parliamentary settlement of royal finances, from the 1620s to the Short Parliament of 1640, where he was the only MP openly to suggest a grant of supply to the king. Sir Nathaniel Rich, a kinsman of the Earl of Warwick, held similar views, as did the great John Pym, who was distinctive in many ways, and not least in his lack of loyalty to any county community. Pym's patron was the Earl of Bedford, while his knowledge of government finance owed much to his practical experience as a receiver for crown lands.

Russell argues that most MPs were uneasy at voting the king taxation in peacetime, relying on the medieval commonplace that the king should 'live of his own', pay his way with the revenue from the crown lands, feudal dues, and the traditional customs. In time of war they refused to acknowledge the sums required and taxation was agreed to with a very bad grace. As MPs in Westminster the gentry voted subsidies very reluctantly; as subsidy commissioners at home they shamefully underassessed themselves and their neighbours so that the yield of a parliamentary subsidy had fallen in absolute terms despite inflation since the start of Elizabeth's reign. A 'subsidy' was not worth a defined sum: subsidymen – those listed in the lists or rolls as liable to the levy – paid 4s. in the £1 on landed wealth, or 2s. 8d. in £1 on annual income from personal property. They paid only in one place, where their main residence was, and were granted certificates of exemption on property elsewhere. Commissioners could fill up their assessment rolls with the names of people who did not in fact pay the subsidy in their areas. In general, of course, commissioners were easy-going in levying the subsidy in their local communities. There was no attempt to keep the rolls of those liable or the assessments of wealth up to date. In Essex in 1566, 6700 subsidy men paid £7000 for a subsidy; by 1628, 3700 men paid only £2016. This was a period of rising population and rising real wealth amongst those ranks liable to the subsidy as well as a period of inflation. Subsidy assessments bore little relationship to real wealth: modern historians multiply subsidy assessments by 50 to get any indication of actual income. Yet in 1621 the Lincolnshire subsidy commissioners explained to the Privy Council that they had not obeyed their instruction to rate JPs at £20 per annum at least, because it was in many cases 'too burthensome for their small estates ... considering the daily charge they undergo by their pains in his Majesty's several services'. In 1628, 32 Essex JPs, members of the landed elite in one of the most prosperous of English counties, claimed an average annual income of £10 p.a. In both countries few JPs would have been worth less than £1000 p.a. It was no wonder that the costs of war proved a shock for local people: the Earl of Warwick claimed that the people of Essex had paid £4000–5000 for the upkeep of Harwich garrison in 1625. No wonder also that ship money was an unpleasant novelty: 12,000 people in Essex paid a direct national levy for the first time. Looking at the national picture, in the early sixteenth century one subsidy had been worth £130,000; by 1628 it had declined to £55,000. MPs were conscious of the great number of subsidies granted by the parliaments of the 1620s, which amounted to twelve in all: two in 1621; three in 1624, two in 1625, and five in 1628. Elizabeth had never received so many in the 1590s, but MPs were less aware that Elizabeth's parliamentary grants had been worth over £90,000 per annum, while in the 1620s all the subsidies equalled only some £82,000 per annum.[12]

In Russell's view the Commons' reluctance to vote the king adequate subsidies or to consider reforming their collection, was compounded by parliamentary attacks on impositions and monopolies. The Commons thus threatened the most profitable sources of royal revenue without offering anything worthwhile in return. Their refusal to grant tonnage and poundage to Charles except for one year in 1625, and thereafter not at all forced the king, in his own and Russell's opinion, into collecting it without parliamentary sanction. A variety of quasi-legal expedients had to be adopted if the war effort was to be carried on. In the 1626 Parliament subsidies were voted but the bill was not completed before the attack on Buckingham forced Charles to dissolve the Parliament. The king's largely successful attempt to collect a 'forced loan' in lieu of these lost subsidies was, Russell suggests, essential for the defence of the realm. The attacks on soldiers and especially on billeting which erupted in the 1628 Parliament are further indications of MPs' refusal to accept the administrative necessities of waging a war. The Petition of Right itself was not simply a ringing declaration of a particular view of the English constitution based on Parliament and the rule of law; the attacks on billeting, martial law and unparliamentary levies again showed lack of concern for the war effort. 'The reactions of the 1628 House of Commons to the soldiers sharply illustrate the difficulties of running a war with an amateur, unpaid local government whose first loyalty was to their county and not to the country'.[13] Only by drastically infringing the independence of the localities, Russell argues, could England have fought an effective war in the 1620s. The wars exacerbated a pre-existing functional breakdown; divisions over and opposition to the war again made things worse, but the fundamental causes of the crisis of 1628 were long-term financial and administrative problems, rather than the ideological divisions stressed by 'Whig' historians. In the 1620s, Russell would argue, there were no ideological divisions serious enough to bring about breakdown.

War put intolerable pressure on the English system of government, and so inevitably increased internal tensions. In Russell's interpretation, there is thus no inevitable process of steadily increasing division until 1642, for the 1630s, which saw no wars (and no parliaments where grievances could be aired) were more tranquil than the war-torn decades of the 1620s or the 1590s.

The 1630s revealed how wise it was for Charles to keep out of European wars, and also how it was possible, even profitable, to do without parliaments. Charles's annual income rose from about £550,000 in 1630 to just under £1m by the end of the decade. The customs brought in over a third of that figure, especially through the impositions so opposed by earlier parliaments; while income from the Court of Wards was between two and three times greater than it had been in the early 1620s. Profitable expedients such as the fines on gentlemen who had not been knighted at Charles's coronation, or the swingeing penalty on the City of London for mismanagement of their plantation lands in Ulster, were much easier to resort to when no immediate parliaments were contemplated. But Charles did not establish a financial and administrative structure that would enable him to fight a war without the cooperation of local governors and money from Parliament. In 1639 the equivalent of over a third of annual revenue had been anticipated, while the alienation of the City of London through the Londonderry fine had reduced the pool of people willing to lend the crown money to those intimately bound up in the regime, such as the customs farmers and prominent individuals like Sir William Russell, the treasurer for the navy, or Thomas, Lord Wentworth. When Charles tried to raise an effective army against the Scots 'rebels' in 1639–40, he faced widespread non-payment of taxes, inefficient levying of unsuitable troops by local governors and an inability to raise loans in the City without calling a Parliament. With the Scots occupying the north of England, the parliament which met in November 1640 was the only means by which sums to pay off the Scots could be raised.

The 'Long' Parliament met amidst great hopes of reconciliation between king and people, hopes that were to be sadly disappointed. In his analysis of the failure of settlement between 1640 and 1642, Russell again stresses the irresponsibility of many members of parliament in refusing the crown a secure, parliamentary-based revenue. As in the 1620s, a minority of MPs, led especially by John Pym and Oliver St John with the backing of the Earl of Bedford, took a responsible attitude to the crown's financial problems. Their aim was an aristocratic coup d'état whereby they would become members of the government, in order to reverse the political and religious policies of the 1630s. In return Charles would receive sufficient sums from Parliament to pay off his debts and secure an adequate annual revenue for the future. The problems of subsidy would be overcome through the adoption of the assessment practices used in ship money for the new parliamentary taxes. Under this system a fixed sum was decided upon and then apportioned between different parts of the country, and so the uncertainty of the subsidy was avoided. Finally, Pym and Bedford planned to take over the farm of the customs, so completing the financial stranglehold on Charles, but hoping thereby to strengthen both Parliament and the monarchy.

There were many reasons for the failure of these proposals, not least Charles's refusal to have his powers so limited. Equally crucial though, argues Russell, was the inability of Pym to deliver the financial settlement because of obstruction in the House of Commons. Most MPs did not want to become part of the government, they wanted simply to limit its exactions for the sake of their local communities. Again, as in the 1620s, the opposition to Pym included prominent MPs and critics of Charles such as Denzil Holles, William Strode and the son and son-in-law of Lord Saye, Nathaniel Fiennes and Sir Walter Earle. This was a formidable group, especially as Saye assumed a dominant position in the opposition to Charles after Bedford's death in 1641. The whole abortive negotiations further poisoned the relationship between the king and the parliamentary leadership and increased Charles's resolve to regain his position through force. In Russell's account it is Charles who had the most reasons to fight a civil war, and Charles who in fact makes most of the running in bringing armed conflict to England.[14] His financial position is one vital reason for his having to fight: in the 1620s Charles had been willing to work with parliaments but he had been disillusioned by their persistent and illegitimate attempts to deprive him of Buckingham, his closest adviser and favourite, and particularly by their refusal to pay for his wars; in the early 1640s Parliament outlawed ship money and other expedients of the personal rule, failed to settle tonnage and poundage, but failed also to grant a decent revenue in return.

The civil war is thus, in part at least, Charles's attempt to achieve a financial base and freedom of action comparable to that of continental 'absolutist' monarchs.

Parliament and Finance: 2. Principle

Much of Conrad Russell's analysis of the 'functional breakdown' is from the monarchs' point of view: their financial problems were intractable and the failure to solve them is attributed mainly to the localism and irresponsibility of members of the House of Commons. There are, however, other ways of looking at the problems of royal finance and administration. Some of the disagreements between historians appear very detailed and technical but in fact are part of significantly different analyses. Most accounts agree that Elizabeth left debts of £400,000 at her death. Russell goes on to argue that James's extravagance is not mainly to blame for the crown's problems: of his debts of £900,000 at their peak in 1618, half had been bequeathed by Elizabeth. In any case a monarch from a new, and foreign, dynasty had to spend money on pensions, gifts and the like in order to establish himself. David Thomas and A. G. R. Smith disagree: on Elizabeth's death there were £300,000 of parliamentary subsidies still to be collected and so James inherited a crown that was virtually solvent. They are thus much more critical of James's increased spending which they do not regard as justified by the political needs of a new dynasty, or the practical needs of a monarch with a wife and growing children. Although peace was made with Spain and the wars in Ireland were over, James's doubling of the crown's ordinary expenditure meant mounting debts. Prestwich is equally critical of James: she writes of the 'pollution' of standards in his reign; that the king's financial and administrative problems were 'great but not insoluble' and that he was 'financially irresponsible'. Where Russell uses continental comparisons to emphasise the crown's problems, Prestwich uses a similar technique to stress royal inadequacy. Her comparison is between the wise king Henry IV of France and his reforming minister Sully, and the corrupt, extravagant and inefficient James and Cecil. For these historians parliamentary attitudes cannot be separated from the problem of royal extravagance: when James spent a fortune on hunting or jewels or showered honours on Buckingham it was not simply a practical addition to the royal debts, but had political implications that made Parliament much less likely to believe royal protestations of poverty and less inclined to do anything about the crown's problems. A greater commitment to reform by the government was an essential element in any solution of these problems.

If Russell's argument is too charitable to monarchs it is also rather pessimistic about the contribution of Parliament, and about the seriousness of the 'functional breakdown' itself. David Thomas emphasises the enormous sums voted by parliaments in the 1620s; the five subsidies granted in 1628, after the forced loan and the expenses of billeting, are especially noteworthy. Richard Cust further points out that it was *not* impossible for England to fight a war in the 1620s: the problems that arose were not part of the functional breakdown, for men and money were raised by local governors and by borrowing, but the simple incompetence of the government's deployment of their resources at Cadiz or the Isle de Rhé, where the expedition's ladders were too short to scale the walls of the fort.[15] Russell's argument that the 'functional breakdown' meant Charles was unable to fight a war is not in fact supported by the European comparisons he uses: the Spanish government repudiated its debts in 1557, 1575, 1599, 1607, 1627 and 1647 but was still able to find credit to finance its wars; in neither France nor Spain did the internal political collapse of the 1640s fatally weaken the external war effort. The Commons' reluctance to vote sufficient money for the war effort was not a straightforward reflection of localist dislike of taxation: the government's mismanagement of the war effort plus the broader folly of engaging both France and Spain in war in 1627 were important influences, as were serious divisions over tactics. Many members opposed the projected continental land campaign to recover the Palatinate as too hazardous and expensive; their preference was for a naval war on the Elizabethan model, attacking Spain's colonial strongholds, with potential profits to be plundered from Spanish treasure ships.

Elizabeth did manage an effective war effort in the 1590s, and as Anthony Fletcher has recently emphasised, the Commons did make great strides in rectifying the functional problems of English government in 1641.[16] They did not vote taxation with great enthusiasm – which should not surprise us since no one likes paying taxes – but Russell's picture of a House of Commons simply avoiding unpleasant realities is extremely partial. The existence of the Scottish army occupying northern England, Scottish Commissioners on hand in London to push their case, and the idle, badly paid and ill-disciplined English army concentrated MPs' minds sufficiently to raise vast sums of money. The subsidy bill took three months, but further subsidies were soon voted, while the £400,000 tax, voted in May 1641, took over from ship money the practice of levying a fixed sum. Finally, in June 1641, with further crisis in the north, a poll tax was rushed through the Commons barely two weeks after the London MP, Isaac Pennington, had first suggested it, to great opposition.

The examples of the 1590s and of 1640–1 reveal the import- ance of the political context of financial problems. As Derek Hirst has stressed, it is not possible to separate the practical, structural weaknesses of the English monarchy from ideological divisions in the political nation. Men's religious and political principles profoundly affected how they saw questions of finance and administration.[17] Ideological issues will be fully considered in the next chapter, but it is necessary to indicate here how they influenced the attitudes of members of the House of Commons, in particular, to the functional breakdown. Many in the Com- mons saw the struggle in Europe as a cosmic struggle between good and evil; any war should be a Protestant crusade against the papists led by Anti-christ, the Pope. With good reason they felt uneasy about the capacity of the government to head such a crusade. Between 1616 and 1624, James followed a studiously neutral foreign policy which culminated in the highly unpopular attempt to secure a Spanish bride for Charles as a means of securing a general European peace. In practice this approach chiefly benefited the Spanish monarchy. In the first years of Charles's reign, England was at least at war with Spain, but there were other disquieting trends: the use of the 'loan ships' intended to relieve the beleaguered French Protestants, the Huguenots, to help the French king's campaign against his Protestant subjects in 1625; and particularly the worries about Charles's own religious affiliations. The Commons were correct to fear royal attitudes for James and Charles did not share the view of evangelical Protestants that foreign policy should be a crusade against the Anti-christ. Charles did have a brief period as a Protestant champion during 1624–6 but he returned to his father's pro-Spanish policy in the 1630s, hoping to win back the Palatinate for his nephew through Spanish favour. Besides their different ideological stance, James's and Charles's increasing reliance on customs revenue further inclined them to a pacific foreign policy that would be good for trade.

Divisions over internal politics were another vital element in the failure to solve the crown's financial difficulties. It has already been indicated that religious divisions intensified from Charles's accession to the throne; attacks on 'Arminian' churchmen were mounted in all parliaments from 1624 to 1628, and prevented united action on the financing of the war. It has also been suggested above, that royal extravagance and the prominence of favourites, particularly Buckingham, encouraged the belief in Parliament that the crown had enough money, and should solve its problems through reform and the elimination of corruption. A more broadly conceived deduction from Buckingham's dominance was that the king's policies were being sabotaged by evil counsellors, who had therefore to be removed before domestic and foreign affairs could go well. In 1626, some promising moves towards financial reform floundered because Charles would not sacrifice Buckingham. Most significantly of all, divergent views of the English political system were coming into conflict in Charles's reign, as will be shown in detail later. Whereas many of the political nation saw regular meetings of parliaments as essential to English stability, the king himself was turning to 'new counsels' which stressed the importance of obedience to royal authority, and increasingly resorted to financial exactions not authorised by Parliament. Members of the Commons were not likely to give the king a generous financial settlement when there were serious doubts about his intentions regarding parliaments.

The fact that a stable financial settlement depended on the support of Parliament was already clear to Salisbury in 1609–10. Although several historians, including Lindquist and Prestwich, have argued that Salisbury was too acquiescent over James's extravagance, and very reluctant to initiate reform, Pauline Croft's edition of private memoranda written by Salisbury to James before the 1610 Parliament reveals a different picture.[18] Salisbury regarded it as vital to arrange some financial settlement in 1610: a financial crisis was looming because Prince Henry (who was as extravagant in his own way as James) was about to become Prince of Wales, and all the crown revenue settled on the prince would be lost to James. In his very frank private advice to James, Salisbury opposed corruption, admired Henry VII and criticised Henry VIII for their attitudes to finance. Henry VII, 'being not born to a kingdom, but having passed his life to mature age in a private and troubled fortune, framed himself to such frugality'. Unfortunately, Salisbury had no notion how unpopular impositions were, although he opposed other ways of raising revenue through the prerogative: 'To suffer your people to be molested and inquired after, upon every claim and obscure title', was unwise and unjust. Salisbury was emphatic that the royal estate could only be maintained with the support of the king's people through Parliament, rather than through the 'sour and harsh supplies' of the prerogative.

The failure of the Contract is not due solely to the Commons' refusal to contemplate the sums involved, which were indeed large: Salisbury asked for £600,000 to pay off debts, and for a permanent settlement of £200,000 p.a. which did not include any compensation for the abolition of purveyance (the system whereby royal households were able to purchase supplies at advantageous rates) and the Court of Wards. The Commons would give no more than subsidies worth £100,000 in response to the request for £600,000, and £200,000 p.a. which was to include compensation for wardship and purveyance. It is true that members of the Commons were worried about how the £200,000 was to be raised, and opposed to any land tax; they were also influenced by the alarm expressed to them in their localities, when they met their constituents during the summer recess. All this is familiar from Russell's interpretation, but other more obviously 'political' factors were also present: the MPs feared that overgenerous grants would encourage monarchs to dispense with parliaments completely, and were very critical of James's favourites and extravagance. In fact it was attacks on the bounty granted to the Scots courtiers in particular that prompted James to sabotage the Contract and the Parliament by asking for a further £500,000 in the new session in November. Salisbury blamed *some* of the House of Commons for the failure of the Contract, but until his death he continued to believe that a solution to royal financial problems could only be found in Parliament. It is worth noting that Salisbury's judgement was shared by Maximilian of Bavaria who believed Charles was hamstrung in Europe by his failure to agree with Parliament. The importance of Parliament to the crown's financial position is equally clear at the end of Charles's personal rule when it was impossible for the king to obtain sufficient credit without a guarantee from Parliament. As Simon Adams has succinctly remarked: it was 'not so much the power of the crown to fight a war that collapsed in 1640, but the power to do so under the prerogative'.[19]

The Centre and the Localities in England and Europe

It has already been shown that the French and Spanish kings also faced serious resistance in the 1640s. The more interesting contrast with Charles I lies in the fact that the opposition to continental monarchs was ultimately overcome whereas the challenge to Charles became more radical and more extensive in the early 1640s. Examining England in a European context can suggest ways in which England was unlike the continent, rather than part of the general crisis of reactions to aggressive central-ising monarchs which was outlined at the beginning of this chapter. Many of these contrasts will be covered as issues in their own right later: the importance of religious zeal and political principle in creating a more cohesive and determined opposition than was found on the continent; the very real sense in which the 'parliamentary cause' was a social alliance including members of the elite, and those from middling and lower ranks, which survived in some qualified form until the Restoration, has no real parallel in France or Spain. Most relevant to this chapter are the nature of central–local relationships; examining these in a European perspective suggests that the notion of the English 'county community' and the view that there were sharp and inevitable conflicts in England between local and national concerns are both improbable.[20]

Compared to the rest of Europe, England had a highly integrated and centralised political system, deriving in large part from the early strength of the English monarchy, both Anglo-Saxon and Norman. Seventeenth century England was made up of various local communities within which people experienced the different aspects of their lives: the village, the parish, the market town, the farming region and the diocese all mattered for personal, economic and religious affairs. The county too was important; the Court of Quarter Sessions was vital for the maintenance of order, the punishment of crime, and the regulation of local administration; the election or selection of knights of the shire to sit in parliament meant the county was a vital political focus. But the county was not the sole or even prime focus of loyalty for most of the population, including the gentry, and all local communities were conceived of as part of a national polity; it was rarely assumed that local and national concerns were inevitably contradictory. Between the separate kingdoms of Spain, and the highly autonomous provinces of France, several of which had been part of the crown's possessions for barely a century, there were great variations in the legal system, in the privileges and procedures under which taxation was levied, and in administrative practices. Some kingdoms and provinces had powerful representative assemblies with proud traditions; others weak bodies, or none at all. England had one common law, with minor local quirks; it had a national framework for local administration, again with comparatively little local difference; and most important of all, it had one national representative body which voted taxation for the whole kingdom. The English

Parliament was also more cohesive socially than French Estates, for example. The House of Lords included lay and ecclesiastical peers; the House of Commons comprised representatives of the towns and the countryside. Although differences did arise between Lords and Commons, they were capable of presenting a united front at times of crisis, and English monarchs had less success with a policy of 'divide and rule' than the French government had in playing off the clergy, the traditional nobility, and the office-holders in the Estates General of 1614.

England was a centralised, but not a bureaucratised country; monarchs were therefore dependent on the cooperation of local elites to raise taxes and soldiers, and enforce order, with the consequent problems that have been discussed in this chapter. These local elites were in turn, however, dependent on the crown and the central government for their appointments to local office, and often for help against local rivals. Sir Robert Phelips of Somerset was a frequent critic of the government in the parliaments of the 1620s but he usually tried to avoid antagonising the authorities so much that they would deprive him of his local offices, which in turn would have meant a decisive set-back in his long rivalry with Lord Poulet, another member of the Somerset elite. Again compared to continental Europe, England had a comparatively uniform national culture and system of higher education, accessible mainly to the upper classes, but open to some members of those middling groups who were also part of the 'political nation'.

Indeed, the centre and the localities were so inextricably intertwined in English politics that even using the separate terms can suggest a polarity that contemporaries did not recognise. This close interrelationship was a vital element in political culture and practice, and in the nature of the opposition to Charles I. There was an almost insatiable hunger for news of rivalries at court or factions in the Privy Council, and a wide interest in international affairs. A significant proportion of the male population had broad knowledge of the workings of government, and experience of participation in it at a number of levels, as will be shown in the next chapter. Local communities were capable of sophisticated lobbying and petitioning over a variety of issues: they mobilised contacts at court and in London generally to reduce their ship money assessments, for example. From the 1580s and 1590s, when counties and villages collected information on the poor condition of the clergy to support the Puritan-parliamentary campaign for reformation of the church, to the petitioning campaigns over episcopacy and the Grand Remonstrance, in the first years of the Long Parliament, we can see local communities involved in general issues and using local pressure to influence national alignments.

In France or in Spain the separate provinces and kingdoms negotiated and disputed with the crown individually because their privileges, especially in taxation, and their histories and traditions, varied enormously. There was no united representative body in either monarchy in the 1640s that could legitimate generalised opposition as the English Parliament could. Even where the continental struggle was an ideological one, at least in part, ideology did not prove capable of overriding particularist local interests. La Rochelle has a deservedly heroic reputation as the centre of the Huguenot struggle against the Catholic policy of the French crown, yet David Parker has shown how Protestant solidarity was weakened by the rivalries of different local and privileged interests. The urban elite of La Rochelle were suspicious of the ambitions of the Huguenot nobility; the city's rural hinterland resented its urban privileges; these and other resentments were mutual.[21] Continental monarchs usually faced divided opponents and were able to overcome them. In England, at crucial periods such as 1628 and 1640–2, the resentments of the provinces could coalesce in the national Parliament into a united opposition. The House of Commons, writes Kevin Sharpe, 'became the seminar of the English localities'. Partly this was facilitated by the very existence of this national institution; partly it was a product of cultural uniformity and agreement over the religious and political issues to be discussed in chapter 2; but it was also a result of structural factors. It was not just that localism was overridden by a common ideology, but that the centralised nature of the English political system meant that local grievances were common to all, or most localities. In the 1620s subsidies had been levied and soldiers and the forced loan raised in broadly similar ways; by 1640 ship money, religious innovations and the burdens of the Scottish war were experienced in all counties. Hence the opposition to Charles was not particularist, concerned only with a variety of local or privileged interests, but general, concerned with the nature and direction of one central government. This was a much more serious situation for the monarchy, and was worlds apart from the problems in Catalonia, or even from the Huguenot struggle based on La Rochelle.

The British Problem

The model of central–local relationships on which Russell's *Parliament and English Politics* is based is thus flawed, and in general the attempt to see the English civil war as part of a European reaction against ambitious centralising monarchs is inappropriate. It was recalled at the start of this chapter that Charles was not merely king of England, but king of Britain, ruler of the very different kingdoms of England, Ireland and Scotland. As the experience of kings of Spain vividly demonstrated, it was very difficult to rule over heterogeneous multiple kingdoms, especially in an era where monarchs felt obliged to establish more uniformity in their domains. Charles and his advisers were themselves conscious of the Spanish parallels, and Secretary of State John Coke proposed in 1627 that Charles I 'unite his three kingdoms in a strict union and obligation to each other for their mutual defence', as attempted by the king of Spain. As early as 1607 the Scots had opposed James's suggestion of the appointment of a viceroy, because it would reduce them to, 'a conquered and slavish province . . . like such of the King of Spain's provinces as your Majesty . . . made mention of'. In the 1640s, Nathaniel Fiennes, one of the leaders of the opposition to Charles in England, was following events in Catalonia closely.[22] The last section of this chapter will thus provide some account of Charles as king of Scotland and Ireland and show something of the ways in which problems in the three kingdoms were interrelated. It may be that the European comparisons have much more relevance to the 'British' problem than they do to the English civil war.

In a series of compelling articles, Conrad Russell has stressed the importance of the 'British dimension' to an understanding of the English civil war. In an early version the Scots intervention in 1639–40 is virtually an outside blow, creating a crisis which could not have been generated from within England. Again, it is only Dutch intervention in 1688–9 that can account for the later transformation in the English monarchy. More recent work presents a more complex picture and draws fruitfully on European examples.[23] In Europe problems in multiple kingdoms tended to focus on conflicts over foreign policy and the sharing of the costs of war; on suspected discrimination in the direction of trade and colonial policies; on resentment at exclusion from patronage and office on the part of nobilities of subordinate kingdoms faced with an absentee monarch. Many of these issues were present in Britain. During the wars of the 1620s fears that Ireland might be used as base for the invasion of England meant that increased Irish taxation was needed to finance additional troops there. In order to obtain this money the English government entered into negotiations over various 'matters of grace and bounty', mainly concessions to 'Old English' Catholic opinion on freedom of worship and security of landed property. The 'graces' were not in fact implemented in the 1620s but they remained an aspiration for loyal Irish Catholics and were an important issue in the emerging Irish crisis of 1640–1. As the Scots prepared for armed resistance of Charles I in 1639, they issued a tract justifying their proceedings, the 'Instructions for Defensive Arms' which distinguished between:

> the king resident in the kingdom, opening his ears to both parties, and rightly informed; and the king far from us, in another kingdom, hearing the one party, and misinformed by our adversaries.

Neither war and finance, nor the grievances fostered by an absentee monarch were at the centre of the 'British problem', however. Russell argues very convincingly that the crucial elements were religious divisions combined with the policy and personality of Charles himself.

Charles was unique amongst European rulers in that he governed multiple kingdoms which were all divided over religion, and 'in all of which there existed a powerful group which preferred the religion of one of the others to their own'.[24] Thus there were almost unending opportunities, when crises came, for both Charles and his opponents in one kingdom to seek allies in another, and conflicts became ever more serious, longer lasting and harder to untangle. Religious diversity was, of course, a problem for all monarchs, given a belief that disunity in religion bred instability and subversion, but Charles's methods and policies were particularly inept and provoked resistance in all his kingdoms. James VI and I had little liking for the Presbyterian structure of the Scottish church, but he broadly shared the Calvinist theology of that church; his basic aim for a uniform religious settlement of his kingdoms would have been Scottish doctrine and English episcopal government. In working towards this he showed patience and caution and thus in Scotland an episcopal layer was added to church government. The Scottish church since the Reformation had been ruled by the 'kirk session', ministers and lay elders acting at a parish level, and by an ascending system of regional and national Councils – presbyteries, synods and the General Assembly – on a Presbyterian model above this. Now bishops were made moderators of the synods and controlled admission to the clergy. This compromise did not inflame Scottish opinion, but there was more opposition to the introduction of a more elaborate English style of worship. Changes in the liturgy were embodied in the Articles of Perth, pushed through the General Assembly of 1618 and the Parliament of 1621 but James characteristically left difficult issues unresolved and the Articles were not enforced. In Ireland Protestantism was the 'religion of conquest' delivered in 'the language of the conqueror' but the Church of Ireland in which the powerful English and Scottish colonists worshipped was a staunchly evangelical, Calvinist church, envied by the English Puritans.

As will be shown in detail in chapter 2, Charles took an anti-Calvinist stance in England, and his attempt from 1633 at least to impose similar views on Ireland and Scotland was a disaster.

In 1634 Thomas Wentworth, Lord Deputy of Ireland, and his ally Bishop John Bramhall of Derry forced the Thirty Nine Articles and the English Canons of 1604 on an unhappy Irish church. Their policy was a 'novel and unpopular insistence upon conformity ... to a norm that was unrepresentative of Irish Protestant opinion', and in the process they excluded the Calvinist James Ussher, Archbishop of Armagh, and in theory Primate of the Church of Ireland, from any influence.[25] The explosive consequences of similar policies in Scotland, where Charles was not, as he nonetheless believed, supreme head of the Church, will need further coverage below.

The formal, constitutional relationship between the British kingdoms was diverse. England and Scotland were independent kingdoms united only in the person of their common ruler; early in his reign over England James failed to persuade the English Parliament to support a legislative and administrative union. Scotland had its own Parliament and its own Privy Council over which the English Council had no jurisdiction; it was not until June 1638, for example, that the English Privy Councillors were informed officially that there were problems in Scotland. Ireland, on the other hand, was a colonial kingdom, subordinate to the English king and Privy Council (but emphatically not to the English Parliament). Ireland too had its own Council and Parliament, but the Council was subordinate to its English counterpart and the Parliament was hedged about with restrictions: all measures to be submitted to it had to be approved in advance by the king, the Lord Deputy and the Councils of England and Ireland. There was, however, no formal connection between all three kingdoms, and no general council for Britain as a whole as there was in the Spanish monarchy. Thus British policy was essentially Charles's own policy, and he received 'British' advice only when he chose to solicit it from individuals he trusted, particularly Laud, Wentworth later in the 1630s and sometimes the Marquis of Hamilton.

The existence of some general body advising Charles on all his kingdoms is unlikely to have made any difference to his attitudes; all the failings of the king as a political leader which will be evident at several points in this book are starkly highlighted in the British context. In 1637–8, as the authority of his Privy Council in Scotland crumbled and the Covenanters gradually took control of the country, Charles refused to discuss matters with his Councillors and simply reiterated orders that they return the dissidents to their proper obedience. His unswerving belief in his divine authority, and in the ultimate justice of his cause, meant that in the short and medium term, any stratagems were permissible if they might help restore his positions. Thus his initial stubbornness in Scotland was succeeded by generous concessions intended to gain time so that he could defeat the Covenanters by force; in Scotland and in Ireland he engaged in dishonest intrigues in the hope of obtaining support against his enemies in all three kingdoms. All his tactics were unconvincing, added to his reputation for untrustworthiness, and simply strengthened the commitment of his opponents.

There was no formal constitutional connection between Ireland and Scotland but it would be a mistake to consider the British problem simply in terms of the interrelationships of England and Scotland, on the one hand, and England and Ireland on the other. There were a multitude of practical, cultural and religious connections between Ireland and Scotland, which had independent implications for the British conflicts.[26] Since the thirteenth century soldiers from the Scottish Highlands, known as 'gallowglasses', had served Irish lords, and many settled permanently in Ireland. More recently, and of the utmost importance for the 'British crisis' of the 1640s, large numbers of the MacDonald clan from the western Highlands and Islands had come to settle in Antrim, Ulster, in the fifteenth century. Indeed, as Stevenson suggests, the distinction between Ireland and Scotland had little meaning for the MacDonalds and MacDonnells, as the clan were known in Ulster; a Gaelic and Catholic culture was common to both sides of the Irish Sea. There was longstanding rivalry between the MacDonalds and the Campbells, their neighbours in the Western Isles; the Campbells were a more securely Protestant clan and usually had the backing of the Scottish government in their struggles for dominance of the Highlands. Although their chief in the 1630s, the seventh Earl of Argyll, had been a Catholic his son was to become the leader of the Covenanters. Randall MacDonnell, the second Earl of Antrim, led the Irish MacDonnells in the 1630s; under his protection Catholics from the Scottish Highlands could obtain the sacraments in Antrim during this decade. The Earl of Antrim, who had married the widow of Charles's murdered favourite, Buckingham, was to claim extensive involvement in intrigues between Charles and Irish Catholics, which aimed to recover the king's authority in all his British kingdoms. Though Conrad Russell, the latest historian to examine Antrim's role, is sceptical about some of the earl's wider claims, rumours of these murky intrigues played a wholly disproportionate part in the British crisis.

As well as the Highland Catholics, lowland and Protestant Scots played an important part in developments in seventeenth century Ireland. Large numbers of Scottish Protestants settled in Ulster after 1603, often acquiring land at the expense of the MacDonnells, and were at first regarded as a loyal bulwark against the Catholic Irish, although Wentworth in particular was suspicious of their Calvinist and Presbyterian religious leanings. In the 1630s the religious atmosphere in Ulster remained freer than in Scotland and some radical ministers went into exile there after opposing religious developments in Scotland. The rising against Charles in Scotland transformed the Ulster Scots in English eyes from loyal allies against the Irish into a subversive fifth column, with consequences to be discussed below.

The Background to Revolt in Scotland and Ireland

Examination of the more precise interconnections between developments in Scotland, Ireland and England from the late 1630s must be based on some discussion of the origins of discontent in Scotland and Ireland. On his first visit to Scotland as king in 1633 Charles I insisted on the ratification of all previously passed religious measures (such as the Articles of Perth) by the Scottish Parliament.[27] In the following year Lord Balmerino was sentenced to death when he was discovered with a copy of a 'Supplication' of grievances drawn up at that Parliament. The sentence was not carried out but Charles had amply signalled his determination to transform the Scottish church on an English model. It was typical of Charles that this Parliament was the first of his reign; in contrast the Scots Parliament met seven times between James VI's inheritance of the English crown and his death in 1625. Charles's policy towards the Scottish landed classes was equally maladroit. The Scottish aristocracy recovered in the early seventeenth century from serious economic difficulties experienced during the sixteenth century inflation, but heavy taxation and trade depression threatened this recovery in the 1620s. Charles intensified aristocratic insecurities: he cut back on court patronage and distributed what remained to a narrow clique; and he engaged on a wide-ranging programme for the 'Revocation' of all grants of church and crown lands made since 1540, which affected up to half the landed income of Scotland. The king did not intend to seize these lands for himself, but to improve the tithe (or 'teind') income of the church, and remove the feudal authority of lay lords over ex-church lands. Most of the grants were simply to be confirmed, and compensation was paid for any losses. In a stance typical of Charles, however, he insisted that landowners declare their willingness to surrender their lands to the crown simply as an acknowledgement that he had the power to demand this.

Nobles, lairds (the gentry), ministers and indeed a broad range of Scottish society became increasingly outraged about religious developments. In 1636 a new Book of Canons was introduced in Scotland; it was modelled on the English Canons of 1604, ominously made no reference to Presbyteries and promised or threatened a new Scottish prayer book. Charles thus gave his opponents time to plan resistance: since 1633 discontented elements centred especially around ministers like Alexander Henderson, David Dickson and Samuel Rutherford, had been meeting to coordinate their views. The king did not take the same opportunities to prepare his government for the enforcement of his policy or even to secure his ministers' support: his Lord Treasurer, the Earl of Traquair, was certainly no friend to the bishops, and through fear or perhaps a more sinister double dealing, did not let Charles know of the mounting resentment at his religious policies. On 16 July 1637 the Bishop of Edinburgh ordered that the new prayer book, prepared by Laud and a group of Scottish bishops, be used in all the city's churches on the following Sunday. On that day there were well organised demonstrations (presented as spontaneous outbursts) at the services, with a major riot at the principal church, St Giles', in the presence of the judges, the Privy Council and most of the Scottish episcopate.

The situation rapidly escalated as the Council prevaricated; Charles sent angry orders from London and an opposition movement was mobilised – against the prayer book at first, but soon a challenge to the Canons and to episcopacy itself emerged. Committees known as the 'Tables', consisting of all the nobility and representatives of the ministers, the lairds and burgesses from burghs eligible to send members to parliaments, organised the petitions and responses to Charles in the winter of 1637–8. At the end of February 1638 a national Covenant for the defence of the true religion, drawn up by Henderson and an influential lawyer, Archibald Johnston of Warriston, was endorsed by the leaders of the opposition movement and subsequently carried round Scotland to be signed by all men admitted to the sacrament, as symbol of, and means of effecting a great national crusade. The Scots drew on a religious covenant of 1581 for precedent, but that had been a covenant between individuals and God; in 1638 the signatories were bound also to each other and all were bound to God. It was 'a public Covenant of the collective body of the kingdom with God and the king'.

Gradually the Covenanters took over the government of Scotland while Charles first did nothing, and then granted insincere concessions, including the withdrawal of the prayer book and a meeting of Parliament and the General Assembly of the church. In private he complained, 'so long as this Covenant is in force ... I have no more power in Scotland than as a Duke of Venice; which I will rather die than suffer'; and military preparations were begun by both sides. In November 1638 the General Assembly, although repudiated by Charles, proceeded to abolish episcopacy, and establish a full presbyterian system of government of the church by synods. Minor royalist resistance was crushed by the Covenanters in Scotland while Charles's preparations in England were hampered by obstructions in the localities, and defiance from Lords Saye and Sele and Brooke. Inconclusive skirmishes on the border in early June 1639 were succeeded by vague negotiations at Berwick and a 'pacification' that both sides regarded as temporary. The reckoning came in August 1640: on 20 August, the day Charles left London to join his army at York, the Scots forces crossed the border; by 30 August the Scots were in Newcastle. In terms of English politics the impact of the Scots invasion was to secure the meeting and continued sitting of an English Parliament. The Scots wanted a settled, permanent peace and so insisted on a treaty sanctioned by Parliament; the Armistice agreed in October allowed the Scots army £850 per diem; and Charles's attempts to raise men and money in the summer had shown clearly that such sums could only be acquired with the guarantee of a Parliament.

The challenge to his government in Scotland prompted Charles to attempt in a variety of ways to obtain help from Ireland. His opportunities to acquire allies were created in part by Ireland's own recent history, while the often contradictory schemes undertaken by the king and his Lord Deputy, the energetic Thomas Lord Wentworth, had in turn their own ominous impact on Irish and British developments.[28] The centuries-old lordship of the English crown over Ireland had been transformed under Tudor and Stuart monarchs into a more direct and intensive legal, administrative, and economic domination. This process inevitably had drastic implications for the two major groups inhabiting sixteenth century Ireland: the 'mere' or Gaelic Irish, and the 'Old English', the descendants of the early Anglo-Norman lords who had settled in the area around Dublin known as the 'Pale' to which direct English authority had hitherto been confined. The Irish were Catholic, and the failure of the Protestant reformation in Ireland had intensified the feeling in England that the Irish were an alien and uncivilised people. The Old English were more ambiguous in their religious affiliations, although they were mainly Catholic;

their defining characteristic was acceptance of the authority of the English crown and a confidence that they were part of the governing class in Ireland. The distinction between the Irish and the Old English was not a clear-cut ethnic division; those who refused assimilation into the English system of rule were overwhelmingly Gaelic, but some of those who were 'Old English' in political terms came from 'Irish' families. A further complication, mentioned already, was the presence of old Catholic Scots settlers who retained links with fellow clansmen from the Scottish islands and mainland. In 1603 the rising by the Gaelic Irish of Ulster was finally defeated; the political power of local lords was broken and the province was subject to the English law and the English crown; Gaelic legal traditions of inheritance and landholding were eliminated. The Old English regarded themselves as amongst the victors of 1603, but important elements amongst the English ruling elite regarded convinced Protestantism as essential to political reliability, and the period from 1603 to 1641 saw a traumatic process whereby these Old English came for the first time to realise they held interests in common with the despised Irish.

'New English' settlement by Protestant adventurers and officials became significant in the sixteenth century; the most successful or rapacious colonist was Richard Boyle, the second son of a Kentish yeoman who arrived in Ireland as a twenty-two year old in 1588. Through exploiting the offices he held in the colonial administration, and manipulation of the legal uncertainties surrounding Irish landholding, he acquired estates worth £20,000 per annum, and the earldom of Cork by the 1630s. He kept most of his fortune despite Wentworth's determined investigations into his corruption. The English regime's initial response to the victory of 1603 was a policy of 'acculturation', attempting to 'civilise' the Irish by outlawing their own cultural and legal traditions, and promoting Protestantism. In 1607 the earls of Tyrone and Tyrconnell, the leaders of the Ulster Irish, fled in despair to the continent; their extensive estates were forfeit and the government switched to a thoroughgoing policy of plantation, settlement of Ulster by loyal, hardworking Protestant Scots and English. Very few Irish landholders could present a legal title to their lands satisfactory to English law, and by the 1630s Protestants owned about a third of Irish land and the new settlers included some 13,000 adult men, half English and half Scots. Most of the occupiers of the Ulster estates were still Irish, however, although the intention had been to clear the planted areas of Irish and bring in new tenants. It proved easier and cheaper to exploit the existing tenantry, and this illegal situation was accepted and legitimised by the government in 1634.

The religious policies of the English government were less straightforwardly punitive. There were intermittent campaigns against Catholicism after 1603, but Wentworth in particular deemed it expedient to allow Irish Catholics to practise their religion. In politics the Old English were alarmed at the increasing Protestant element in the Irish Parliament after the incorporation of new boroughs in 1613, but the European wars of the 1620s highlighted the importance of Ireland to English security, and the Old English used their bargaining strength to put the concessions known as the 'Graces' on the negotiating agenda. To the staunchly Calvinist bishops of the Irish church the government's proposed leniency over such matters as Catholic office-holding and property rights was to 'set religion to sale', while the fact that the graces were not yet implemented remained an Old English grievance when Wentworth arrived to take up his position as Lord Deputy in July 1633.

Wentworth's aim was to create a financially stable and well ordered Ireland that would serve as a model for England and perhaps make practical contributions to England's own revenue. The actual result of Wentworth's regime was an Ireland where almost no one outside his own immediate circle was a committed supporter of the government. Initially Wentworth allied with the Old English, using their support in the 1634 Parliament to obtain additional subsidies and customs revenue, against the opposition of the New English who argued that effective execution of the penal laws against Catholics would raise sufficient revenue. Once the revenue had been voted, however, Wentworth broke with the Old English and with Protestant backing the crucial Graces were not given legislative backing. As mentioned before, this alliance with the New English was equally short-lived as Wentworth's Arminian religious policy alarmed Protestant opinion, especially as it was combined with a campaign to recover former church property from laymen. He alienated most of the New English governing elite by a no doubt justified attack on the corruption of men such as Cork, and contrived a remarkable unity amongst New and Old English groups through attacks on property rights. In Wentworth's proposals for the plantation of Connacht he refused any concessions over Old English property in Galway but initiated the unprecedented and horrifying policy of treating them exactly as he treated the 'mere' Irish. When a jury refused to validate the royal title to Old English estates in Galway, Wentworth imprisoned them for their impertinence along with the sheriff who had appointed such unsuitable men. A further insight into Wentworth's views of politics is found in his comment on the lobbying at the English court of prominent Old English figures like the Earl of Clanricard. Wentworth had no time for this 'unbecoming way of remonstrating and negotiating their grievances' which was more suitable to a republic than a monarchy.

The new settlers were also made painfully aware of the insecurity of their property rights under Wentworth's rule. In 1635 the City of London was fined £70,000 and forced to surrender its patent to colonise Derry because of various infringements of the original agreement with the government. In the process the land titles of all the settlers of Derry became void; they were made subject to commissioners who managed their estates and threatened to impose a much higher rent level. The leader of these aggrieved settlers, Sir John Clotworthy, was an associate of John Pym, and unsurprisingly was to be prominent amongst the opponents of Wentworth in the early months of the Long Parliament. The complex recent history of landholding in Ireland meant that very few people could prove a clear-cut title to their estates, and consequently Wentworth could use investigatory commissions and other legal organs of the state to harass all landowners for the government's profit. Such measures had long been used against the 'mere' Irish with the enthusiastic endorsement of New English opinion, but Wentworth's extension of this approach to other groups was a thoroughly alarming novelty to Old English and new settlers alike.

The Three Kingdoms 1638–1643

The Scottish challenge to Charles I, particularly from the signing of the Covenant and the commencement of military preparations in the spring and summer of 1638, had a major and complex impact on Charles's other kingdoms. More discussion of England itself will be found in chapter 4; here it is necessary to discuss the Irish and Scottish influences on England and on the British situation in general, and to elaborate further on the British context for events in each individual kingdom.[29] The demands of clear analysis require that very closely interconnected matters are unravelled; it must be emphasised that the reality was more complicated than the discussion can be. The various groups in Ireland were particularly aware of the British background to their situation; in a clearly subordinate kingdom they were most aware of the impact developments in the other kingdoms could have. The Ulster Scots, as described above, were in the most sensitive situation. Most of them had been opposed to Wentworth's Arminian religious policy, and were enthusiastic about the new Scottish reformation of their church. To Wentworth the Scots in Ireland were dangerous subversives; by 1639 he had stationed 1500 troops in Ulster to watch over them, and imposed an oath requiring them to renounce the Covenant or to leave Ulster. Many went into hiding to avoid this 'Black Oath', and it was the later boast of staunch Protestants that it was those who fled their estates for conscience sake, who avoided the worst suffering in the 1641 Irish rising. The imposition of this 'Black Oath' was to be stressed in 1640–1 by the Scots commissioners who called for punishment of the Lord Deputy.

Wentworth's broader aim was still to use Ireland to back up Charles's power in the whole of Britain. He hoped his dominant position would ensure an Irish Parliament in March 1640 that would set a good example to the forthcoming English Parliament, and raise the men and money for an army to defeat the Scots. The Parliament dutifully did what was required but when Wentworth, now Earl of Strafford, returned to England to advise the king, Catholic and Protestant opposition to the collection of the subsidies delayed the raising of an Irish army so that it was not ready to face the Scottish invasion in the summer. To Strafford's dismay, Charles was apparently engaged from 1638 in obscure intrigues with the Earl of Antrim to use the Irish MacDonnells against the Covenanters with the restoration of former MacDonald land now in Campbell hands as a reward for their aid. These plans came to nothing, and may never have amounted to much, but suspicions of such plans were amongst the factors that propelled the new Earl of Argyll into support for the Covenanting cause late in 1638 although the undoubted religious zeal of the eighth Earl was at least as important. The possibility of an invasion from Ireland thus gave Argyll an excuse to drive the MacDonalds from their last strongholds in the Hebrides in June 1639. By 1640 Argyll was ready to invade Ireland if Strafford's Irish army, composed mainly of Catholics, had supported Charles against the Scots. The Irish and both the Old and New English were more indirectly affected by the success of the Scots; the weakness of the monarchy emboldened all into hoping for some redress of their own grievances although Catholics obviously gave no support to the Scots' particular demands. The New English and, for the time being, Old English elements also, looked to an English Parliament to deal with the hated figure of Strafford.

The position of the English Parliament that met in November 1640 was secured by the Scots army in the north; but there is a great deal more to say about the interrelationships of events in Scotland and England. There had been mutual encouragement between English and Scottish opposition groups from the mid 1630s. The Scots began their resistance to Charles's religious policies in the confidence that they had support in England while English opposition was emboldened by the Scots' success. In February 1637, Eleazar Borthwick, the London agent of the Scots opposition group, returned to Scotland with encouragement from English groups; throughout their struggles with the king the Covenanters directed carefully considered propaganda towards the godly in England. They asked that their case be put to an English Parliament, and stressed the common interests of the two kingdoms in promoting true religion. Scots propaganda circulated widely in England. The Scots, writes Stevenson, had 'a poor and provincial nobility' but their clergy were generally better educated and better paid than their English counterparts, and there was a great nostalgia for the sixteenth century when the Scottish church was the 'best reformed church in the world'. The reformation of the church could not therefore be confined to Scotland; it was the Scots' duty to promote true religion in the whole of Britain. Thus in the Glasgow General Assembly of November 1638 episcopacy was declared unlawful, that is unacceptable everywhere, and not simply inconvenient for the Scots (which was a perfectly respectable reformed Protestant opinion). The Scots' determination to generalise the religious struggle was of course a fundamental challenge to the powers of Charles in his other kingdoms, and made it even more imperative, in Charles's view, that the Scots be crushed. Furthermore, the Covenanters' rising was for Charles clear proof of his belief in the subversive implications of 'Puritan' religion; this inevitably affected his attitude to opposition in England.

The increasingly radical demands made by the Scots in civil matters were equally dangerous to Charles. The king prorogued the Parliament that met at Edinburgh under the terms of the pacification of Berwick because he could not control it, but before it rose in November 1639, the Covenanters won the right to appoint a committee to sit and deal with business in the interim. This 'Committee of Estates' consisted of 12 each of nobles, lairds and burgesses and was, as Russell has pointed out, the first example of parliamentary government in the British Isles. It governed Scotland between 1639 and 1640; organised the Second Bishops' War; and was the model for the recess committee of the English Parliament set up in the summer of 1641. The Scots lacked a parliamentary tradition comparable to the English: it was in church government and the powers of the General Assembly that they took most pride, but in 1639–40 dramatic changes took place in the composition and aspirations of the Scots Parliament which again had an influence on England. Traditionally the general body of the Parliament was controlled by the 'Lords of the Articles', a committee which included representatives of the officers of state, the bishops, the nobility and the representatives of the shires and burghs. Through the complicated process by which these representatives were chosen, it was usually possible for the king to keep a tight rein on Parliament's deliberations. In 1639, and especially in June 1640 when the Scots Parliament reconvened on its own initiative despite Charles's prorogation, royal control was broken. It was declared that the Scottish estates consisted of the nobility, and the representatives of the shires and burghs; the bishops and the officers of state were not part of a parliament, and thus the principal supporters of the royal government were removed. The members of the Lords of the Articles were to be chosen directly by each estate, while the powers of this committee were drastically curtailed by the decision that all issues were to be aired in a full parliament.

The Scots further declared that parliaments should meet every three years, and began to claim that officers of state should be chosen with Parliament's approval. This last claim was granted by Charles with great reluctance in September 1641; in an attempt to prevent his concession having implications for England the king stressed that it was necessary in Scotland because there he was an absentee monarch who was not fully acquainted with the candidates for high office. Stevenson argues that the radicalisation of the Scottish demands was mainly a pragmatic response to circumstance – particularly the need to defend their gains against an untrustworthy monarch. Their knowledge of English parliamentary traditions may also have been important, although Russell suggests that the influences ran in the other direction in the 1640s: many of the Long Parliament's demands were stimulated by the Scots example. The views of church government, derived from Andrew Melville, in which power was derived from the whole membership rather than from a divinely ordained hierarchy, also played a crucial role, for if the king had no power of veto in church affairs it was easier to challenge his secular authority.

Within a week of the Scots taking Newcastle twelve English peers petitioned Charles for a meeting of Parliament and the redress of religious and secular grievances. This Remonstrance had been under discussion for several months, and clearly shows the stimulus to the English opposition given by the Scots' success. The English Parliament that met in November had its powers massively enhanced by the Scottish invasion, and the responsibility given to it to settle with the Scots. Indeed the Scots commissioners refused to allow Charles even to be present at negotiations, a humiliation that could not fail to influence his English opponents. The presence of these Scots commissioners and preachers in London for the treaty ensured that there were very direct contacts between the two opposition movements, especially as the English negotiators included men with long-standing links with the Scots, among them several peers who had written vaguely but perhaps treasonably to encourage the Scots invasion in July 1640. The Triennial Act, the Protestation Oath, the Recess Committee, and attempts to obtain parliamentary approval of the great officers may all have owed something to the Scots example. The close relationship between the Scots nego-tiators and the English Parliament was not without its tensions. In February 1641 a supposedly private declaration drawn up for the Scots commissioners by Henderson found its way into print, to royal fury and parliamentary resentment. This attacked 'prelacy' and called for justice on Strafford whose Irish policies threatened the security of the new Scottish regime and the safety of Scottish Protestants in Ulster. Serious divisions over the Scots intensified in the English Parliament where there was already some resentment that the Scottish occupying forces were better supplied than the forlorn English army. Although Pym and other leaders managed to head off any direct condemnation of Scottish meddling, the Scots thought it wise to issue a hasty statement denying any wish to interfere in English affairs.

Strafford's policy in the 1630s had shown a consistent aware-ness of the British dimension of his master's rule; in 1640–1, the downfall of this hated British politician was thus the product of a British campaign. The Irish were more directly concerned than the Scots. In the first week of the Parliament's sitting, Sir John Clotworthy, the settlers' leader, attacked the Lord Deputy and the Catholic army he had raised in Ireland. A committee of thirteen, including Catholics and Protestants, was sent from the Irish Parliament to deliver evidence against Strafford and pursue general grievances. This was a fragile alliance; the committee's members included a future 1641 rebel, and a future regicide and colonel in the New Model Army. It seems that the Catholic Old English later regretted encouraging the English Parliament to interfere in Irish matters. It was through royal favour, rather than the Parliament, that they could expect to improve their position. The expenses of Strafford's army, and the examples of Scotland and England, increased the pretensions of the Irish Parliament in turn, while Charles's weakness in his other two kingdoms prompted concessions to the Old English. Thus the Galway plantation was abandoned and in April 1641 Charles finally confirmed the 'Graces' whose implementation would have ended the policy of Protestant plantation. Although Poynings Law was not repealed, the Irish Parliament was given greater powers. Within three months, however, Charles once more delayed the implementation of the Graces; he probably realised the concessions would greatly lessen royal revenue in Ireland, although publicly he declared he was acting on the request of the English House of Lords.

The hopes of the Catholic Irish was thus raised, and then dashed. By the end of 1641 the worst nightmare of English Protestants, an Irish Catholic rising, had occurred and the Old English, for the first time, had joined the 'rebels'. More serious for Charles was the fact that the Irish claimed to be acting under his orders; and worst of all for the king was the fact that his own religious policies, and suspicion of his intrigues with Antrim and others since 1638 made this claim very plausible in England and Scotland. It might be thought that the sufferings of the Gaelic Irish since 1603 were sufficient to cause a rising against the English, but to explain the precise timing and nature of the events of 1641 it is again necessary to reflect on the British context. Stevenson puts many of the issues succinctly:

> The success of the Scots in the Bishops' wars had simultaneously inspired the Irish to revolt, created circumstances in which they could hope revolt could be successful, and made their revolt necessary.

The Scots proved an encouragement to the English Parliament, while Irish Catholics too could see the concessions the Scots had won from Charles and hope for similar gains if they themselves resorted to force. The Gaelic Irish of Ulster had been hit very hard by the plantations but they had not been driven out of the province, and from early 1641 they were plotting a rising. The king's weakness in Scotland and England, and the execution of the once all-powerful Strafford, increased their resolve. The success of the staunch Protestant opposition in Charles's other two kingdoms was in most respects very ominous for the Catholic Irish, however. As later chapters will show at greater length, anti-popery was amongst the defining characteristics of the opposition to Charles in Britain as a whole. The Scots desire for a reformation that would bring all of Charles's kingdoms into line with the Scottish church was potentially disastrous for Irish Catholics while the English Parliament discussed crusades that would extirpate popery in the British Isles. In March 1642 the Catholic clergy of Armagh declared the rising a just war, and excommunicated those Catholics who had not yet joined it. It was a war against the 'Puritans' who 'have always, but especially in recent years, plotted the destruction of the Catholics, the destruction of the Irish, and the abolition of the King's prerogatives'.

The king's own role in stimulating the rising is still debated by historians. One of the accusations of the Long Parliament against Strafford was that the army he had raised in the spring of 1640 had been intended to subdue England, rather than Scotland. This was not initially the case, but as his position in England worsened Charles may indeed have wanted to call this army to his aid. The Irish army was formally disbanded in May 1641, the month of its creator's execution, but it was not completely dispersed as there were plans for the troops to join the service of the king of Spain. Charles, through the Earl of Ormonde and the inevitable Antrim, perhaps wished to use it against the English Parliament or the Covenanters. Most of Charles's intrigues were aimed at the Old English, but Antrim, the grandson of the 'great' Earl of Tyrone, had extensive Irish connections in addition to his own leadership of the

MacDonnells, and some of this meddling may have encouraged the delusion that the king would welcome a rising by the 'mere' Irish. Men and officers of Strafford's army did play an important part in the Ulster rising but the complete background to this involvement will probably never be known.

The Ulster rising began on 23 October 1641 and within two days much of central Ulster was under Irish control although a plan for the simultaneous seizure of Dublin had been betrayed on 22 October. The momentum of the Irish soon slackened but not before there had been slaughter of the Protestant settlers, atrocities which were enormously magnified in the propagandist accounts of the London press. The Old English at first remained aloof and some participated in the condemnation of the revolt by the Irish Parliament, but many joined the rising at the end of 1641 as the insurgents moved south. The motives of the Old English were many, and included their perceptions of the broader British situation. They believed, or could convince themselves, that it was a rising sanctioned by Charles and intended to strengthen his position; consequently they were not abandoning their traditional stance of loyalty to the English crown. Like the Irish they had every reason to fear that a Britain dominated by Scots Presbyterians and English Puritans would endanger their religion and their estates. Finally, they greatly resented the claims of the English Parliament to authority in Irish affairs, particularly as English pressure had again lost them the confirmation of the Graces.

The Irish rebellion intensified the political crisis in England, as will be indicated in chapter 4. Charles himself heard the news of the Irish rising in Edinburgh, having journeyed to Scotland in the summer of 1641 in another attempt to win support. The king's projected visit to Scotland had caused great alarm amongst English politicians, still digesting the revelations that men close to Charles had planned to use the English army to save Strafford and coerce the parliament. The king's journey would take him through the two armies, English and Scots, which still waited idly on the border for disbandment. Consequently, the treaty with the Scots was rapidly completed so that the soldiers could be soon dispersed. Charles arrived in

Edinburgh on 14 August, by which time the Scots Parliament had ratified the peace treaty and the Scots army finally left Newcastle on 21 August, almost a year after they had taken the city. Charles's precise intentions concerning Scotland are unclear, and were very probably contradictory as usual. It is perhaps unsurprising therefore that modern historians have differed in their assessment of the king's aims and his success in achieving them. Russell suggests that by September 1641, Charles had succeeded in breaking the alliance between the Covenanters and the English Parliament, and had obtained a promise of non-intervention in England from Argyll. However, there were also some murky plots, against Argyll and Charles's ambiguous adviser Hamilton, by men close to the king and in touch with enemies of the Covenanters such as Montrose. The half-baked intrigue was inevitably betrayed and the 'Incident', as it became known, was added to the Army Plots in England as examples of the perfidy of Charles's intimates and perhaps of the king's own dishonesty. Stevenson puts less emphasis on Charles's attempts to mobilise anti-Covenanter elements in Scotland, but he also argues that the king's rapprochement with the Covenanters was extremely superficial. Charles agreed to most of the Scots demands, and showered their leaders with honours and offices, but the Covenanters knew that if Charles did recover his authority in England their own position would be perilous. Both historians agree that Charles's proceedings were confused and contradictory.[30]

What is certain is that the Irish rebellion had a disruptive impact on the political situation in Scotland as it did in England. Charles immediately asked the Scots Parliament for aid against the Irish rebels but the response was cautious, partly for fear of offending the English Parliament, 'the kingdom of Ireland being dependent upon the crown and kingdom of England' which was thus 'first and most properly concerned'. The Covenanting leadership also had serious doubts about Charles's own position, and whatever had been settled in September, the Irish rising made any longlasting amity between themselves and the king improbable. To Argyll and the other Scots leaders the rumours of Charles's complicity in the rising were easily believed for they were aware of the king's intrigues against them from 1638. The Scots were intimately concerned with events in Ireland. Not only were their co-religionists and fellow-Scots in Ulster amongst the targets of the rising; it was even possible that the Irish Catholics would be so successful that the nightmare of an Irish invasion of Scotland might occur, with particular dangers for Argyll's Campbells. Thus the Scots offered the English Parliament help in suppressing the rising, and although some English MPs regarded the need for Scottish help as a reflection on their honour (and feared Charles might make use of a new Scottish army) there was little alternative. By April 1642 a 'New Scots' army had landed in Ireland where it formed a major barrier to Irish success until the English could themselves deal with the Irish.

When examining the origins of the English civil war in isolation, 1642 is the natural and obvious date at which to finish. In a British context, it makes more sense to continue the narrative to the end of 1643 by which time the impact of Ireland and Scotland on the English war was clarified. In September 1643 a cessation of arms was agreed in Ireland with the New English forces commanded by Ormonde under the authority of the king. This freed elements in Ormonde's army for service in England although it did not lead to floods of Irish Catholic troops joining the King as anti-papal hysteria had predicted. Charles did continue to hope for Irish help, and negotiations with the Confederation of Kilkenny, the organisation of the Irish, rambled on without coming to a final settlement before the king's execution. As ever Ireland and Scotland were closely connected. In November 1642 the English Parliament had asked for Scots aid, but the Covenanters were divided with a royalist element gathering around Hamilton. Argyll and his pro-parliament wing became sure of success, however, when Antrim was briefly captured in May 1643 carrying compromising letters which revealed yet more royal intrigues to bring Irish Catholics and Catholic and royalist Scots to Charles's aid in England. In May 1643 also the Scots summoned an informal parliament, the Convention of Estates, which by August had negotiated the 'Solemn League and Covenant' as a seal of the alliance with the

English Parliament. In January 1644 the Scottish army crossed the border. This particular configuration of alliances was not necessarily inevitable. The Scots were divided over the English civil war, while in Ireland divisions amongst the Protestant settlers were very complex. The parliamentarian supporters amongst the New English were not expelled from Dublin until 1643, and the New English fought initially under Charles's authority mainly because he seemed the most likely victor in England in the early months of the war, and thus most likely to bring help to beleaguered Protestants in Ireland. Nonetheless developments in the British monarchy since 1603 suggest that the pattern that emerged in 1643 was the most natural and likely result.

Russell's examination of the British context to the English civil war has led him to stress Charles's own responsibility for the conflict: the king's policies, and his means of enforcing them, 'invited resistance'. It has also underlined his earlier view that the divisions in England were not the product of any long-term, serious, ideological or social divisions. England, argues Russell, was the most resilient and least revolutionary of Charles's kingdoms. It was only after five years of British crisis in Scotland and Ireland that England moved reluctantly towards civil war. The Scots, with a stronger tradition of resistance from the sixteenth century and their Melvillian theory of church government, were the ones who broke the taboo of active resistance to the monarchy in 1638–9, and were a vital influence on both English and Irish opposition to the crown. The English civil war was more serious than the Scottish because it was in England that Charles won the greatest support, and so the sides were more evenly matched. In Scotland, in contrast, no convincing challenge to the Covenanters was mounted until the campaigns of Montrose in 1644–5.

In the next two chapters English ideological and social developments will be discussed in their own right, and it will be argued that Russell's account needs modification. Here it is worth noting the irony that Russell, coming to Scottish history from an English point of view, gives the Scots more credit for initiating British developments than does David Stevenson, the specialist historian of Scotland. Stevenson emphasises Scottish hesitation, the pragmatic reasons for their increasingly radical positions, and their desire for the security of English support. It is usually the case that there are English precedents for some of the moves which paralleled Scots initiatives; regular parliaments is one demand with respectable medieval origins. Oaths of Association which were also loyalty tests were a feature of all British resistance movements, and the Scots National Covenant was obviously a major influence on the English Protestation of May 1641, on which in turn the Confederation of Kilkenny modelled their oath. For England, though, there was also the example of the Bond of Association, a manifestation of loyalty to Elizabeth in the dangerous days of 1584. Another Scottish historian, Keith Brown, has recently challenged the common sharp contrast made between James and Charles as good and bad British monarchs. Brown argues that James shelved problems, he did not solve them. 'What made Charles I so dangerous', then 'was that he clumsily touched already very raw nerves'. Furthermore, the 'British' context, or at least the Anglo-Scottish dimension of it, had deeper roots than the union of the crowns or the short-term cooperation of wily politicians in the late 1630s. There had been cooperation, albeit sometimes tense, between lay and clerical Protestant elites in the two kingdoms ever since the accession of Elizabeth to the throne of England in 1559 had secured the reformation in Scotland also.[31]

More generally and more positively it is clear that an interpretation of the English civil war which ignores Charles's other two kingdoms is no longer satisfactory. Historians of England have too complacently assumed that the important initiatives in resisting the king must have come from the now-dominant element of the British Isles. The earlier and successful resistance of the Scots, and many of their specific measures and theoretical positions were clearly important to later developments in England. Looking at the 'British problem' as a whole does produce closer parallels with European developments than were found with the English civil war specifically. Nonetheless European comparisons still suggest as many differences as similarities. The burdens of war were not important triggers of revolt in

Scotland, in sharp contrast to events in France or Spain. The multiple conflicts in Britain were different in crucial respects from contemporary events in the Spanish monarchy. As Russell has stressed, religious commitment was vital to the complicated alliances and influences, and nowhere else in Europe had the reformation and counter-reformation had such a complex impact. Shared religious commitment was the basis for the remarkable degree of unity between the English and Scottish oppositions to Charles, unity which was not matched or aspired to in the Spanish monarchy, where the revolts remained isolated from each other. Unlike the Catalans or Portuguese, the Scots did not want secession or independence from England, but greater unity and uniformity. As Charles especially, but also James, had wanted to anglicise Scotland, the Scots wanted England to become like Scotland. They wanted 'unity' in religion to establish 'perfect amity' and 'peace for ever'; and triennial parliaments in both kingdoms so there could be regular meetings between them. Only thus could the Scots feel that their own position was secure, and that their duty to generalise their godly reformation would be fulfilled. In 1640 the Scots appealed to 'all good Christians and patriots in this isle' to 'join with united arms against the whore of Babel and her supports'. It was England, the metropolitan kingdom, which was most sceptical about closer union; again this is strange in a European context.

The Scottish minister, Robert Baillie, dreamed of a 'British' army that would intervene to help Protestants in Germany but there were of course supporters of the whore of Babel much nearer at hand, in Ireland. As religious ideology brought influential elements in Scotland and England to conceive themselves as fighting a common struggle despite their divergent cultures and political traditions, so it led them to see events in Ireland as part of a world-wide struggle against the evils of popery.[32] In addition, the colonisation of Ireland by English and Scots Protestant settlers meant that events in Ireland could not be regarded coolly as occurring in an autonomous kingdom, as the Catalans could regard the Portuguese. It is taken for granted that Charles's opponents in Scotland and England were committed to the suppression of the Irish rising but it is remarkable in a

European perspective where rebels were more likely to see parallel risings as additional blows to a ruler's position which they could exploit. It is not enough to look at bare structures of government; the political and religious ideas which people brought to their understanding of the processes of government are also vital. The next chapter will examine these issues in the English context.

2

HIERARCHY, CONSENSUS OR CONFLICT: POLITICS AND RELIGION IN EARLY STUART ENGLAND

Laurence Stone's *Causes of the English Revolution*, published almost twenty years ago, provided a summation of the best existing work on the period as well as providing its own subtle and intellectually dazzling contribution. Stone's book indicated very aptly the broad thinking of historians on the role of political and religious division in bringing England to civil war. The 'Rise of opposition', 'New ideas and values' are amongst his section headings; he writes of Puritanism creating 'a burning sense of the need for change in the Church and eventually in the State'. Intensifying religious and political divisions were exacerbated by the prevailing atmosphere of insecurity: social mobility amongst elites and the vulnerability of poorer groups wrenched men away from 'familiar associations and surroundings'.[1] Since the publication of this book almost all of its presuppositions and many of its conclusions have been subject to searching and wide-ranging criticisms, as this and the following chapter will show. In the place of a polarised society and politics, many historians have presented England as a deeply hierarchical and deferential society with political practices and attitudes to match. The role of the monarch, the peers and the court have all been stressed in recent work.[2] It has been argued, by Mark Kishlansky, that the political process was marked above all else by a hatred of division and a desire to preserve harmony and consensus; Kevin Sharpe and Conrad Russell have denied that there were sharp, long-term divisions over political principle in the early seventeenth century; Russell has questioned the validity of the term 'opposition'. And, as demonstrated in chapter 1, it is the monarchy that has often been credited with the adoption of new ideas and values and those who obstructed Charles I seen as conservative.[3] There has been much debate about the nature, or even the existence of something called 'Puritanism'. For some commentators Puritanism has disappeared into a broader Protestant consensus, united by Calvinist theology and staunch opposition to popery; its social and political implications have been linked to a concern for hierarchy and order, rather than to any burning zeal for change. Any opposition Puritanism provided was a conservative and defensive reflex to the pressure of a novel and fashionable Arminianism. For others, however, Puritans are a small band of unpopular zealots whose political role and religious influence is negative until the breakdown of 1639–40.[4]

This chapter will examine the specific political and religious issues which exercised the politically active in early seventeenth century England but it is important also to discuss more generally the context and nature of politics in this period, in the light of current disagreements among historians. Who made up the 'political nation'; who participated in political activity; whose views needed to be taken into account? What were the general assumptions and ideas about how the political process should operate; the frameworks within which people experienced and understood day to day issues? These complex but important elements are usually summed up as the political culture of a society.

Politics and Social Hierarchy

Historians often use Sir Thomas Smith's comments on hierarchy in sixteenth century England as an insight into the nature of the political process:

the fourth sort of men which doth not rule ... day labourers, poor husbandmen, yea merchants or retailers, which have no free land, copyholders, all artificers as tailors, shoemakers, carpenters, brick makers, bricklayers, masons etc. These have no voice nor authority in our commonwealth, and no account is made of them, but only to be ruled and not to rule other.[5]

Politics is seen as working from the top down and only a minority had any influence. It was the monarch and his closest associates, the titled aristocrats, or at most the landed elite as a whole who really mattered. Indeed, it is a misnomer, an oversimplification, to speak of 'political life' at all, for 'politics' was not a clearly separate sphere of activity; authority and government were part of the social world or the natural order. The right to rule came from personal, inherited social position – from being the heir to the throne, or the owner of a landed estate. The exercise of government was not a right earned through abstract, specialised characteristics such as particular political skills or opinions. People understood the political process through natural metaphors or comparisons with the body or the family. The kingdom made up a 'body politic' where the king was compared to the head that governed the other members of the body, or commonwealth, who all had their fixed, subordinate, but accepted and cooperative positions and roles, appropriate to their inherited status. Obedience to monarchs and other superiors was modelled on the 'natural' subordination of children to parents. Instructed by the catechism, a young person promised to 'love, honour and succour my father and mother: to submit myself to all my governors, teachers, spiritual pastors and teachers'. Here religion joined with nature to encourage obedience within an ordered hierarchy, while rebellion was condemned. The *Homily against Disobedience and Wilful Rebellion*, one of a series read in churches when no sermon was available, described Lucifer as the 'first author' of rebellion; anyone following his example was condemned to death and 'damnation eternal'. The general consequences of disobedience were horrendous:

Take away kings, princes, rulers, magistrates, judges, and such estates of God's order, no man shall ride or go by the highway untroubled, no man shall sleep in his own house or bed unkilled, no man shall keep his wife, children or possessions in quietness, all things shall be in common.[6]

In early modern England, then, it has been argued, there was great anxiety about order and hierarchy; while, as the *Homily* suggests, all hierarchical relationships were seen as inextricably connected. The patriarchal authority of fathers over their children and their wives, the rule of kings over their people, and the rule of God the father were all alike in nature, and each type of rule was a model for, and helped to justify, the others. A challenge to monarchy could threaten the authority of landlords and local governors, or disrupt the dominance of fathers in their families. The patriarchal model for authority was a particularly effective guarantee of political and social stability, for men of all social classes were inevitably sensitive about threats to their authority in the household. In general, it is suggested that hierarchy and obedience were sanctioned by nature and God, by custom and tradition, while the frameworks of thinking about politics left little room for the development of justified challenges to authority.

At the head of this social and political system was the monarch and access to his person at court was the best way of acquiring personal profit and political influence. A good king ruled with the advice of the great noblemen of the kingdom and met periodically with parliaments. For the most part historians, especially from within the 'Whig' tradition, have concentrated on the activities of the Commons but more recently, as part of the renewed emphasis on hierarchy in the political process, attention has been drawn to the importance of the peerage as a social and political elite. Again we see a startling shift of historical interpretation over the last twenty years: where Laurence Stone argued that the decades before the civil war witnessed a crisis of the aristocracy – a shaking of their military, economic and political power – one leading young historian of the 1980s regards the civil war itself as a baronial war. Clearly the peers dominated as 'politicians' at the king's court and in his Council but it is now argued that they also dominated, less directly, the House of Commons and provincial political life. After the crown, the peers were the major source of patronage and protection, and their great houses were centres of local political authority. Peers could provide places of profit and influence in royal service or their own households; they controlled many local offices, through their own influence and that of their friends and kin, and often nominated urban representatives to Parliament; they could help speed a law suit or get a local grievance raised at court. In return their subordinates provided political support and practical expertise, through their legal and financial skills, or their promotion of particular issues and suits in the House of Commons and at county Quarter Sessions. Thus, it has been argued that prominent members of the House of Commons, independent heroes of the Whig tradition, were in fact the agents, clients and spokesmen of peers, as John Pym was for the Earl of Bedford. Until 1649 most parliamentary initiatives came from leading members of the House of Lords with the Commons in a supportive role.[7]

Similarly recent work on the electoral process has emphasised its hierarchical nature, albeit that broader local elites than the peers are seen as the crucial political actors. It had come to be widely accepted that the seventeenth century witnessed an expansion in the size of the electorate and also a significant increase in the frequency with which elections were contested so that many from the ranks below the gentry – the 'middling sort' of yeomen, small merchants, substantial craftsmen, and even some humbler men – were able to exercise political choice and influence. There has been disagreement over the degree to which this electorate had a sophisticated awareness of national political issues, but only recently has the whole nature of the system been challenged.[8] Mark Kishlansky has written of a process of parliamentary *'selection'*, arguing that 'election' conjures up too great a sense of conflict and competition. Until the mid seventeenth century, contests were extremely rare, and represented a traumatic breakdown in the normal process whereby the county gentry and urban governors selected the 'natural leaders' of their community to represent their interests in Parliament. Parliamentary selection was not a specific political means of achieving honour and status, or of pushing a particular political standpoint. Rather it reflected or confirmed the honour a man already had through his personal and social status in his community. Contests were abhorrent and shameful for defeat was a slur on a man's personal honour and standing; it was not a setback in some separate, more impersonal, political struggle. The united acclaim of one's community was what mattered: success was not worth 'the loss of a friend' declared one aspirant knight of the shire in the 1614 Somerset 'selection'.

The process of selection was controlled by the leading gentry in the counties, who aimed to make a consensual choice of two candidates who would simply be confirmed by the freeholders on election day. The electorate had no initiative, or even influence; their role was to provide a ritual affirmation of the will of the united community. This was 'assent', not consent in its modern sense. Urban selections showed greater variety, but again they reflected the local power structure so that one typical pattern was that a noble patron nominated to one place while the corporation chose one of their own number for the other. Where earlier historians highlighted competition for votes and polls of voters on election day, Kishlansky aruges that early Stuart landed elites sought at all costs to avoid a poll. In Essex in 1640, Lord Maynard protested bitterly against elections 'where fellows without shirts challenge as good a voice as mine': a poll affronted all ideas of social hierarchy by counting each man's vote as equal.

Within this framework the 'lower orders' knew and accepted their place. Kishlansky writes of the 'natural leaders' of an 'organic' society where traditional vertical links of protection and obedience operated throughout the social scale. Social and economic grievances provoked unrest in food riots or protests against enclosure, but these arose from specific discontents, not from rejection of the social hierarchy as a whole. In any case England was more stable socially than many other European states. The lower orders were not only unwilling to challenge the social and political authority of landed and urban elites, they were unable to do so. The majority of the population lived in 'stable poverty' which encouraged passivity rather than political activism. The increasing efficiency of the poor law was a further stimulus to conformity and dependency on the part of the poor. Most English people were isolated in their local communities and they were largely illiterate. In one study based on the ability of participants in ecclesiastical court proceedings to sign their names, it has been calculated that 93 per cent of husbandmen in Norfolk and Suffolk were illiterate in the 1580s, and the figures had fallen only to 86 per cent in the 1630s. In this latter period 57 per cent of tailors, and 52 per cent of weavers, were illiterate, belying to some extent the reputation of these crafts for high literacy rates. Over 90 per cent of women appearing before these courts were unable to sign their names. On illiteracy, Peter Laslett has written:

> without access to books, without usually being able to write as much as their own names, how could the husbandmen of a village where the politically active gentlemen lived be expected to develop and defend a political opinion?[9]

Much recent work thus describes a closed, hierarchical, political system, dominated by the monarch, the peers and the greater county gentry. There is much truth in this: seventeenth century English society was based on massive inequalities of wealth, power and political opportunity. In a day to day sense, as important recent work has shown, early Stuart politics was focused on the king's court, where elites took advantage of their access to the king's person. In a personal monarchy, the king's personality and style of rule were crucial. (Although it is important to remember that the links between titles and government service worked in both directions: while some men were active in government because of their titles, others only acquired titles because of their service to the monarch.) However, if the possibilities open to the political elite are looked at more generally, including the practical structures and patterns of the ideas which influenced their behaviour and policies, the picture becomes more complex. As described in chapter 1, the English state lacked a strong army and a large central bureaucracy; its activities were thus dependent on the more or less willing cooperation of men from a broad section of society who participated in local administration and law enforcement. It will be shown below that there were influential beliefs about how the political system should function which did give a major role to the House of Commons, and which resisted any moves to control the Commons by the monarch or the peerage.

The 'Political Nation'

The view of the political system as closed is misleading not just because it misrepresents the nature of the relationships between Lords and Commons, peers and gentry, but also because it seriously underestimates the capacity of those below the ranks of the landed elites to influence early seventeenth century politics. There is, in fact, a great deal of recent work which challenges the framework already discussed, by showing how many humbler men had extensive experience of, and information about the English political system. We can return again to Sir Thomas Smith.[10] It is insufficiently noted that Smith included the yeomanry amongst his three sorts of men by whom the common-wealth was governed, along with the monarch and the gentry (who *included* the peers). Of yeomen he wrote: 'each of these hath his part and administration in judgements, corrections of defaults, in elections of offices, in appointing tributes and sub-sidies, and in making laws'. Smith also qualified the pessimistic remarks with which this chapter opened by pointing out that day labourers, poor husbandmen and artificers:

> be not altogether neglected. For in cities and corporate towns, for default of yeomen, inquests and juries are impanelled of such manner of people. And in villages they are commonly made churchwardens, aleconners, and many times constables which office toucheth more the commonwealth.

Law, administration and politics were intertwined in seven-teenth century England. Much political debate was centred on legal concepts such as the rule of law or the historical liberties of Englishmen. Experience of law enforcement made a crucial contribution to political consciousness; hence the broad nature of participation in the legal process had significant implications for politics.[11] 'The legal system exemplifies the participatory nature of English government in the seventeenth century', writes Herrup. Legal authority was confined to men with some property but this definition incorporated a wide range and could include up to half the adult males in some communities. In one East Sussex village 111 individuals contributed to the collection for the relief of Irish Protestants in 1642; only the very poor were excluded. Of this 111, 40, plus the fathers of 11 more, had participated in the enforcement of the law. Almost anyone could be a witness or a victim appearing before the courts; any householder could serve as a parish constable; any freeholder as a trial juror or a grand juror. Grand jurors at Quarter Sessions were frequently middling rank yeomen, rather than gentry; their role was not simply to give verdicts in individual trials, but to decide whether cases should go to trial and often to draw up presentments of a county's general problems and grievances. Village constables' difficult responsibilities brought them into contact with broad national issues, particularly through their revenue-collecting duties, while they were also charged with the enforcement of the law at village level. 'Legal decisions reflected not gentry values, but the common ground between the values of the legal elite, the gentry, and the local men of middling status'; these comments of Herrup are suggestive also for the analysis of politics in this period.

Other experiences helped form the political consciousness of those below the elite. As churchwardens, comparatively humble men were forced to reflect on the controversial religious developments of the period, and to take responsibility for local decisions on the enforcement of religious change. Experience of collective action, especially in local government, could be useful in political and social protest. Ordinary property-holders cooperated in mediating local economic and social relationships through manorial courts; they trained with the representatives of other communities in the county militias; in towns they participated in the deliberations and ceremonies of their craft guilds and trading companies, and often in the choice of urban governors. In the City of London in the mid seventeenth century some 15,000 male freeholders voted in ward elections. The habits of collective organisation in fen villages were shown both in protests against drainage projects and in more directly 'political' activities: in the Lincolnshire fens delegations were sent to Lincoln to protest against the forced loan and 'common purses' raised to support those in prison, mirroring techniques used in fighting the drainage schemes. When Derbyshire leadminers fought a long campaign against the tithes levied on their product, or London traders and apprentices thronged around Parliament in 1640–2, calling for religious reform and justice against Charles's ministers, they were drawing on habits and attitudes developed in their 'ordinary' lives.[12]

There is much evidence that the ranks below the gentry were perfectly capable of independent collective activity to redress practical grievances, attack religious enemies or defend local customs and rights. It is also true that, before the 1640s at least, most 'high political' events were initiated by members of the elite – at court, in parliaments, or in meetings of the county gentry. But elites' freedom of action was circumscribed by the involvement of a broader political nation which included the groups often described as the 'middling sort' – yeoman, small merchants, prosperous husbandmen and craftsmen – as well as humbler men. These members of the broad political nation were well-informed about political and religious issues. While some historians have suggested that even the provincial gentry were ill-informed about national developments, Richard Cust has demonstrated that there was a hunger for news amongst people from many social groups, a hunger that was satisfied in a variety of ways.[13] The gentry relied on sons at Inns of Court, or neighbours up in London on legal business to send back news from Parliament and the royal court, and gossip from St Paul's and the Exchange, for London was the 'melting pot' for news from all over England. The semi-professional newswriter who provided specialised newsletters for a provincial audience emerged by the 1620s, reflecting an increased interest in news in this troubled decade. From this period also, there is an expansion in the survival of 'separates', copies of set-piece parliamentary speeches, or legal judgements, in gentry family collections. This access to news was not confined to the prosperous gentry.

The news diary of a Suffolk clergyman, John Rous, shows that much of his information came from oral sources – rumour, or 'country intelligence' which circulated amongst his contacts from the minor gentry and yeomanry. This was not just local news, but national information very similar to that found in the written news media. Ballads and scurrilous verses dealing with national and international affairs circulated widely in alehouses and market places; these were accessible to a very wide audience, including the illiterate, and seem to have operated on a variety of levels. They included vulgar abuse, and simple stereotypes, such as that of the 'evil counsellor', which would appeal to the unsophisticated as well as obscurer, classical allusions and more detailed discussions of current debates, which presumably meant more to the educated. Some verses against Buckingham in 1627, for example, referred to specific prominent Arminians at the University of Cambridge, where the duke was Chancellor, while also attributing Buckingham's early, ignominious return from the Isle de Rhé, to the 'want of wenches'. Illiteracy in a predominantly oral culture did not imply ignorance, precisely because in such a culture the means of oral transmission of information, and the capacity to remember it, are much better developed. The mother of a London artisan, Nehemiah Wallington, was born in the 1560s, and it is most unlikely that she could read, yet her son recorded that she knew from memory, 'the stories of the martyrs', and much history from 'the English chronicles'. She thus had a simple context of religious and political history within which the public affairs of her own times could be interpreted. The religious experience of humbler people in early Stuart England was not confined to catechizing and repeated homilies, but for many included attendance at rousing, 'godly' sermons which made reference to contemporary events as part of the unfolding of God's purposes for his people, and for England.

Political Participation

There existed then a comparatively large, well-informed, experienced, 'public', capable of political action and influence. Everyone, so far as is known, agreed that politics was a matter for male heads of households (allowing for the occasional anomaly of a female monarch). There was, however, much less agreement over how many of this potentially numerous body of men should be active in politics, and in what ways. Kishlansky has identified an important set of attitudes: that political decisions were a matter for local elites, with lesser property owners having a passive, acclamatory role. At a more elevated level, Charles I himself had a similar view of politics as operating strictly from the top down, with any initiative from below threatening the anarchy of 'popularity'. Elites themselves were, however, divided over attitudes to 'popular' participation; it will be seen in chapter 3 that these divisions can be connected to differing reactions to the complex processes of social change. The differences can be illustrated from work on elections which contrasts with Kishlansky's. Some commentators argued that the individual choice and active participation of freeholders was crucial as a guard against the corruption which court dominance or popery threatened. The Puritan pamphleteer Thomas Scott lamented traditional patterns of deference: freeholders should, '(neglecting both their landlords or great neighbours or the Lord Lieutenants themselves) look upon the wisest, stoutest and most religious persons, ... for he that is religious will stand for the country's good.'

In practice attitudes were frequently muddled or compromised. A Northamptonshire gentleman, Sir John Pickering, applauded the agreement amongst the county's leaders to choose knights of the shire in 1626, but argued that the pact should be kept secret, 'lest the freeholders whose birthright it is to elect should take it ill, conceiving themselves concluded thereby'. For elements within the elite, there were considerations which overrode the deference which was normally due to social superiors. The senior Cheshire gentleman, Sir Richard Grosvenor, addressed the freeholders in the 1624 election, urging them to accept the county magistrates' choice of knights, but he emphasised that their assent was due because the men nominated were 'untaynted in their religion ... without fear to utter their country's just complaints and grievances'. If the candidates had not been godly and independent – if they had been papists, for example – then it was the freeholders' duty to reject them, to 'have their voices', and eschew deference. Grosvenor's views on how politics should work included potentially conflicting emphases, on hierarchy, but also on godliness; if the social elite failed in their duty to true religion and in their service to the commonwealth, then it was essential that a broader, politically active group existed to remind their superiors of the correct path.

There will be further discussion of the ideals that Grosvenor espoused; here they can be briefly summed up as adherence to staunch Protestant religion and opposition to popery; standing for the interests of the 'country', distinguished from those of the 'court'; support for Parliament and the rule of law against arbitrary power, unparliamentary taxation, and the monopolising of patronage by corrupt courtiers such as the Duke of Buckingham. It was not as obvious as Kishlansky suggests who the 'natural leaders' of a county were; the men regularly chosen as knights of the shire were not always from the most wealthy families or the most ancient lineages. Riches and respectable pedigrees were not sufficient; in many counties it was also necessary to be seen as a zealous Protestant, and a defender of the 'country's' liberties; such a reputation secured a regular county seat for Sir Clement Throckmorton of Warwickshire, for example, despite his comparatively lowly position in the 'pecking-order' of the county gentry. It is true that explicit, political criteria were not used in the choice of MPs; Kishlansky has made the important point that a fully fledged, specialised political realm of life did not yet exist. However, the contrast drawn in Kishlansky's work between the first half of the seventeenth century as a pre-political era, and the period after the traumas of the civil wars as a time when politics suddenly emerged, is much too stark. Abstract ideological criteria were implicit in much early seventeenth century political life: godliness, and support for the public good were seen by many as essential attributes of a true gentleman or an acceptable local leader. In other words, politics was gradually developing as a sphere distinguished from personal or social relationships.

There is evidence that in many counties, the freeholders or the broader 'political nation' did indeed support a general Protestant and 'country' position. The freeholders were not merely 'voting fodder' in elections, rubber stamping the magnates' choices, but had definite preferences of their own. This emerges most obviously in counties where there were open contests for seats. In Yorkshire, for example, the long electoral feuds between Sir Thomas Wentworth, later Earl of Strafford, and Sir John Savile were marked by extensive, but varying, appeals to religious and political principle. In the early 1620s Savile directed his campaign particularly towards the freeholders in the clothing areas around Leeds, Halifax and Wakefield, emphasising the need to combat popery and to be wary of courtiers. Wentworth preferred to rely on the gentry. As the decade wore on, however, the stances changed. Savile's credit with the 'country' waned as his close association with Buckingham became known while Wentworth's reputation waxed after his (reluctant) opposition to the forced loan. Ideological divisions in Yorkshire had not become solidified into two 'parties'; there were instead a variety of issues which could be exploited or manipulated in particular circumstances. A similarly opportunist pattern is seen in Somerset which became 'the field of battle in a struggle between ... two county giants', Sir Robert Phelips and John, Lord Poulett, which lasted a quarter of a century. The feud originated in a contested county election of 1614 but involved all organs of local government, not simply access to Parliament. Again each man appealed to a wide variety of county opinion; both claimed to represent the 'country' and the 'godly', and angrily refuted accusations of 'turning courtier'.[14]

Open feuds and contested elections provide obvious and important means of exploring differences in political attitudes. Even in the absence of contests, however, the ideological preferences of potential voters helped to structure gentry actions and initiatives. Staunch Protestants were preferred to those suspected of popish leanings; independent champions of their country's liberties were chosen before those who could be described (as one candidate was in 1628) as 'altogether a Dukeist, or Duckling ... a Buckinghamist'. Of the 42 county MPs chosen in 1628 whose attitudes to the forced loan are known, only 11 actively supported the loan, 13 abstained from its promotion, while 18 opposed or refused it. This does not imply a straightforward, consensual choice of 'natural', social leaders. County leaders' positions over the loan were a crucial test of their standing amongst the broad political nation. Twenty years later the biographer of Lord Montagu, the dominant influence in early Stuart Northamptonshire, claimed that 'his paying the loan lost him the love of the country' in contrast to Sir Nathaniel Barnardiston in Suffolk, who opposed the exaction, 'standing up for his country and the defence of the just rights and liberties thereof'. Broader popular struggles reveal a commitment to Parliament and the rule of law on the part of the 'middling sort'. In the East Anglian fens, there was most resistance to drainage schemes where the fen dwellers had most confidence in their customary rights; the least trouble occurred where the schemes were backed by parliamentary statute. The Derbyshire leadminers struggled for a decade, through the courts and through direct action, against the tithes levied on their production; when the 1624 Parliament declared the levy legal, open opposition ceased.[15]

Law, History and Political Division

One important thrust of recent work on early Stuart politics has been to emphasise its hierarchical nature, but it has been argued here instead that the activities of the landed and urban elites were influenced to a significant extent by the actions and opinions of a broader political nation of male householders who had definite opinions about religion, Parliament, taxation and the law. Some historians see the political process as both hierarchical and involving conflict. On this view, conflict comes from problems in the relationships between the monarch and the great men who made up his court and council, or aspired to do so. The civil war can even be seen in the tradition of medieval struggles between incompetent kings and their barons, as will be seen in chapter 3. Here the discussion will be focused on the work of historians who describe early Stuart politics as a hierarchical and a consensual process, dominated by the drive for unity and harmony.[16] The habits of seeing political authority as sanctioned by religion, nature and tradition, as discussed at the start of this chapter, limited the possibilities for challenge or change. In addition, it is argued, all aspects of political life were structured by a hatred of division. The object in parliamentary 'selections', according to Kishlansky, was a unified choice which represented and reinforced the solidarity of local communities under their natural leaders. Kishlansky holds that 'adversary politics', a system where division and conflict was acceptable and the aim of political actors was to achieve a majority position for their party, emerged only in the upheavals of the 1640s. Before this, parliaments, for example, sought unanimity; their procedures were not developed to facilitate opposition to royal government (as earlier 'Whig' historians had argued) but rather to produce cooperation and agreement amongst their own members. Unity was essential to order, division brought anarchy, and came about when selfish, private interests overrode the common good.

This view of the political process as consensual is founded on a belief that there existed, in fact, in early Stuart England a fundamental ideological consensus. Broad religious agreement amongst English Protestants is seen as surviving until the accession of Charles I, at least; while a wide measure of common ground on political principle lasted until the very eve of armed conflict, and even beyond it.[17] Religious developments will be discussed below but here the focus is on the content of the supposed political consensus. The monarch ruled with God's divine approval and had unquestioned responsibility for governing the kingdom, and for waging of foreign war. He would, it was hoped, rule according to the laws of the land; and take advice from the great noblemen of the kingdom whose inherited wealth and experience made them ideally suited for this task. He would not, in other words, rely on small factions, or obscurely born favourites solely dependent on the crown for advancement. A good monarch would also meet, from time to time, with parliaments where he could obtain the collective help of the lay peers and the bishops in the Lords, along with the Commons who represented the broader rural and urban communities of England. King, Lords and Commons were seen as working together for the mutual benefit of king and people, not as potentially, or actually, opposed entities. They cooperated to pass legislation, but in a pre-industrial, traditional society, it is argued, the making of new law was rarely as much of a preoccupation as later historians have imagined. Hence the 'winning of the initiative' in legislation with which Wallace Notestein credited the Commons, was not as important as has been supposed; no statutes were passed by the parliaments of 1614, 1621 and 1626. More important functions of the Commons included the provision of information on local grievances and financial support and demonstrations of unity at times of foreign war. Above all it was understood that Parliament was clearly subordinate to the monarch; it met at his bidding, to do business he referred to it.

It was argued in chapter 1 that the problems within the English political system arose from divisions over matters of principle and not simply out of practical issues. In the previous section it was suggested also that there was significant conflict within the political process. Political news inevitably tended to stress division and conflict rather than the more mundane agreements and compromises of political life. In the first session of the 1621 Parliament the headlines were made by the attack on the 'evil projector' or monopolist, Giles Mompesson, who was denounced in newsletters, verses and early cartoons, while bread and butter solutions to local problems were ignored. We need therefore to modify the current emphasis on consensus. While some elements in early Stuart political culture stressed unity and agreement, others implied that conflict was normal. The law was perhaps the most important framework for understanding seventeenth century politics and society, and Derek Hirst has stressed that the law was founded on a contrast between the guilty and the innocent.[18] Christianity suggested human experience and history were based on conflict between God and Satan, good and evil, heaven and hell; and these contrasts were most striking in Calvinist theology with its sharp cleavage between the elect and the damned. In a natural metaphor, the political system was compared, as we have seen, to a body whose parts all worked together well. But if the body politic fell sick, medical ideas often suggested that its cure should come through drastic methods of purging or purification.

Expressions of general agreement over the nature of politics in fact masked serious disagreement over specifics. Government might be natural, or ordained by God, but this did not necessarily imply anything very precise about forms of rule. Johann Sommerville has commented that, 'men agreed that it would be wrong to change existing political and constitutional arrangements, but disagreed on what these arrangements in fact were'. Indeed twentieth century historians who believe in an early Stuart consensus themselves often disagree on the precise nature of the political arrangements that were apparently generally accepted: some emphasise the powers of the royal prerogative, others stress that the king was limited by the laws. [19]

The commonplace belief that the political order was sanctioned by history had double-edged implications. The classic work of J. G. A. Pocock explored the widespread belief in the early seventeenth century that England's common law and government, its 'ancient constitution', were immemorial; they had existed 'time out of mind' and literally went back before human record or memory and, because of this, were excellent and should not be changed. [20] This adherence to custom and tradition implied both adaptation and preservation. In the words of the great common-lawyer, Sir Edward Coke, 'the laws have been by the wisdom of the most excellent men, in many successions of ages, by long and continual experience, (the trial of light and truth) fined and refined.' Adaptation was an almost unconscious, natural process, while preservation was an automatic instinct. No single act or individual had created the English laws and so no one should alter them; it was the duty of Englishmen to hand them on unchanged to their successors. In form this was obviously a very conservative mode of thought, but its practical implications were by no means conservative. The belief in the 'ancient constitution' for men like Coke implied a belief that the laws were immune from interference by the king; John Pym declared in the 1628 Parliament that: 'The law of England, whereby the subject was exempted from taxes and loans not granted by common consent of Parliament, was not introduced by any statute, or by any charter or sanction of princes, but was the ancient and fundamental law, issuing from the first frame and constitution of the kingdom.' As Pocock has commented, Englishmen of the sixteenth and seventeenth century 'were capable of extraordinary radical action while remaining highly conservative and even traditionalist in their modes of perception and behaviour'.

Opposition or resistance to royal policies could be justified where they were felt to contravene the 'ancient constitution', especially if they were a threat to property rights which it was the prime function of the common law to protect. Patriotic pride in the law as English was also important in promoting suspicion of royal interference. There was some disagreement over whether the Judges or Parliament were best fitted to protect the common law but the judges were often seen as vulnerable to royal pressure, especially in Charles's reign. The forced loan, imprisonments, billeting and other measures taken to prosecute the wars of the 1620s, fostered a widespread fear that the laws were in danger and only parliamentary action could preserve them. Thus in the 1628 Parliament John Selden refused to accept the validity of martial law: 'All the law you can name, that deserves the name of law, is reduced to these 2: it is either ascertained by custom or confirmed by act of parliament.' Selden was emphasising the supremacy of the common law in reply to Secretary of State John Coke. Coke agreed, 'there is no man but desires to live under the law, and we all hold the common law our inheritance that does preserve us', but felt also that, 'martial law is an essential law of the kingdom, and the whole government consists not in the common law, but in others'. The attack on the war effort in this parliament culminated in the Petition of Right, a general declaration of 'their rights and liberties according to the laws and statutes of this realm', which it was hoped would prevent future abuses.[21]

Many recent commentators have taken seventeenth century appeals to tradition too much at face value. History was used as 'a normative past' whose values justified much practical resistance to present-day authority. This approach was widespread throughout society: popular resistance to enclosure or changes in use of fens and forest was often legitimated by appeal to ancient custom while noble opposition to Charles was justified by 'aristocratic constitutionalism'. This involved a general belief that the peers, as a long-established, independent landed elite, had a vital role to play in the government of England and that therefore monarchs should rule with the help and advice of the leading nobility. More specifically, precedents from earlier reigns where the inadequacies of monarchs had led peers to take over their functions were used to support measures taken against Charles in the early 1640s. This was a more sophisticated and historically precise programme but it was similar to the way the fen dwellers of the manor of Epworth in the Isle of Axholme appealed to a fourteenth century 'Mowbray deed' which they believed granted them 'many and great privileges' and justified their resistance to the drainers. The deed was, writes Holmes, their 'Magna Carta'.[22]

A belief in tradition could thus involve dissent from the status quo; while other elements in the political culture of the early seventeenth century further suggest that consensus was not its major characteristic. In the first place there was profound disagreement over the foundations of politics: did kings rule according to law, or meet parliaments because they were graciously pleased to do so, or because the nature and origins of their power obliged them to? Secondly, there were different diagnoses of the problems of politics: if things went wrong was it the fault of ungrateful and unruly subjects, or of monarchs exceeding their lawful powers (probably under the influence of evil counsellors)? These disagreements were based on different ways of thinking about politics; and recently historians have been much concerned to understand these contrasts. Richard Cust and Anthony Fletcher have shown how in the 1620s and the early 1640s two rival conspiracy theories were elaborated which explained political breakdown and were associated with divergent remedies for the kingdom's ills. It is sometimes argued that beliefs in conspiracy were superficial or irrational, but Johann Sommerville argues that these cleavages arose from two very distinctive beliefs about the English constitution, and that

Pocock has underestimated English capacity for abstract political theorising. Overlapping with Sommerville's work has been a rehabilitation of the division between 'court and country' as an important framework within which early Stuart politics was understood, after a period when historians denied the division any reality.

Sommerville contrasts a royalist or absolutist view of the constitution with ideas based on notions of contract, law and consent.[23] In the absolutist framework kings were subordinate only to God and were unfettered by any human authority. Kings should not wield arbitrary power; they should rule according to the known laws of the land, and for the public good. James and Charles felt that kings might allow their subjects to influence them on specific matters but they denied that the law in general and by right influenced royal power. Most importantly, it was up to kings to decide to rule justly, with God's aid; subjects had no redress if they did not. In 1610 James argued that 'prayers and tears' were the only legitimate weapons against an unjust king; and the duty of non-resistance was very widely emphasised throughout the period. The rival tradition (which owed as much to continental natural law influences as to ideas derived from a view of English history) held that royal power was derived from the community who had given it up on conditions and could resist if these conditions were broken; the statutes of the realm and the coronation oaths of monarchs were surviving evidence of these conditions. Such power that monarchs had acquired through the Norman conquest had become modified by later compacts to obey the (ancient) laws of England. The position was expressed often in the terms of the influential medieval lawyer Sir John Fortescue, that England was a constitutional monarchy, a *dominium politicum et regale*. Kings were therefore obliged to rule according to law, and as discussed earlier, many also argued that it was Parliament that had the supreme power to interpret the law. It is clear therefore that there were currents in English political thinking that could promote opposition to royal power; the English were not nearly as dependent on the example of the Scots as some analyses discussed in chapter 1 suggested.

Potential tensions between the role of Parliament and that of common law judges were limited in the case of taxation. It was a fundamental principle of the common law that property rights should not be interfered with by kings without consent; and this consent should be obtained through Parliament. Hence Parliament played a vital role in conflicts over the financial problems of the crown, as demonstrated in chapter 1. It is also important that it was the *Commons'* consent to taxes that was vital, although the Lords shared Parliament's law-making powers and advisory role. Members of the Commons may have had aristocratic patrons but they also had vital links and responsibilities down to their tax-paying constituents who formed a vital section of the broader political nation. The traditional emphasis of historians on the House of Commons perhaps needs qualification, but should not be replaced completely. In contrast 'royalist' theories held that kings had a *right* to their subjects' property if the safety of the realm demanded supply. It was, of course, kings themselves who judged whether an emergency existed. This was argued by the clerics Roger Maynwaring and Robert Sibthorpe in support of Charles's levying of a 'forced Loan' in 1627, while the judgement in the king's favour after the test case on ship money brought by John Hampden declared, 'that the King of mere right ought to have, and the people of mere duty are bound to yield unto the King, supply for the defence of the kingdom'. A thoroughgoing version of 'royalist' ideas was articulated in the Canons passed by the 1640 Convocation of the clergy. Resistance to monarchy was unequivocally condemned:

> For subjects to bear arms against their kings, offensive or defensive, upon any pretence whatsoever, is at least to resist the powers which are ordained of God; and though they do not invade but only resist, St Paul tells them plainly they shall receive to themselves damnation.

The protection of subjects' property rights was part of the kingly office, but

> tribute, and custom, and aid, and subsidy, and all manner of necessary support and supply be respectively due to kings from their subjects by the Law of God, Nature and Nations, for the public defence, care and protection of them.[24]

The Court and the Country

As Sommerville emphasises, divisions were less clear-cut in practice; monarchs needed money and subjects needed office and royal support, so there was a lot of stress on the necessity for king and people to work together. Perhaps also Sommerville underplays traditionalist modes of thought and sees political divisions in too logical and clear-cut a way. Members of the elite were perfectly capable of believing at the same time in both 'ascending' and 'descending' theories of political authority, that all authority came from above, from God, and that power came from below, from the people; the Cheshire gentleman Sir Richard Grosvenor is one well-documented example. Some ways of understanding politics lacked intellectual coherence but could nonetheless foster conflict and division; the polarity between 'court' and 'country' is perhaps the most important. This contrast was an influential and wide-ranging way of explaining divisions twenty years ago. For Perez Zagorin the division between court and country summed up the growing cleavage within the governing elite in the years before 1640. The 'country' was an embryonic political party, 'the first opposition movement in English history whose character transcended that of a feudal following or faction'. It comprised those of the peers and gentry, often known as 'patriots' who stood for the public interest as identified with Parliament, or local government rather than with office at court or in central government. It involved a positive programme of reform, in line with zealous Protestantism and the 'ancient constitution', of a 'court' which was felt to be increasingly authoritarian and tainted with popery; the court-country division is thus not the same as the negative localist suspicion of central government discussed in chapter 1. Moreover, the 'country' conjured up an image of a place and a style of life, naturally healthier and morally superior to a decadent court. Finally, court and country had a cultural dimension seen in the contrast between the cosmopolitan, rarefied sophistication of court culture in Charles's reign and more robust and more English, traditions. At court, Charles's rule was idealised in Van Dyck portraits and masques designed by Inigo Jones and written by

Davenant or Carew. In the country, subjects more used to Hilliard or Shakespeare became more and more alienated from the crown.[25]

Recently, scepticism has been expressed about the validity of a court-country division. Political historians have pointed out that there was no clear institutional separation: many who clearly had what Zagorin would describe as 'country' attitudes held office under the crown. The staunch Puritan Sir Robert Harley was the son-in-law of a Secretary of State and Master of the Mint for life, although he was deprived of the right to exercise the office in 1634; more remarkably John Pym was involved in the administration of crown lands until well into the 1630s.[26] Important new work on culture and politics has also challenged notions of a straightforward contrast between court and country. In place of the conventional view of court culture under Charles as escapist self-regarding fantasy, Kevin Sharpe and Malcolm Smuts have stressed that there was no gulf between art and life. The masques were not escapist, but like all art had a moral purpose, that 'art might elevate men to what they might become'. Thomas Carew's masque *Coelum Britannicum* took the theme of reform and argued that reordering of the court provided the model for reform of the kingdom as a whole. Martin Butler has shown that it was possible to criticise royal policy and advocate alternatives through the drama; support for an active pro-Protestant foreign policy was one issue that was so pressed. Masques could be ways of 'finding bridges between the crown, the crown's supporters, and the crown's critics'.[27]

The ambiguity and complexity of court culture is further apparent in examinations of 'country' ideals. To some extent, the idealisation of the country was itself a product of the court, in art and in practice. Ben Jonson was the collaborator with Inigo Jones on some of the great masques of the early Stuart court; he was also the author of some of the best known pastoral idealisations of country life in poems like 'Penshurst'. In both genres, he, like many others, drew on classical models. The court developed a critique of the London-based, cosmopolitan and urban culture it was itself fostering, a sophisticated nostalgia for the purity of the rural life. The frequent proclamations by James and Charles ordering the gentry out of London and back to their country estates were a practical manifestation of the court's own belief that proximity to it could corrupt the unwary.

The new work which integrates politics and culture demonstrates that a simplistic court-country division is not adequate, but it also points the way to a more subtle interpretation of how the political culture of the court intensified divisions in England.[28] The image of monarchy promulgated at Charles's court was one of 'formality, distance and privacy'; it was characteristic of Charles's reign before 1640 that while a great deal of propaganda emphasised the efficacy of the king's touching to cure the royal evil, in practice Charles was extremely reluctant to touch any real subjects. Charles cancelled the public procession arranged for his coronation and his royal entry into London on his return from Scotland in 1633. The cult of Charles was an elitist, court-based cult, in great contrast to the 'decentralised' image of Elizabeth (and James to a lesser extent) produced through frequent public displays and provincial progresses.

The political implications of court culture were authoritarian. The early Roman empire was an important model in Charles's reign, producing a stress on restraint and order in a world that was threatening to get out of hand. In reform of his court, as in his attitude to the realm as a whole, Charles believed that authority operated strictly from the top down. He had an almost obsessive concern with detailed investigations and regulations of practices at court, seeing a 'well-regulated court as a shrine of virtue and decorum'. In the court, as in the kingdom, he attempted reform through a tone of 'repeated hectoring enquiry'. The cosmopolitan, baroque art fostered in the 1620s and 1630s linked the court firmly with Roman and European Catholic influences, an international dimension which should not be contrasted with the insularity or provincialism of the 'country' but with a rival internationalism. Smuts, in particular, has stressed the importance of Europe's religious conflicts in the shaping of cultural traditions and views of monarchy. The view of the world as involved in a cosmic struggle between good and evil, Protestant and Papist, was an important current in English educated and popular culture from the sixteenth century, as seen most obviously in the success of Fox's *Book of Martyrs*. Elizabeth and James had an obvious, if idealised, role as leaders of the international Protestant cause, and heroes of this national culture. After the mid 1620s, Charles's image was based on pacific virtues and on love; he was a chivalrous knight, but not the warlike leader of a European struggle. Protestant internationalism became subordinated at court, and a part of 'country' ideology.

This country ideology should be distinguished from the pastoral idealisation of the rural life which emanated from the court. When James and Charles ordered the gentry back to the country it was so they could fulfil their traditional and semi-private responsibilities of hospitality, and not meddle with religious or political affairs. The court's image of the 'country' was one of passivity, privacy and retreat; but it is clear that there were ideals which stressed precisely the opposite – the public and active duty of all to be vigilant in the protection of commonwealth and church. These attitudes were often expressed in terms of the duties of, or loyalty to the 'country'; they are implied in the views of Grosvenor and Scott on elections as discussed above, while an early example is seen in a speech of the Puritan politician Job Throckmorton in the 1586 Parliament: 'When they that should speak be mute, then burst out they that should be still. It is wondered at above, that simple men of the country should be so forward, and it doth amaze us in the country that wise men of the court should be so backward.' These notions of active citizenship derived partly from Protestant and Puritan ideas, as will be shown shortly, but also from the Renaissance development of classical beliefs that men found fulfilment through public life. In more specifically cultural senses this Protestant vision of the public life was embodied, according to David Norbrook, in the zealous Protestant, 'prophetic tradition' of Spenser and his successors, like George Wither, who emphasised the necessity for men to cooperate actively in God's purposes; they felt that the country was purer than the court but also saw it as promoting martial, activist virtues. The restrained, classical style of Ben Johnson was a reaction to the Spenserean tradition; the early work of Milton an attempt to revive Spenser's public concerns in a 'modern' style.[29] The current interest in culture in a political context does thus reveal a divided political culture, albeit that the divisions are more complex than was thought in the 1960s. Furthermore cultural divisions encapsulated different visions of the structure of society, and can be connected to patterns of social change, as discussed in chapter 3.

In its own terms the court was a place of decorum, hierarchy and order; to its country critics it was increasingly a site of popery and corruption. Country ideals were much broader than pastoral nostalgia, and did not imply an institutional or structural separation between court and country; they implied attitudes, prejudices, a way of looking at the political world. Indeed it was possible to be a courtier or a member of the royal government in fact, and still represent a country position, as the careers of the Earl of Pembroke or Archbishop Abbot demonstrated. The rhetoric of the 'country' was vague and ambiguous, which made it all the more effective a motivator in politics.[30] The term 'country' often seemed to indicate a place, but the place could be the immediate neighbourhood, the county or the whole commonwealth of England; the creative imprecision in itself reveals the integration of the localities within the nation as a whole. The 'country' also described the inhabitants of these places, or at least the 'better sort' of them, the male householders who comprised the broader political nation discussed at the start of this chapter. The term 'better sort' could be a moral as well as a social description, referring to those who supported the values the country was supposed to represent. Some of these values were consensual ones – the need for law and order, or social harmony, the desire to keep financial exactions as low as possible – increasingly in the seventeenth century, however, the ideals of the country became more ideologically specific, stressing zealous Protestant, anti-popish positions, and support for frequent parliaments. Parliament was central to all the definitions of 'country'; it united and represented all the places and people implied in the term, and its frequent meetings were seen as the best barrier to court corruption. In a blurred way, country ideas drew on the constitutionalist views of politics discussed in Sommerville's work, and on a belief that Protestant vigilance was essential to prevent the spread of popery. Political leaders who supported these positions were seen as 'standing for the country' and its liberties and were often described as patriots. In turn, the country was often portrayed as a complex entity to which leaders owed loyalty and duty. Examples have already been provided in the comments of Scott and Grosvenor on elections, and the attitude of Barnardiston to the forced loan.

Finally 'country' attitudes included a belief that politics should, at times of danger at least, involve active participation by a broad political nation. There was thus a particular 'country' analysis of England's political problems and a particular country solution. It was intertwined with a conspiracy theory which explained political conflict in terms of an authoritarian popish plot to undermine English laws and liberties as well as true religion, a plot which had alarming support from evil counsellors at court. This view is seen most starkly in the famous phrases of the Grand Remonstrance: 'The root of all this mischief we find to be a malignant and pernicious design of subverting the fundamental laws and principles of government, upon which the religion and justice of this kingdom are firmly established.'[33] The belief in such a plot was perhaps unsophisticated but it was not irrational. As we shall see, religious developments in Charles's reign made it all too plausible while court support for the absolutist tendencies in politics added further evidence. The only way to defeat such heinous conspiracies was to preserve an open and dynamic political process which could maintain the purity of a threatened and corruptible system. The few could be corrupted but broad involvement preserved honesty; deception and secrecy might flourish at court but frequent parliaments would expose it; struggle and even conflict were preferable to a dangerous complacency.

Council Divisions and the King's 'New Counsels'

'Popular' responses to political difficulties were seen by Charles and his most favoured advisers as a subversive attempt to undermine his God-given authority: 'popularity', not popery, was the great threat to the stability of English (and British) politics. This alternative conspiracy theory also had links to more elaborate political ideas – the absolutist views discussed above – and the two conspiracy theories were mutually re-inforcing. As developments at 'court' encouraged country views of a plot against religion and political liberties, so the attitudes of the 'country' encouraged royal fears of subversion. All empha-sised the importance of consensus but while the country believed that harmony could be restored through activism and openness, the 'court' promoted a restrictive political system. The 'court' response to threatened breakdown was to stress the hierarchical, authoritarian elements in political culture: political participation was suspect and politics was to work from the 'top down' with the king transmitting orders which should be obeyed without question or debate. These beliefs found expression in Charles's turn to 'new counsels', as his opponents termed them, in the later 1620s.

From the sixteenth century there were clearly unresolved ten-sions within the English political process. The Henrician refor-mation on the one hand emphasised that royal power was sanctioned by God, but also stressed the supreme role of parliamentary statute in achieving legitimate change. In Eliza-beth's reign it was more generally agreed that the prerogative was bounded by law, and Patrick Collinson has recently drawn our attention to the collective, participatory, 'republican' ele-ments in the Elizabethan political culture which could make the monarch herself seem almost irrelevant. Both James and Charles insisted on their personal authority and stressed royal power to dispense with the usual laws of the land if (in the royal judgement) an emergency existed. John Cowell's *Interpreter* (1607) was attacked in the Commons in 1610 for holding that the king was above the law; James I condemned Cowell for meddling but did not renounce his ideas. Later in James's reign a privately but widely circulated tract held that annual parlia-ments were necessary to prevent the prerogative becoming too powerful.[32] But it was under Charles that the 'court' conspiracy theory became fully elaborated, and divisions intensified.

Notions of conspiracy were central to court culture, as Smuts has shown. The king was seen as the divine guardian of order while the major threats to authority came from demagogues who stirred up the ignorant and unstable populace. In practice this attitude was demonstrated in Charles's dissolution of the 1626 Parliament in the belief that the impeachment of Buckingham was part of a general conspiracy against the monarchy formented by the 'malicious practices of wicked spirits' (as the king described his opponents in a draft proclamation). Charles's action was influenced by a sermon to the parliament by Laud, the future Archbishop of Canterbury, which linked Puritanism, 'popularity', and opposition to monarchy into one conspiratorial framework. Smuts quotes Laud's view of Magna Carta: 'The Great Charter had an obscure birth from usurpation and was fostered and shown to the world by rebellion' – an account which immediately reveals the churchman's distance from conventional English constitutionalist attitudes.[33]

The hectic and confused politics of the late 1620s foreshadow to a degree the divisions of 1640–2. They reveal the increasing gulf between 'court' and 'country', based ultimately on contrasting views of politics, but they also show how practical political conflicts were more 'fudged', less clear-cut than theoretical divisions. As 'revisionist' historians have emphasised, the division was not between king and Parliament, still less between government and opposition; sharp political divisions were present within the Privy Council itself. An important group of moderate councillors – Manchester, Pembroke, Carlisle, and Holland – tried to talk Charles out of the dissolution of 1626 while Lord Keeper Coventry also voiced opposition. The moderates' view was summed up by Abbot's remark that 'in kingdoms the harmony was sweetest where the prince and the people tuned well together'. Other councillors were extremely suspicious of Parliament; some because they were clients of Buckingham like Conway or Dorset and sought to protect their patron, others like Laud out of principle, because they believed parliaments encouraged popular attacks on monarchical authority. Charles's adoption of 'new counsels' showed he shared Laud's view. Parliament had urged him towards an active foreign policy and then refused to pay for it; its members attacked his closest advisers and impugned his authority. Therefore he would henceforth avoid parliaments and collect revenue by other means unless the people showed that they were obedient and trustworthy, no longer the tools of the ambitious, factitious men who had stirred up opposition in the Commons. Thus the 'benevolence' of the summer of 1626 was a loyalty test for Charles's subjects. The four subsidies which had been proposed, but not voted, by the recent parliament were to be collected as a free gift; if they were eagerly paid it would demonstrate that the 'wicked spirits' were only a small minority, and most subjects were loyal. Unfortunately, there was widespread opposition to the benevolence, thus confirming Charles and Laud in their belief in a widespread conspiracy.

It has already been shown how opposition to unparliamentary levies, and specifically resistance to the forced loan of 1626–7, was an important part of 'country' mythology. The loan is also very revealing of the king's approach, and of divisions in the Council. Like the 'free gift', the loan was seen as a loyalty test; as Charles said in the proclamation which accompanied the levy in October 1626, 'by our people's affection now showed unto us in this way of necessity, they shall the sooner invite us to the frequent use of Parliament, being confident in the hearts of our people'. Moderate councillors saw this as a hopeful sign that a parliament could be called, but from other points of view it was a sinister move. Parliament here was not a fundamental part of the constitution, but something which had to be earned, its calling was purely in the monarch's gift. The loan was an embodiment of absolutist views of monarchs' rights to their subjects' property in cases of emergency, as the sermons of Sibthorpe and Maynwaring stated; such views made parliaments irrelevant. The king regarded the loan as a crucial test of loyalty to his person; his honour was tied up with its success so he favoured a hard line with resisters. Lord Keeper Coventry, more dubious about the legality of the loan, favoured a more circumspect approach, and Council moderates tried to avoid issues of legal principle. Their policy failed when Charles himself decided to respond to the challenge of the 'Five knights' in October 1627, and with the 'martyrdom' of country heroes like Sir Francis Barrington of Essex and Sir Edmund Hampden of Northamptonshire who were among the prominent loan refusers who died during, or soon after, imprisonment. In part of course, the problems of the 1620s derived from the pressures of foreign war, but it was the contrasting ideological frameworks within which the problems of war were understood that led to conflict.

The lobbying of moderate Councillors, and the pressures of foreign policy did bring Charles to call the 1628 Parliament but the king's view that the purpose of a parliament was to endorse royal policy was hardly fulfilled. The attacks on Buckingham and Maynwaring, the criticisms of 'Arminianism', and the passing of the Petition of Right, followed by the abortive 1629 session, confirmed the king's worst fears. His approach in the 1630s was thus to avoid Parliament through the use of financial expedients and a limited foreign policy, although moderates in the Council survived to hope intermittently for a change of tack. The attitudes forged in the 1620s were evident in his relationships with local governors and in his intervention in local disputes. Kevin Sharpe has suggested that the major problem for the 'personal rule' was a lack of communication between the central government and the localities. In some ways, however, there was a great deal of communication; it was rather the nature of the process that was the problem. The king believed that ruling was a matter of issuing commands and that disobedience to God-given authority was inexcusable and attributable to the factiousness of the common people and the incompetence, if no worse, of his subordinates. Late in the 1630s hapless sheriffs trying to collect ship money from a reluctant people were bombarded with reprimands and reminders from London: in February 1640 many hard-pressed sheriffs were threatened by the Privy Council with Star Chamber proceedings if arrears were not collected. Their failures showed, 'your ill affections to his Majesty's service besides your disobedience to the directions of the Board'.

The king was consistently suspicious of corporations, especially those which allowed a measure of popular participation in their government, as centres of subversive Puritanism. In 1633 John

Workman, a lecturer at Gloucester since 1619, was suspended from his post, excommunicated and imprisoned at Laud's instigation for factious preaching. He was said to have opposed the Book of Sports and preached against images but also to have prayed for the States of Holland and the king of Sweden before Charles I, and to have argued that ministers should be elected by the people. Laud and Charles were also the driving forces behind the prosecution of the Puritan Recorder of Salisbury, Henry Sherfield, for destroying a 'superstitious' stained glass window when other members of the Privy Council proposed leniency. A last example shows how from a provincial perspective the exploitation of the king's prejudices was a means of winning disputes if local people could brand their enemies as popular men, or Puritans. When disputes in Great Yarmouth came to the attention of the Privy Council, Attorney General Robert Heath wrote sternly of the corporation: 'There is a great party in this town of sectaries, averse to all government but their own popular way which must be reformed . . . the government of the whole stands but upon the well-ordering of the parts which made up the whole.' With Council backing anti-Puritans were able to wield great power in Yarmouth. The legacy of the 1620s is clear in Charles's denunciation of the Scots rebels in a proclamation to his English subjects in February 1639. The 'disorders and tumults' raised in Scotland were 'fomented by factious spirits, and those traitorously affected, begun upon pretences of religion, the common cloak for all disobedience; but now it clearly appears, the aim of these men is not religion (as they falsely pretend and publish) but it is to shake off all monarchical government'. Other characteristics of Charles were consistent throughout his reign. As he believed that the people were too easily swayed by factious demagogues so he held that the removal of a few embittered leaders would restore his subjects to their natural obedience and prevent conspiracy succeeding. The attitude which led him to 'prick' potential leaders of the Commons as sheriffs in 1625 (so disqualifying them from serving as MPs) reappears in attempted coups against the leaders of the Covenanters in 1641, or the botched arrest of the 'Five Members' of the Long Parliament in January 1642.[34]

The first of Charles's articles of treason against the Five Members was,

> that they have traitorously endeavoured to subvert the fundamental laws and government of the kingdom of England, to deprive the King of his regal power, and to place in subjects an arbitrary and tyrannical power over the lives, liberties and estates of his Majesty's liege people.

In very similar fashion, the House of Commons in its protestation of May 1641, requiring an oath of loyalty to true religion, the king and the Parliament, wrote of

> the designs of the priests and Jesuits ... to the undermining and danger of the true reformed religion ... and finding also that there hath been, and having cause to suspect there still are, even during the sitting in Parliament, endeavours to subvert the fundamental laws of England and Ireland, and to introduce the exercise of an arbitrary and tyrannical government by most pernicious and wicked counsels, practices, plots and conspiracies.[36]

The structural similarity of these arguments is support for the arguments of Mark Kishlansky that there was a great desire for unity and harmony in seventeenth century politics, and a tendency to explain division through the conspiracies of evil men. Political principles were not expressed in as clear-cut a fashion as in more recent times; ideas were more intertwined with social and personal considerations; notions based on custom and tradition were much more pervasive. It is equally important to stress, however, that there were sharp contrasts in the content of the two conspiracy theories, and that these contrasts were based on complex and conflicting approaches to politics and on fairly sophisticated understandings of divergent political theories.

Understanding Religious Divisions

In February 1633 an order of the Exchequer court outlawed the 'feoffees for impropriations', the means by which a group of Puritan merchants endowed preaching lectureships especially in corporate towns. Charles and his authoritarian associates feared a popular subversive attack from Puritans stirred up by factious lecturers. Similarly, James I told the House of Lords in 1624, 'I think it is all one to lay down my crown to the Pope as to a popular party of Puritans ... I commend my Lord of Norwich for suppressing of popular lectures within his diocese. I mean such as are nowadays most frequented, being supplied and held up by such ministers as have not cure of souls where they preached, for such must flatter and cog and claw the people and therefore I will never allow them.' On the other hand, by 1640 there was a widespread belief in a popishly inspired plot to undermine the English constitution. The country feared that papists had infiltrated the court: the 'Jesuited Papists' were the main villains identified in the Grand Remonstrance. Much of what has been covered already has shown the inextricable connections of religion and politics, both domestic and international. That religion and politics were linked is accepted by most historians of the civil war, but there is less agreement on the precise nature of the links. For S. R. Gardiner, and other nineteenth century historians, the civil war was a 'Puritan Revolution', a view that derived from a particular analysis of the overall impact of the Protestant Reformation. The Reformation, in this framework, affirmed the importance of the individual conscience against the dogmas of priests; it attracted much 'popular' support from those no longer willing to accept authority without question. In the English context, Puritans held that the Elizabethan settlement of the church was not adequate, and worked from the 1560s against the ecclesiastical establishment for further reformation. They were often harassed or persecuted by authority and their religious sufferings, plus their sturdy individualism, meant they also led the struggle against political oppression and arbitrary government.

Much recent work has been sceptical about a 'Puritan Revolution'. In parallel to discussions of politics, many historians have argued that a rough and ready consensus on religion existed amongst ruling elites, at least from the 1560s to the 1620s. They suggest that it is not possible to divide English Protestants neatly into an 'Anglican' establishment and a Puritan opposition.

There was instead a broad spectrum of opinion, and much on which Protestants were united.[36] Most importantly, the vast majority were Calvinist in their theology, that is they believed that God had predestined some to salvation but most to damnation. People were sharply divided into elect Saints and the reprobate or damned although only God knew for certain who these were. Human effort was irrelevant to salvation and only impious papists had the presumption to believe that humans had free-will or could influence the Almighty through good works. Although a small minority had campaigned for a Presbyterian system of church government in Elizabeth's reign, most Protestant opinion accepted that government by bishops was a perfectly legitimate framework for a reformed church. Only a tiny minority countenanced separation from a national church. There were, of course, some differences of emphasis. All Protestants professed to hate popery, and wished to encourage the preaching of the word, but some were more enthusiastic about this than others. There were divisions over whether it was valid or necessary to conform to the ceremonial which the Elizabethan church enjoined. In this spectrum, though, Puritans were not an alienated opposition, but simply the more enthusiastic wing, the 'hotter sort' of Protestants. Indeed, many with Puritan tendencies were at the heart of local and central power structures: Sir Edmund Lewkenor in Elizabethan Suffolk and the queen's close associate the Earl of Leicester are obvious examples. Unsurprisingly, in this account, Puritan approaches to politics are not seen as subversive. Puritans wanted to strengthen the existing social and political order by morally reforming it, so that godly magistrates and a godly prince could lead a struggle to eliminate popery. Many in the ecclesiastical hierarchy sympathised with much of the 'Puritan' programme, here the classic example is presented of James's Archbishop of Canterbury, George Abbot. Abbot was an uncompromising Calvinist in theology, he hated popery and worked zealously to defeat it in Europe; he promoted preaching and did not search out nonconformists for punishment although he dutifully admonished those who opposed the ceremonies if they were brought to his attention or if James complained of the insolence of 'Puritans'.

It is argued that this broad consensus was wrecked by the rise of English Arminianism in the 1620s. Arminianism challenged the theological certainties of Calvinism by arguing that predestination was not absolute: the elect could fall from God's grace through sin. This seemed to suggest that human beings had free-will, and that works could contribute to salvation. English Arminians stressed ritual, ceremony and the sacraments rather than the preaching of the word. They had a very elevated notion of the importance of the clergy. All of this seemed alarmingly like popery. Arminians were obsessed with conformity and uniformity and branded anyone who opposed them (and all Calvinists) as dangerous Puritans. In this approach to the religious history of the early seventeenth century, it is only the pressure of Arminianism, backed enthusiastically by Charles I and his Archbishop William Laud, that turned hitherto conventional, conservative English Protestants into opponents of the crown. Again, there are parallels to analyses of politics in the description of innovative royal policies provoking defensive resistance. Furthermore, this analysis stresses short-term, almost random factors. Arminianism is almost a bolt from the blue, while Charles's support for it is seen as a simple matter of a personal preference with appalling consequences.

Some historians have, however, denied that 'Arminianism' was so distinctive.[37] Peter White and Kevin Sharpe have argued that there was no clear theological break with Calvinism and that Laud and Neile were firmly in the tradition of Elizabethan conformists such as Archbishops Whitgift and Bancroft. Their main concern, it is alleged, was with conformity and order, and, if they had been understood, their policies should have been fairly acceptable. This view is not convincing. Nicholas Tyacke's recent study of the rise of English Arminianism has comprehensively shown that the late 1620s did see notions of religious orthodoxy transformed.[38] The early 1620s were a good time for Calvinists. At the Synod of Dort in 1618 which discussed divisions between Calvinists and Arminians in the Dutch church, the official British delegation took the Calvinist side. George Carleton, one of the Calvinist delegates to the synod, was elevated to the bishopric of Chichester in 1619, and his colleague

John Davenant went to Salisbury in 1621. In August 1625, however, Bishop Davenant wrote to his friend Samuel Ward, of Sidney Sussex College, Cambridge, that Richard Montagu's views on predestination were contrary to what had been the doctrine of the English church 'ever since we were born'. By February 1629 the House of Commons was complaining that 'prelates near the King, having gotten the chief administration of ecclesiastical affairs under his Majesty, have discountenanced and hindered the preferment of those that are orthodox, and favoured such as are contrary'. The turnround is demonstrated also in Tyacke's analysis of the prestigious set-piece sermons preached at St Paul's Cross in London, and frequently printed afterwards. Only one clearly anti-Calvinist sermon from Elizabeth's reign was published; while 27 printed sermons from James's reign include support for Calvinist teaching on pre-destination although it is significant that none were published after James's 1622 directions to the clergy, condemning all 'popular' preaching about 'pre-destination, reprobation, or of the universality, efficacy, resistibility, or irresistibility of God's grace'. There is no evidence of anti-Calvinist sermons in James's reign. The last Calvinist sermons were published in 1628, thereafter Arminian ideas were publicly promoted while Calvinists were silenced.

Clearly, conflicts between Calvinists and Arminians poisoned the political atmosphere from the 1620s onwards. Some historians, however, regard these divisions as a matter for small minorities only. John Morrill, who has described the civil war as a war of religion, thinks the most serious religious conflicts were rather different. His analysis is based on a very different view of Puritanism, and of the Protestant reformation itself, from that associated with Gardiner.[39] Here the Reformation is not seen as a movement of liberation, rather its elitist and repressive elements are stressed. Protestantism was a religion of the word and of the mind; to be a member of the godly it was a great advantage to be literate, and it was essential to understand complex intellectual issues (to internalise doctrine, in the jargon of historians). Protestantism, especially in its Calvinist form, harped on sin in hell-fire preaching, yet because it denounced

99

good works as a means to salvation, it gave little practical guidance on how to live a Christian life in this world. Many were left only with the despairing notion that the majority of mankind was condemned to irretrievable damnation. The Reformation in England was not promoted by a popular movement against a corrupt and spiritually bankrupt medieval church; instead the emphasis is on the vitality of the church and on the positive adherence of much of the population to it. The medieval church was accessible to unlettered people through its images, its local saints and shrines, and the multiplicity of organisations in which lay participation was encouraged. Its priests were not distant intellectual moral reformers but mediators in local communities. Consequently, the process of inculcating protestantism into the bulk of the population was difficult, slow and often resented.

By the seventeenth century, Morrill suggests, there was popular support for protestantism, but little for its Puritan variety. Puritanism was too demanding, and bred despair; Puritans were busybodies and kill-joys. They believed that God's purposes would be served by a thorough moral reformation of society, thus they tried to eliminate the harmless recreations and festivals of ordinary people and caused divisions by their interference. Puritans did not oppose monarchy until Charles attacked their notion of reformation; they were elitists who attacked the traditional unity of village society. The opponents of Puritan reform were those 'prayer-book' Anglicans who emerged into prominence with the petitioning campaign to the Long Parliament in favour of espiscopacy and the Book of Common Prayer in 1641–2. These, more easy-going protestants, believed complex preaching of the detailed issues of predestination was futile. Religion should be accessible, practical and support communal solidarity in the parishes. The Book of Common Prayer thus had elements of ritual and ceremony and stressed a regular pattern of worship through the year which brought the parish together at great festivals like Christmas, Easter and Whitsun and matched the rhythms of the agricultural year. Puritans, in contrast, opposed 'set prayers' and elevated the sermon above outward observances of ritual and participation in the sacraments. These parish Anglicans should not be identified with Laudians or

Arminians although it can be seen that elements in the religious policies of the 1630s had general appeal. The Laudians circumvented the Calvinist preoccupation with predestination; they believed that images, sacraments, rituals could lead people to religion as well as the word; they promoted 'lawful recreations' through the Book of Sports. But Laudianism was also disliked for its divisiveness. Its leaders interfered too much in the affairs of parishes and imposed expensive and controversial changes in church decoration and furnishings; it elevated the clergy to far above the laity and promoted too much clerical involvement in secular government. It is thus only after the fall of Laud and his allies in 1640–1, that great enthusiasm emerged for the Church of England and its bishops; an enthusiasm that was to frustrate the godly crusade of Puritan reformation in the 1640s and 1650s.

Calvinism and Puritanism

The emphasis on anti-Puritanism and anti-Calvinism in recent work has added much to our understanding of the religious divisions which contributed to the cleavage of 1642, and of how these divisions can be connected to broader cultural and social contrasts, as will be discussed in chapter 3. However, the intention here is to challenge the currently influential views that Puritanism appealed only to a small minority, and that this minority was usually a social as well as a religious elite. It is often argued that Puritanism appealed particularly to the 'middling sort' of small merchants, yeomen and prosperous husbandmen; it was a means by which independent but modest property holders acquired a discipline which helped them to survive and prosper in difficult economic circumstances and provided a cultural identity which enabled them to distinguish themselves from the poor masses of the population. Puritan zeal also gave the methods and motivation for an attack by parish elites on the recreations and morals of the poor which affronted God and undermined social order.[40] Puritanism required an understanding of the word of God embodied in the Scriptures and clearly the literate and leisured had an advantage here. But many

humble people made great efforts to acquire reading skills –
John Bunyan, the poor artisan, is a famous illustration – while
the importance of oral transmission of ideas and information in
early Stuart England has already been emphasised. Enthusiastic
protestanism was spread by preaching not reading.

As will be shown below, Puritanism emphasised the individual's responsibility to be active in this world, to root out sin
and popery, and build a society in accordance with God's word.
It was an important element in the creation of a new self-image
of governors, whether these were Privy Councillors, JPs or
parish constables, but it could also appeal to men and women
from humbler social groups. Christopher Hill's classic study
Society and Puritanism outlined the appeal of zealous Protestantism to the middling sort but it also had a consciousness of
contradictions and complexities, of a greater radical edge or
potential which has been lost in some of the work that has built
on Hill's analysis. The sharp Calvinist contrast between good
and evil, the elect and the damned, had close parallels in some of
the stark distinctions between heroes and villains, good and bad,
in popular literature and ideas, and Puritan preaching could find
a wide audience. Theoretically and often in practice, the distinction between the godly and the reprobate was a moral and
religious distinction, not a social one. Thus, as Patrick Collinson
has shown for the Elizabethan period, there was an organised
Puritan movement which included substantial support from
those outside gentry ranks. These people recognised each other
as being involved in the same enterprise and facing the same
enemies. The collecting of information for the parliamentary
petitions and surveys of the ministry drawn up in the 1580s and
1590s as part of a campaign for further reformation of the church
was an important element in the politicisation of sections of the
lower orders. This phenomenon was matched in the Puritan
petitions against ecclesiastical abuses in 1640–2, which also
obtained widespread support.[41]

Puritanism was not of course a majority movement but the
available sources do not enable us to discover what 'majority'
opinion was in early modern England, and the system was one
which depended anyway on the opinions and position of crucial

minorities. Puritanism was, however, a well supported movement with a wide social base although it was also a movement which provoked serious opposition. Puritans were not an isolated minority but neither should it be suggested that they should simply be identified as the most influential, mainstream Protestants until the 1620s. The work discussed at the start of this section has demonstrated that Puritans were not a clear-cut opposition movement, completely alienated from the existing religious or secular order. Protestantism in the late sixteenth and early seventeenth centuries was a broad and complex spectrum of opinions rather than a group of distinct parties. This work has added a very valuable subtlety to our understanding of religious developments. However, we should not take the notion of a broad spectrum to imply that there was simply a broad, cosy 'Calvinist' consensus destroyed by the rise of an alien, novel Arminianism. There were more serious tensions amongst Protestants before the 1620s than many historians now suggest, and it is in these tensions that we can see the rationale for the rise of Arminianism which was not simply an accidental factor promoted by the personal preferences of Charles and some of his closest associates.

English Protestants in the early seventeenth century were both largely Calvinist, and seriously divided; one useful way in which historians have approached this paradox is through a distinction between credal and experimental (or experiential) Calvinism.[42] Credal Calvinists were those who believed in Calvinist doctrines of predestination as a matter of theory or belief, but did not see these beliefs as the basis for their religious practice or a detailed guide to the rest of their lives. One important example is Elizabeth's Archbishop Whitgift who shared the broad theological beliefs of his Presbyterian opponents. Whitgift took seriously the strict Calvinist belief that it was not possible to distinguish between the elect and the reprobate in this life, and therefore people could not be sure that they were elect. The visible church, the church as an institution in this world, consisted of both sheep and goats and only God could distinguish them. The purpose of the church in this life was not to divide the world between the godly and the ungodly, but to encourage order, obedience and conformity. It was futile and dangerous to encourage elaborate preaching about the complexities of Calvinist doctrine. It was futile because God had already decided who the elect were before they had ever heard any sermons: and it was dangerous because it would promote despair in those listeners who feared they were damned and presumption in those who assumed they were elect saints. The ceremonies and rituals of the established church were to be obeyed because obedience and conformity were religious duties in themselves – there were few specific spiritual benefits from the ceremonial of the established church.

Puritans, in contrast, were experimental predestinarians. Unlike Whitgift, men like the Presbyterian Thomas Cartwright or the more moderate William Perkins argued that the doctrines of Calvinism had direct and dramatic implications for individuals and for society in general. Their preaching suggested that in practice it was possible to discover who was amongst the elect although they acknowledged that in the last analysis only God knew for certain. For individuals they stressed the doctrine of assurance: the belief that it was possible to obtain some security of salvation through searching one's heart, conscientious attention to religious duties such as hearing and discussing sermons, or studying the scriptures, and active, conscientious zeal against evil in the world. In simple terms you could demonstrate to yourself and to others that you were an elect saint by living a godly, religious life. More collectively, two aspects of Puritan religious impulses had a crucial effect: the drive to create a community of the godly in this world, and a determined anti-popery. For zealous Puritans, the preaching and the discipline of the church was intended to make a distinction between the godly and the wicked; the saints would come to recognise each other and work together through their responses to true doctrine while the easy-going and the sinful would be exposed and chastised through a church with an effective structure of reproof and correction. Some radical Puritans came to identify the true church with those who were visibly godly, and almost to separate from the ungodly – a process which gave rise to the independent congregations of saints in the 1640s, or in New England. Puritans espoused most strongly a world-view that distinguished sharply between true religion and popery, and held that Protestants had a compelling duty to struggle against popery. Again this is a useful way of distinguishing Puritans from more conformist Protestants such as Whitgift for whom anti-popery was an intellectual commonplace with few practical implications.

The most fruitful studies of anti-popery have denied that it was an irrational impulse.[43] Sociologists have helped us to understand that labelling enemies in a simple, stereotyped manner is a common means by which societies cope with, or control, the anxieties which emerge in periods of change. Zealous protestants were only too conscious of the partial and contested nature of the reformation in England: attributing the resistance of the people to the machinations of papists made failure more acceptable and suggested a programme for overcoming difficulties through attacking popish doctrines, practices and their supporters. For Puritans the Pope was literally anti-Christ; popery was at the bottom of all the evil in the world: it appealed to human beings' basest, sensual instincts, seducing them into a false church with imagery and empty rituals. Its operation could thus speak to people's intimate worries about disorder in families, as well as more public anxieties. The wiles of papists provided an explanation of why the idle wasted their lives in the local ale-house, as well as of the tribulations of the Protestant cause in Europe. True Protestantism, on the other hand, was seen as a religion of enlightenment which developed the higher rational faculties; again its triumph would transform everything from family life to the nature of European politics.

Thus God's elect saints should seek each other out, and work together to fight popery and reform the sinful world in accordance with the word of God. This activism in the world was spurred on by the quest for assurance (especially as there was always an edge of anxiety because it was not possible to be absolutely sure). Puritans were troublemakers because they could not quite be presumptuous about their salvation. The staunch Protestant predisposition to activism blended with Renaissance humanist teaching that it was through public life that men found fulfilment to produce an influential exemplar for members of the elite – the model of the godly, Christian magistrate who was incorruptible, and dedicated to the defeat of popery and evil. It could give meaning as well to the duties of people in humbler walks of life and provide a more general concept of active citizenship than humanism could offer. The political implications of Puritanism are superficially contradictory. Puritans were clearly concerned about order, and blamed papists for disorder but they wished for a morally improved purified order, and so worked for transformation of the world as it was. This in itself was potentially disruptive while the stress on individual responsibility and commitment, on citizenship, could be extremely alarming to some in authority. Puritan ideas suggested that there might be times when it was more important to be conscientious and diligent against evil than to be obedient or conformist to authority. These impulses were a very important element in the 'country' ideas of political activism and participation discussed earlier.

We can now understand the motives which could lead Puritans to initiate division and disorder in local communities as they sought to root out sin and promote godliness. Puritans were not necessarily hostile to monarchical authority. Zealous Protestants often showed great enthusiasm for a godly prince who would promote true religion and lead the struggle against popery. At the level of the history of ideas of course it is ironic that popery was identified with absolutist monarchy because so much of early modern European resistance theory came from Catholic theorists, especially from late sixteeenth century France. However, in the context of English political developments the connection is not an accidental one. In the first place the concept of the godly prince was implicitly conditional because if the monarch did not act in his appointed role, the obedience of subjects was not necessarily forthcoming. This had an increasingly obvious and ominous relevance to Charles I. Furthermore, the activism of the prince against popery was to be matched by the participation of many others in the vigilant defence of the church. Hence in country ideas defence of the church was linked to defence of English constitutional ideas of government, and to participatory notions in law and government. The papists would win by destroying civil government which was the bulwark of the church. The recent suggestion that there was the potential for Protestant absolutism in England is thus implausible.[44]

The importance of a notion of a religious spectrum must be reiterated. Experimental Calvinism and dynamic anti-popery informed the attitudes of many who would have been horrified at being considered Puritans. Another way of exploring the range of religious opinions is through the issue of conformity to the ceremonies and liturgy of the established church. Some Puritans saw the ceremonies as offensive, and suffered for their nonconformity, others would accept them with various degrees of reluctance in order to avoid the evils of separation. Members of the ecclesiastical hierarchy like Abbot who shared a zealous protestant world-view did not have scruples over the ceremonies but Abbot usually avoided making an issue out of nonconformity and for the most part defined Puritanism in a very narrow sense as involving separatism or Presbyterianism. On a range of practical, political issues, notably opposition to the Spanish match or to royal patronage of men like Montagu, Abbot had much in common with men who could broadly be seen as Puritans. Conformist members of the church had a wider definition of Puritanism and a harsher approach to it. Experimental predestinarian preaching and activism was seen as dangerously popular and subversive; in practice, conformist Calvinists often saw Puritanism as a greater danger than popery. As was suggested above, however, the Calvinism that conformists like Whitgift shared with their dynamic opponents limited the effectiveness of their anti-Puritanism. Seventeenth century conformist Calvinists such as the prominent Lincolnshire minister Robert Sanderson, or, amongst the laity, Charles's Attorney-General Robert Heath, quoted above, tended to stress the importance of obedience for social and political stability. Conformist dominance of the church, contested anyway by men like Grindal or Abbot, was a product of political patronage, not of victory in a battle of ideas. Conformist Calvinists lacked an alternative religious vision of the nature of the church or the way to individual salvation. Arminians, who broke with predestinarian theology and did have an alternative, positive vision of religion, provided a much more effective response to the popular and participatory implications of Puritanism, and to its stress on the preaching of the word and the drawing together of the godly. Arminianism did not come as a bolt from the blue, then, but is explicable in terms of earlier religious conflicts and political tensions in England.[45]

Anti-Calvinism and Arminianism

Alternatives to Calvinist divinity before the 1620s were incoherent and isolated. Richard Hooker developed a notion of the Christian community very different from the Puritan stress on the godly. For Hooker, the visible church had a spiritual significance as part of Christ's mystical body; its sacraments and rituals were not 'things indifferent' or popish survivals as Calvinists variously held, but vital religious practices the performance of which provided entrance into the Christian community. A little later the preaching of Lancelot Andrewes offered an implicit challenge to Calvinist divinity by stressing that faith depended on the senses and feelings, not just the mind. Worship therefore should involve the actions of the whole body – sacraments, rituals, and imagery as well as the hearing of the word. Neither Hooker nor Andrewes openly attacked Calvinist doctrines on salvation, a caution that in Andrewes' case is partly due to dependence on the protection of the king. For much of his reign James I's religious policy involved a complex balancing act which reflected his own ambiguous views.[46] James was fiercely anti-Puritan but for much of his life he was a credal Calvinist; indeed in his own view, he was one of the leading Calvinist intellectuals of Europe. As such he set himself the task of restoring religious unity to his kingdoms and the continent by detaching moderate evangelical Calvinists and Catholics from their more extreme co-religionists. At times he promoted zealous Protestants like Abbot or Davenant, at others he favoured crypto Papists like the Howards in the hope of isolating Puritans or open Papists. He did not permit attacks on the doctrines of

Calvinism but, as we have seen, he was a great opponent of popular preaching about these doctrines.

As has been hinted already, there are significant shifts in attitude towards the end of the reign. The wide-ranging opposition to the proposed Spanish match for Prince Charles in 1622, encouraged by Puritan preachers, reinforced James's sense of the subversive populist implications of dynamic Protestantism. It is also possible that the king's own approaching death lessened the attraction of a strictly predestinarian theology. Changes in the patterns of promotions in the church have been illustrated above; other evidence of change includes the 1622 restrictions on preaching, and the permission given for the publication of Richard Montagu's *A New Gagg for an Old Goose* in 1624. In this volume Montagu argued that Rome was a true if flawed church, and denied the doctrine that the elect would always persevere in grace.[47] The new king's more committed anti-Calvinism soon became clear although at the outset of his reign, when Charles and Buckingham were at the head of a zealous Protestant foreign policy, some Arminians feared for the future. There is the famous story of when the Arminian Matthew Wren was chaplain to Prince Charles, Lancelot Andrewes summoned him to a meeting in London attended by Laud and Neile who asked Wren 'how the Prince's heart stands to the Church of England, that when God brings him to the crown we may know what to hope for'. Wren assured them that Charles would do more than his father towards the 'upholding the doctrine and discipline, and he right estate of the church' and their hopes were not disappointed.

The dominance of the Duke of Buckingham provided continuity despite the change in monarchs. The duke had links with Arminians from at least 1622, and by 1624 was closer to Laud than to his 'Puritan' chaplain John Preston. Very shortly after James's death Laud gave Buckingham a list of leading clergy classified as orthodox or Puritan, showing clearly how Laud saw divisions in the church. In February 1626 Buckingham presided over the 'York House' conference called at the request of the Puritan peers Saye and Warwick to discuss Montagu's work. Here Buckingham made plain his support for an outright attack on Calvinist orthodoxy. The Calvinist Bishop Thomas Morton of Coventry and Lichfield, supported by Preston and Saye, denied that the sacraments could confer faith, and argued that the Church of Rome erred on fundamentals; but Montagu held that good works had a part to play in salvation, that the ceremonies were obligatory under divine law and were by no means things indifferent, while Francis White, dean of Carlisle, proposed that Christ had died for all mankind. Montagu reiterated his view that the Church of Rome was a true church.

Montagu was bitterly attacked in every parliament from 1624 until 1628, especially for his denial of the crucial Calvinist doctrine of perseverance, but Charles took him under his protection and made him Bishop of Chichester in July 1628. In June 1626, Charles had issued a proclamation 'for the establishing of the peace and quiet of the Church of England'. Partially drafted by Laud, it outlawed 'any new Opinions, not only contrary, but differing from the sound and orthodoxal grounds of the true religion, sincerely professed, and happily established in the Church of England'. Calvinists believed that it was Arminianism that was innovatory, as the 'Protestation' forced through the House of Commons by hotheads at the end of the abortive 1629 session implied: 'whosoever shall bring in innovation of religion, or by favour or countenance seek to extend or introduce Popery or Aminianism, or other opinion disagreeing from the true and orthodox Church, shall be reputed a capital enemy to this Kingdom and Commonwealth.' It became clear, however, that Charles's notion of orthodoxy was anti-Calvinist and the 1626 proclamation, more thoroughly than James's 1622 restrictions, hindered the promotion of Calvinist doctrine. The king retained important Privy Councillors who were Calvinists, notably the third Earl of Pembroke who as Chancellor protected the University of Oxford from the full force of the 1626 proclamation. Tyacke regards Pembroke's death in April 1630 as a crucial turning point, as the preacher at the earl's funeral suggested with his sermon on Isaiah 57.1: 'Should the abomination of desolation, the idol of the mass, be set up again in the holy place ... happy he his eyes should behold none of all this'.[48]

Arminian dominance was confirmed in the promotion of Laud

to the Bishopric of London in 1628, and finally his appointment as Archbishop of Canterbury in August 1633 although in practice Abbot had been in disgrace for many years. Neile became Archbishop of York in 1632; both Primates were Privy Councillors. Arminian clergy were never a majority in the church but there were many reasons why they could mount a more successful attack on Puritanism and zealous Calvinism than earlier conformists had. The break with Calvinism itself made possible a more confident and coherent challenge than that of Whitgift, for example. Archbishop Richard Neile was the organiser rather than the intellectual of the Arminian party but his comments on predestination are far removed from the views of the godly Calvinist:

> I will not take upon me to open the mouth of the clay to dispute with the potter why hast thou made me thus, or to enter into the secrets of God's unrevealed counsels, farther than in fear and reverence to apply the comfort of God's goodness and general promises of mercy to all penitent sinners laying hold thereof by faith in Christ Jesus.

As important was Neile's building up of the 'first organised opposition to English Calvinism', the 'Durham House' group formed while he was bishop from 1617 to 1628. Neile was already Laud's patron: contact was made in 1608, on the recommendation of John Buckeridge. The group included prominent Durham clergy such as John Cosin along with important associates like Laud, Buckeridge and Francis White. Richard Montagu first became associated with the Neile group, when he sent the manuscript of *A New Gagg* to Cosin in December 1623, to 'read it over privately, or at most with Austen [Lindsell, another Durham Arminian] and get it licensed, but of no Puritan'. Again the sharp consciousness of allies and parties in the church should be noted. All the Arminians at York House were part of this network, and it formed a 'rallying point' for the clergy who came to power in the 1630s, when their systematic use of contacts and clerical patronage was made easier by royal backing and important links at court. In the decades of Calvinist dominance the 'Durham House' men had developed a sense of themselves as persecuted outsiders and they retained this consciousness in the balmier days of the 1630s; this only sharpened their determination to transform the church and emerged also in bouts of vindictiveness towards opponents. Finally the Arminians benefited from the fierce anti-Puritanism of many Calvinist conformists who allowed the aggressive Laudians to take the initiative in harrying the godly in the localities and so to acquire more influence than their numbers alone warranted.

In the 1630s, the interiors of churches were transformed more than at any time since the Elizabethan settlement. Neile and Laud had long shown their commitment to a ceremonial and sacramental worship. Neile moved the communion table at Durham from the middle of the choir to the site of the pre-Reformation altar in 1617, the same year that Laud, then Dean of Gloucester, came into conflict with his bishop for establishing an altar. In 1633 Charles, with Laud and Neile present as Privy Councillors, judged in favour of the authorities of St Paul's Cathedral who wanted to move the communion table 'altarwise' in the adjoining St Gregory's church. Laud's metropolitical visitation of 1636 enforced this as a general policy while a 1637 speech of the archbishop showed the basis of this sacramentalism:

The altar is the greatest place of God's residence upon earth . . . yea greater than the pulpit, for there 'tis *Hoc est corpus meum*, 'This is my body'. But in the pulpit 'tis at most but *Hoc est verbum meum*, 'This is my word'.[49]

Laud requested in his will of 1644 that he be buried under the altar of the chapel of St John's, Oxford; a sharp contrast to his Calvinist predecessor Abbot who had wished to die in the pulpit. For Calvinists, preaching was the means by which the 'foreknown of God' were effectually called. The sacraments, as the debate at York House showed, were not seen as important to salvation. Peter Lake has described Arminianism as a broad theological, cultural and political reaction to the populist elements in activist, Puritan Protestantism. It was thus by no means a 'bolt from the blue' but built on, and developed earlier stresses on the sacraments and on the importance of the visible church and of conformity to its ceremonies. Neither was Charles's adherence to it a matter of coincidence or accident. English Arminians stressed order and hierarchy, seemliness and obedience to the established practices of the church as an institution; they decried individual activism and initiative. As Tyacke has put it, 'against the incipient egalitarianism of Calvinism, Arminians stressed the hierarchical nature of both church and state in which the office not the holder was what counted'. These ideas obviously connected with the authoritarian 'new counsels' adopted by Charles in the realm of politics. On Charles's accession Montagu promised the king, 'defend me with the sword and I will defend you with the pen' while the Calvinist George Carleton said 'defend the truth and faith, whereof God hath made you the defender and God (who only is able) will not fail to defend you'. It is not surprising that a king who did not believe his subjects had the right to remind him of his duties preferred Montagu. Neither is it accidental that English Arminians were authoritarian in their politics (although the Dutch anti-Calvinists were not).

As Tyacke has stressed, the awareness which grew during the 1630s that Calvinism was no longer the orthodoxy of the English Church had a drastic impact on religious divisions. Some Calvinists who had conformed in the 1620s felt driven to non-conformity or even separation. John Davenport, an influential London conforming Puritan in the 1620s, regarded Arminianism as an attack on the fundamentals of the church and fled to Amsterdam in 1633. Henry Burton, a chaplain to Prince Charles, described himself as conformable in his reply to Montagu's *Apello Caesarem* in 1626; by the 1630s he was a nonconformist, by 1640 he was working for the abolition of episcopacy. Zealous Calvinists who differed on details or tactics drew closer together in common horror at the developments of the 1630s although their overt reactions varied. The diaries of the very moderate Puritan schoolmaster of Warwick, Thomas Dugard, and the more daring steward of Northampton, Robert Woodford, both reveal broad circles of opposition to the Laudian church, including those who emigrated in despair to New England, or who had lost livings through refusing to read the Book of Sports, men who would express open support for the Scots in the late 1630s and others whose more muted or conventional opposition involved no more than private meetings to discuss sermons. When Stephen Marshall, a prominent Essex Puritan harassed by Laud in the early 1630s, summed up the evils of the archbishop's regime in a sermon preached to the Long Parliament in November 1640, he stressed the 'miserable defection' in doctrine, the 'high affronts' to the Lord's Day, the suppression of preaching, the corruption of worship by 'idolatory and superstition', and indiscriminate admission to the sacrament. Only the last complaint would have been seen as particularly Puritan before the 1630s.[50]

Religion and Politics

It has been argued recently that the civil war was a war of religion, rather than a struggle over politics, that political divisions were not sufficiently serious to cause breakdown. Whilst religious divisions were crucial in motivating people and in poisoning the political atmosphere, it is a mistake to imply such a clear separation between religion and politics. On a day-to-day practical and tactical level, men did distinguish between religious and political matters. John Adamson has argued that for Viscount Saye and Sele, constitutional issues about Charles's rule were the most pressing grievance although radical Puritan ideas were also crucial to Saye's political style. Looking back on the civil war in the 1640s and 1650s, Saye wrote: 'It is true, it was not for a Service-Book or for abolishing Episcopacy, that this war was made . . . it was indeed a war made to destroy the Parliament of England, that is the Government of England . . . and hereby it appears, what it was we defended.' In his famous speech at the opening of the Short Parliament, Pym described the Commonwealth's grievances under three heads, 'liberties of parliament', 'matters of religion' and 'affairs of state or matters of property'. Religion should not be stressed in a way that downgrades political division. At a more general level, however, there were very close links between political attitudes and religious outlooks. Activism and participation were characteristic

114

of zealous Puritanism, and of 'country' ideas; order and hierarchy were crucial aspects of English Arminianism and of Charles's new counsels.[51]

Because these connections were drawn by opponents as much as by adherents of such positions, religious divisions played a vital role in the rival conspiracy theories already discussed. Through anti-popery, in particular, politics and religion were integrated through the way (common in many cultures besides that of seventeenth century England) of describing and understanding the world through dichotomies or contrasts. The contrast between popery and true religion was an overarching dichotomy which stood for the ultimate contrast between good and evil as well as more local divisions between court and country. Arminianism played a crucial part in convincing many that Charles was himself implicated in a popish conspiracy. Again it was neither irrational nor implausible to make these connections. Caroline Hibbard has shown how Charles's diplomacy in the 1630s, along with the growing influence of Catholics at court suggest that fears of a popish plot were justified. The role of the Scots Catholic George Con, the papal agent at the Queen's Court 1634–9, was especially suspected. James's Queen Anne, a Catholic convert, had lived mostly in retirement, so Henrietta Maria's household provided the first focus for English Catholics since Queen Mary's reign. Con dined with Juxon, Lord Treasurer and Bishop of London, while the king delayed an installation of new Knights of the Garter while he showed the pope's agent around his picture collection. These were vivid insights into court intimacy with the servants of anti-Christ.

Understandably, Con and other Scottish Catholics prominent at court were seen as a malign influence on Charles's policy towards Scotland so that it was indeed unfortunate that Con's friend, the crypto-Catholic Earl of Arundel, rode in Con's coach, complete with the papal arms, to meetings with the king. Arundel was made commander of the army sent against the Scots in the first Bishops' War. A Commons Committee in 1641 heard how Peterhouse chapel in Cambridge held Latin services with chanting, elaborate singing, incense and bowing to an altar in a marble-floored sanctuary. Good works and free-will were stressed in sermons at the university. All this 'local' evidence clearly suggested a view of the church rooted in Catholic tradition. Finally the existence of a broad internationally backed papist conspiracy to undermine all that was upright in British life was horrifyingly demonstrated to many in the Irish rebellion of 1641.[52]

Anti-popery both fuelled and fed on Charles's own version of conspiracy theory, the popular-Puritan conspiracy against order and hierarchy in general and monarchy in particular. A minor example of the connections Charles and Laud made between religion and politics has already been given in the charges against the lecturer Workman of Gloucester. On a broader level this conspiracy was evident to Charles in all three of his kingdoms, with the rebellion by the Covenanters in Scotland providing the most terrible and convincing evidence. Thus in the late 1630s and early 1640s there existed two rival conspiracy theories which explained religious and political conflict; both were rational and each reinforced the other.

Arminianism in England provided a focus for elite fears of the populist implications of zealous Protestantism, but through the stress on communal parochial ceremonial and recreations, it also chimed in with popular resentment of the interference and demands of the godly. Religious divisions like the cultural cleavages also discussed in this chapter had intricate connections with attitudes towards social relationships. The political and religious divisions which have been analysed reveal widespread anxiety about social order, although there clearly was no consensus on the sources of the most serious threats to order or on the best means for preventing or controlling disorder. Contrasting religious and political ideas imply different visions of how society should be organised and different notions of good government and legitimate rule. The next chapter will examine ways in which these ideological divisions can be placed in a social context and linked to the processes of social change in early modern England.

3

A SOCIAL AND CULTURAL CONFLICT?

Exploration of the social context of the civil war is extremely unfashionable in the current historiographical climate. Changing historical fashions can be illustrated from the titles of two collections of sources covering early modern social history. In 1965 Laurence Stone published *Social Change and Revolution in England 1540–1640*, whereas in 1988 Barry Coward produced *Social Change and Continuity in Early Modern England 1550–1750*. The coupling of continuity rather than revolution with social change in the latter work reveals a more qualified assessment of the extent of transformation in early modern England, but the different choice of chronology is also significant. Where Stone saw social change as crucial to the political breakdown of 1640–2, Coward refers only briefly to the civil war and in the main does not find it valid to tie social developments to a timescale defined by political conflicts.[1] There are many reasons for this change in the approach to the origins of the English civil war, ranging from shifts in the general intellectual atmosphere to problems with the specific attempts to discover a social context for the divisions of 1642. As was suggested in chapter 1, it is much less common now for historians to see the English civil war as a major landmark in the 'modernisation' of traditional society, and this has affected views of social change as well as encouraging scepticism about the emergence of modern liberty

117

or the rise of religious toleration. Furthermore, although the emergence of a 'modern world' has been the focus for historians and sociologists working in several traditions, in its social and economic aspects this has often been expressed in Marxist terms as the shift from a feudal to a capitalist society. Distrust of social explanations of the civil war has thus been encouraged by a broader attack on Marxism in the social sciences.

A Bourgeois Revolution?

It is also true that the difficulties of constructing a Marxist interpretation of the causes of the civil war, theoretically coherent and supported by evidence, have themselves contributed to a move away from Marxist styles of analysis. The most common Marxist interpretations have centred on the civil war as a crucial element of a 'bourgeois revolution' although the precise descriptions of this revolution have varied. Sometimes the stress has been on the external or structural aspects of revolution: the civil war was both a product of the tensions accompanying the emergence of capitalism within a feudal society and, through the victory of Parliament, its 'outcome was the establishment of conditions far more favourable to the development of capitalism than those which prevailed before 1640'.[2] Historians are often not very precise about what is intended by terms like 'feudal' or 'capitalist', but the following brief and oversimplified account may add clarity to the discussion.

Within a feudal society it is assumed that most economic production is by peasants who farm their land more for subsistence and to provide a surplus for their landlords than for sale through markets. Landlords acquire their profits through legal and political power, not directly through economic enterprise, and for the elite land is a source of social influence, and a means for conspicuous consumption, not for the maximisation of economic profit. Social relationships are marked by deference and paternalism and there is little consciousness that society is made up of competing classes defined by their economic position. In a capitalist society waged labour is the characteristic form of economic production; production is for the market in a money economy. Elites concentrate on accumulation and the maximisation of profit; social stratification is more clear-cut, and takes the form of class divisions although capitalism is also a system which stresses individualism, rather than communal ties. In an English context agricultural changes are at the heart of this transformation, but the emergence of capitalism also witnesses increasing investment and involvement in industry, trade and colonisation.

There has been a two-pronged attack on the general notion of the English civil war as part of the transition from feudalism to capitalism. It is denied that such a transformation took place; and secondly it is argued that economic changes cannot anyway be closely linked to political or religious stances (which are not considered innovatory or revolutionary). One can cite the famous remark of Conrad Russell about Stone's *Crisis of the Aristocracy*, that it 'attempts to explain events which did not happen in terms of a social change for which the evidence remains uncertain'.[3] Two sharply contradictory arguments have been presented against the view that the seventeenth century was a period of decisive transformation in the English economy: some historians argue that the crucial changes had already taken place, others that they were yet to come. Alan Macfarlane has claimed that England had been an individualistic, market-orientated society for centuries before 1640, while within a Marxist tradition, Robert Brenner has implied that the result of social conflicts between peasants and landlords in the medieval period was more important to the development of agrarian capitalism in England than anything that happened in the seventeenth century. In contrast Peter Laslett's very influential social history, *The World We Have Lost*, describes a 'traditional society' that endured into the nineteenth century while for J. C. D. Clark, England was an *ancien régime* dominated by the landed aristocracy, the established church and divine right monarchy until political reform and industrialisation destroyed this old world in the 1830s.[4]

Neither is it clear how far in fact the rule of Charles I acted as a brake on the English economic development that did occur. It has been suggested that Charles's erratic and ineffective foreign policy, in contrast to the vigorous use of national power by the regimes of the 1650s, provided little help for trade or colonisation. There were unpredictable attempts at the regulation of enclosure, or of industrial enterprise (through monopolies) where royal financial exigencies rather than any economic rationale was the most important motive; and general threats to property through levies and exactions backed by prerogative power. Most of these points are accepted, to some extent at least; it is their significance that is disputed. It is argued that these policies were not integral, structural aspects of royal rule; they were often the result of the government's methods of rewarding its allies, and ignoring 'outsiders'. The opponents of royal policies did not want to challenge the whole system; they wanted a share of the spoils or, as with the Earl of Warwick's desire for colonisation and an active anti-Spanish foreign policy, they wanted their views rather than their rivals' to be implemented. Several commentators have questioned whether royal economic policies were sufficiently irksome, or effective, to be worth fighting over, or to require a revolution for their elimination. Some are equally sceptical about the transformation in the relationship between the state and economic development after the civil war. Christopher Hill has stressed the passing of the Navigation Act by which the government backed English trade in a more systematic fashion than hitherto, and the abolition of the Court of Wards which meant that members of the landed elite were no longer at risk of their estates falling under royal supervision if they died before their heirs came of age. This, it is suggested, freed the landed elite to engage more whole-heartedly in agricultural improvement. As both these measures were confirmed at the Restoration, they were among the permanent gains of the civil war years, but whether they amount to a bourgeois revolution is another matter.[5]

The concept of a 'bourgeois revolution' has also been used in a more subjective sense which stresses the deliberate agency of a newly emerging capitalist class, a 'bourgeoisie' which was engaged in novel economic enterprise, and whose advance was blocked by an outmoded social and political system. Consequently attempts have been made by Marxist and Marxist-influenced historians to link elite allegiances in 1642 directly to the emergence of new economic interests. A brief historiographical survey of these attempts will help us understand why they contributed to the current disillusion with social interpretations of the civil war. Two very different interventions in the early 1940s began the modern debate although twentieth century historians drew also on the social analysis of seventeenth century commentators like James Harrington, the Earl of Clarendon and Richard Baxter. In 1940, Christopher Hill provided a rousing analysis: in the 'English Revolution', 'the state power protecting an old order that was essentially feudal was violently overthrown, power passed into the hands of a new class, and so the freer development of capitalism was made possible'. It was, wrote Hill, 'necessary for the further development of capitalism that this choking parasitism should be ended by the overthrow of the feudal state'. The composition of the new class was complex, as it is in most Marxist analyses, although their critics have not always allowed this. It included 'progressive sections of the gentry' as well as a trading bourgeoisie, and sections of the yeomanry, and Hill's later work has emphasised the importance of the 'industrious sort' of people, the 'middling sort', in economic and political change.

Albeit in a less polemical style, R. H. Tawney, the left wing, but not Marxist historian and politician, presented what was in some respects a simpler argument than Hill's. Tawney had already written on many aspects of the 'transition to capitalism' in his important works on the role of religion, and on the disappearance of the small farmer; now he argued that the rise of a new aggressive gentry class and the decline of the old aristocracy was crucial to the outbreak of the civil war.[6] One of his 1941 articles was called 'Harrington's Interpretation of his Age', and developed the view of the conflict outlined by the political philosopher James Harrington in the 1650s. Harrington argued that the civil war came about because the dissolution of the monasteries and the anti-noble policies of the early Tudors brought about a shift in landed power from the aristocracy to a broader group. This upset the balance between landed and political power which Harrington believed was essential to stability, and so required a corresponding shift from a mixed monarchy to a commonwealth or republic. Tawney added statistical backing to this framework by counting the manors held by the peerage, the crown and the gentry in the mid sixteenth century and in 1640. From this he argued that the wealth of the gentry had risen while that of the crown and the peers had declined, in part because the peers remained wedded to the traditional patterns of conspicuous consumption and paternalist estate management whereas the gentry showed greater enthusiasm for new commercial methods. Their increasing prosperity encouraged the gentry to claim a greater role in politics, and the civil war was their drive to achieve political power against the opposition of the king and the peers.

The notion of 'the rise of the gentry' attracted much debate and much criticism. Not much faith was put in the 'counting of manors' as evidence because manors varied so much in their nature and value, and several commentators denied that the gentry had risen, either in numbers or in wealth. Trevor-Roper even suggested that gentry who depended solely on landed income without the profits of court office or a lucrative legal practice were actually declining in wealth. He saw parliamentarians in the civil war as the embittered declining gentry attacking a parasitic court, rather than the confident, prospering leaders of a new class. This argument did not find much support but it at least indicated how difficult it was to make convincing judgements about general developments amongst the gentry, still less to tie these developments to civil war allegiance.

Furthermore there has been widespread agreement amongst social and economic historians (although less unanimity amongst those whose main concern is politics) that it is misleading in an English context to see the peers and the gentry as two distinct groups. Rather they form together one landed aristocracy; although they are divided between nobles and commoners, this is a matter of different legal privileges, rather than an indication of separate economic characteristics or sharp differences in kind in matters such as role, power or life-style.[7] This was a major criticism of Laurence Stone's *Crisis of the Aristocracy*, which discussed the economic, social, cultural and political fortunes of the *peerage* between 1558 and 1641. Stone broadened and modified Tawney's argument but still concluded that the peers suffered a wide-ranging crisis in the late sixteenth and early seventeenth centuries. Their independent legal, political and military power was replaced by dependence on the crown while their economic position did worsen in the inflationary sixteenth century. In purely financial terms the peers were doing better by the 1620s, but often at some cost to their social power as more efficient policies of estate management weakened traditional ties between noblemen and their tenants. Stone's argument will be returned to below in discussing the social and ideological nature of leadership in the civil war.[8]

The most obvious problem with Tawney's and Stone's interpretation was that peers were prominent on Parliament's side as well as on the king's in the 1640s; Charles, as well as Parliament, obtained much gentry support. In the 1950s Christopher Hill approached these problems by developing his own 1940 argument that the landed class was divided, and Tawney's point that the rising gentry had adopted commercially orientated estate management policies in order to profit from inflation. Hill thus suggested that the division of 1642 was not between peers and gentlemen but between 'mere rentiers', with traditional or feudal economic attitudes, and 'those ... actively engaged in productive activities', those who sought the best possible return from their landed estates and who engaged in industrial or commercial enterprise. This 'progressive' group included sections of the 'middling sort' as well as sections of the peerage and the gentry. Noting further that royalist strength was concentrated in the 'backward' north and west while Parliament predominated in the economically advanced south and east, Hill argued that traditional economic interests gravitated to royalism while the economically progressive supported Parliament as the best guarantee of property rights and economic enterprise. Like Tawney, Hill could cite seventeenth century support for his views. The royalist Earl of Clarendon claimed that although 'gentlemen of ancient families and estates' in Somerset were:

for the most part well affected to the King ... yet there were a people of an inferior degree, who, by good husbandry, clothing and other thriving arts, had gotten very great fortunes, and, by degrees getting themselves into the gentlemen's estates, were angry that they found not themselves in the same esteem and reputation with those whose estates they had . . . These from the beginning were fast friends to the Parliament.

The parliamentarian cleric, Richard Baxter, had similar views:

On the Parliament's side were (besides themselves) the smaller part, as some thought, of the gentry in most of the counties, and the greatest part of the tradesmen and freeholders, and the middle sort of men, especially in those corporations and countries which depend on clothing and such manufactures.[9]

The implications of modern research have not been so clear. The varying hypotheses on the fate of the gentry, and on connections with the civil war, prompted much detailed research – into individual families, the economic background of MPs, the civil war allegiances of common lawyers and, perhaps most influentially, into county-wide patterns of gentry allegiance. Little of this research provided support for a convincing social interpretation of the civil war. Alan Simpson studied a range of East Anglian gentry families to discover: 'How far is the English Revolution – the whole of it, or any part of it – to be explained in terms of alterations in the balance of social power?' His conclusions were that there were no general patterns to gentry fortunes; much depended on individual, accidental matters – the hazards and expense of office or the random influence of demography. There was little point in erecting general explanations of the 'English Revolution' on such insecure foundations. A thorough study of the Yorkshire gentry found that there was little difference between the individual wealth of royalist and parliamentarian gentry; there were 'rising' and 'declining' gentry, 'mere rentiers' and active agricultural producers, on each side, and similar proportions of commercial and professional men amongst royalists and parliamentarians. Yorkshire parliamentarian gentry were in slightly better financial shape than their royalist neighbours, but the difference was not great. The most obvious contrast was that almost twice as many gentry families supported the king as sided with Parliament, 242 to 128.

In Lancashire also, most of the gentry were royalists but any differences between royalists and parliamentarians were subtle. Rising gentry and declining gentry were in a minority on both sides which were thus largely composed of families of stable fortunes. There were more prospering families on Parliament's side, while the king's followers included the more spectacular failures, and the most indebted. The Lancashire royalists included reactionary, paternalistic and progressive landlords, coal speculators and 'commercial tycoons'; it is hard, therefore, to characterise them as the defenders of a feudal social order. Furthermore, Lancashire royalists, like royalists in Suffolk or royalist members of the Long Parliament, were younger than their parliamentarian counterparts; a finding which those who associate youth with radicalism have used to support the argument that it was monarchy which represented the *avant-garde*. On the other hand, in many counties royalist gentry came from families established longer in their shires than parliamentarians who were relative newcomers; this is taken to represent a tendency towards conservatism. This research into the gentry and their civil war allegiance thus produced much useful information but also discredited most attempts to draw general conclusions. [10]

Consequently there is now much scepticism about the sixteenth and seventeenth centuries as a period of revolutionary change and about attempts to construct theories of elite allegiance in the civil war which link political division with economic and social transition. It is not necessary though for impatience with stark claims of a transition from feudalism to capitalism to undermine all attempts to examine social change, and its possible links with political, religious or cultural divisions. The rest of this chapter will examine the latest work on social and economic change, and recent analyses of the causes of the civil war which emphasise a social context. Here the conclusions will be less pessimistic. Three important aspects of current work must be stressed. In the first place social and economic change, while not rapid or revolutionary by the standards of later centuries, was nonetheless significant and complex; in particular changes were regionally diverse. Secondly, the most fruitful approaches to the social causes of the civil war do not focus in a crude way on social categories to see how they moved up and down in some concrete entity called society; they examine social relationships, and the *variety* of ways in which different social ranks were affected by, or reacted to the processes of social change which did take place. Finally, work on the nature and social context of aristocratic power enables the types of political leadership that were possible in 1642 to be discussed.

A Century of Social Change

The civil war broke out in a society which had experienced a century of complex social and economic change.[11] This in itself is an important context for the ideological divisions and anxieties about social order revealed in chapter 2. Furthermore, without assuming that individuals' political stances or religious ideas are crudely determined by their economic position, it can be seen that specific aspects of change made plausible or helped to structure some of the positions outlined in the last chapter. In the sixteenth century the English population rose by at least 75 per cent and may have doubled to reach about 5 million by the 1630s. This was a period also of unprecedented inflation: from the late fifteenth to the mid seventeenth century, grain prices rose eightfold; the prices of industrial products lagged behind and peaked later, but still tripled. It has been estimated that the cost of living for an agricultural labourer rose sixfold and that the value of real wages was halved. The pressure of population growth and the quest to survive or profit from inflation encouraged more intensive, market-orientated agricultural practices. The markets served the increasing urban population, particularly of London, and the growing number of people who did not grow their own food. About 25 per cent more land was taken into cultivation; new crops and farming practices enabled more efficient exploitation of the land.

The impact of agricultural change varied from region to

region.[12] Where there was spare land available, and where manorial organisation was too weak to restrict immigration, as in upland and forest areas, especially in northern England, there was an expansion of poor, small land-holdings in response to population pressure. In other areas, particularly in parts of the Midlands where a mixed 'sheep-corn' farming system operated, there were significant shifts from common field and common pasture agriculture to large enclosed individual estates. Enclosure was a controversial and often resisted procedure, especially in the sixteenth century; at first it was carried out mainly for sheep farming, but later for arable too. However, a growing proportion of enclosures was carried out with the agreement of a wide range of land-holders. Middling landowners – minor gentry, yeomen, some prosperous husbandmen – were often amongst the major beneficiaries or even the initiators of such agrarian change; their interests, unlike those of poorer families, were usually protected. At the level of government, and of elites, there was a momentous shift in attitudes towards enclosure in the middle third of the seventeenth century. The 1630s was the last decade when governments tried to enforce the laws against enclosing or engrossing of holdings in the interests of social stability. By the 1650s, enclosure was conventionally regarded by men of property as a means of agricultural improvement which would benefit all, rather than a disruptive and exploitative process.

Agricultural change was crucial to overall transformation in England, but there was also a general expansion of inland and overseas trade and an increase in the numbers who owed part of their living to industrial by-employments. Many industries flourished in upland or forest pastoral areas – south Lancashire and west Yorkshire, the west Midlands 'Black Country' or parts of Somerset, Dorset and Devon. These areas were highly populated, with many small property-holders who could not survive on their agricultural production alone. In addition, a pastoral agriculture or a dairying economy (to a lesser extent) allowed time for additional employment. The availability of industrial employment facilitated the survival of small land-holdings which in other areas would not have been viable, but the industries themselves became increasingly large scale, with complex credit and marketing organisations exploiting the production of the countryside. By 1650, with population growth halted, the basis had been laid for the development of a 'consumer society' which had a fairly broad basis of prosperity.

In connecting economic change to political conflict and division, one crucial point to stress is that the century before 1640 was a time of both risks and opportunities, with winners and losers amongst all social groups besides the poor. Those from the upper and middle ranks of the population who could produce a surplus for the market and whose profits rose faster than expenses such as rents could reap great rewards. Indeed, although political historians have let the matter drop, economic historians have quietly concluded that there was a 'rise of the gentry', both in numbers and in overall prosperity. Thus there was a broadening in the ranks of the landowning classes. Clay's survey shows that while the numbers and size of great estates remained about the same from the mid fifteenth to the late seventeenth century, the numbers and landed possessions of the middling and lesser gentry may have doubled. These generalisations of course mask very drastic contrasts in the fortunes of individual families. In so far as the owners of great estates were often peers there was some adjustment in the relationships between noblemen and gentlemen, but in many ways, as we have indicated, it is misleading to distinguish too sharply between the peerage and the gentry.[13] No great distinctions in economic fortunes or activities can be made between peers and greater gentry. Often the most wealthy landowners were best placed to profit from the opportunities offered in a century of inflation; they invested in trade and industry and sought the maximum profit from their landed estates. Such enterprise did not detract from noble or gentle status although direct involvement in manual or practical activities would. Some large landowners were less flexible and experienced severe problems of indebtedness as prices rose but rents remained static. The very active land market in the late sixteenth and early seventeenth centuries is one indication of the degree of change occurring in the personnel and prosperity of English landowners.

For the landed elite then, there were good causes for anxiety in a period of generally increasing prosperity. The sheer prosperity of the landed elite is an obvious point but one that is too little stressed: most members of the English governing classes had much greater economic independence of the state than their counterparts in the French monarchy, for example. Few relied on royal pensions or concessions for significant elements of their income and this must have played a part in the willingness of some, albeit a minority, of the landed elite to engage in determined, armed resistance of their monarch. The confidence inculcated by broad economic advance is reflected in the political claims of the conscientious, Protestant public servants, the men who ran local government and sat in Parliament. But the precarious nature of the economic advance is also important in a political context. The security of the elite could be threatened by the reordering of relationships with their social inferiors, who were themselves affected by social change in complicated ways.

Both the prospering middling sort and the increasing numbers of the poor were potentially problems for elites. Furthermore, raising rents, and intensifying the exploitation of land and manorial rights inevitably altered landowners' relationships with their tenants and neighbours. The vulnerability of landowners was part of a revaluation of the nature of social and political leadership in England, a revaluation that can validly be seen as part of a 'crisis of the aristocracy', despite the criticisms made of this concept as formulated by Stone. The responses of elites took various forms, and much of the rest of this chapter will elaborate on the differing interpretations of the process by historians. Here some preliminary suggestions can be made. Some peers and gentlemen maintained a dominant place in their localities as the leaders of the 'country', a broad social alliance united by an ideological commitment to godliness, and the defence of English laws and liberties. This was what Charles and his allies regarded as a factious and corrupt appeal to the prejudices of the vulgar, and labelled as the spectre of 'popularity', a spectre that itself becomes much more explicable in the context of the social changes we have discussed. The related attack on Puritanism as a divisive and subversive influence in local society and the consequent support for supposedly communal parish rituals and a more practical, ceremonial religion are also connected with the increased social differentiation that was in fact taking place.

Divisions in social attitudes amongst elites were complicated by developments amongst the 'middling sort'. This vague but necessary term, very widely used by historians, refers as in the previous chapter, to yeomen, and richer husbandmen among landed groups as well as to prosperous craftsmen and small merchants. As the earlier comments on enclosure suggest, the impact of economic change on the middling sort was very complex. Many did not have the resources to cope with rising prices and declined into the expanding ranks of the landless, but probably a majority produced a sufficient surplus to profit from the inflation in agricultural prices, expanded their holdings and became important commercial farmers. This prospering section of the middling sort comprised the most important element of the broader 'political nation' discussed in chapter 2. They participated in law enforcement and local government at parish and often county level; they were increasingly literate and were well informed about national political affairs. Again there are few parallels in the major continental monarchies. For some the arbitrary nature of predestinarian Calvinism could make sense of the practical dangers of their existence, while living sober and godly lives could prevent disaster striking a family whose margins were narrow. It must be admitted, however, that Nehemiah Wallington, the best documented godly artisan of the seventeenth century, so devoted himself to self-examination and hearing sermons that his business was utterly neglected.[14]

The impact of social change on the increasing numbers of the poor was more clear-cut. The rise in population was greater than the increase in production and it was the wealthier elements in society who reaped most of the benefit from economic expansion. In general the gap between the comfortably off and the poor widened. In some sparsely inhabited upland and forest areas ample land or industrial by-employments preserved egalitarian societies, but for the poor in many areas the half-century from the 1590s to the 1640s may have been the worst time in English history. The poor were most seriously affected by rising food prices; they were most likely to lose out as their richer neighbours engrossed larger land-holdings, and exploited their land more ruthlessly. Often the rise in numbers of the poor was equal to the total rise in population from the early sixteenth to the early seventeenth centuries as it was in the Warwickshire parishes of the Forest of Arden, for example. In Terling, Essex, there were 21 households of poor labourers or cottagers in 1524–5, but three times as many in 1671 while the numbers in other social groups had hardly altered. The landless or virtually landless poor comprised as much as a third of the population, many of them dependent on the parish-based poor relief developed systematically from the 1590s. Less fortunate still were those forced by lack of work or home to become vagrants; vagrancy was one of the major fears of governing elites.[15]

The poor themselves rarely appear as direct actors or participants in nationally important political events in the early seventeenth century. More relevant is the political impact of fear or anxiety about the poor on the part of the better off. It has recently been convincingly argued that the threat to social stability posed by the poor was more apparent than real. The Elizabethan poor law – a concession won from an alarmed propertied class – made widespread social conflict both less necessary and more difficult to achieve. Poor relief took the edge off the desperation of the very poor – although it is rarely the most desperate who rebel – and it institutionalised the dependency of the poor on the good opinion of their more prosperous neighbours. Furthermore the machinery of poor relief solidified divisions in local communities, between those who administered and paid for, and those who received poor relief. By the seventeenth century the prosperous villagers who had been prominent in earlier popular movements were now part of the machinery of local government. Jim Sharpe has written that the two centuries after the extensive risings of 1549 saw a transition from popular rebellion to rioting by the poor. Disorder became smaller in scale, and involved a more limited section of the population. Rather as elites are seen as becoming more tamed, or mannered, the threat from the poor was becoming domesticated, and

defined as crime not as rebellion. There were important exceptions to this trend still in the 1620s to the 1640s, but they were
special, localised cases where many ranks of the community were
affected by economic change – the large-scale drainage schemes
in the fens, or the forest clearances in the West Country.[16]

These structural changes were of course less apparent to
contemporaries than they are to historians and the unrest caused
in the 1620s by poor harvests and depression in the cloth
industry, as well as by the burdens of war, intensified elite
anxieties about royal levies and policies. In the early 1640s also
fear of popular disorder was an important part of the political
context. Unrest continued in the fens and the West Country, and
economic discontent in London hardened the resolve of the
crowds who demonstrated on political and religious issues in
1641–2. Alarm at the impact of the London crowds in particular
may well have contributed to support for the crown in the civil
war as a way of bolstering social and political hierarchies in
general. But the qualified nature of the threat from the poor is
also important in that it meant that there was room for disagreement within elites over the nature of social problems, and the
most appropriate responses to them. It was seen in chapter 2
that there were serious divisions amongst elites over the extent to
which broader social groups should participate in politics;
equally there was no uniform programme of 'social control'.

One final general point about the social context of the civil
war is worth emphasising: according to most economic indica-
tors it occurred during a period of reverse or stagnation after a
longer period of economic expansion. The upward movement of
prices, population and rents was coming to an end by 1642,
although by that time rents had generally risen faster than
inflation. The war itself exacerbated economic distress but from
the 1650s real wages began at last to improve and a more
broadly based prosperity stimulated further agricultural and
commercial advance. Sociological explanations of a 'revolution',
popularised particularly by Laurence Stone in the 1960s, post-
ulated that it was in just such periods of readjustment that elites'
anxiety about their own status, and their relationships with
other groups contributed to serious political divisions and

unrest.[17] Although general concepts of revolution, and the use of sociological models rarely find much favour now, events in Britain (and in Europe also) in the 1640s suggest that this particular point has much validity.

Social Relationships and Political Conflict

Social and economic change thus involved complex readjustments at all levels of society, and led to new problems in the relationships between different social groups. The most convincing specific attempts to explain the social context of the civil war have focused on social relationships and reactions to the problems of social change. The important studies of Manning, Hunt and Underdown all seek to connect these issues with the ideological divisions discussed in chapter 2. Brian Manning's *The English People and the English Revolution*, first published in 1976, has been the most controversial.[18] For Manning the civil war was not a 'struggle . . . between a declining feudal class and a rising capitalist class, but a conflict between the aristocracy or governing elites and the independent small producers', this last group comprising both the peasantry and artisans and small traders in towns. The conflict occurred in a society that was still essentially feudal, although capitalism was developing and affecting all social groups. An 'aristocratic reaction' occurred in the decades before the civil war as landlords attacked the peasantry by raising rents, and taking into their private possession the forests, fens and other common lands, essential to the economic survival of small producers. At the head of this reaction was the king, the greatest landlord of all; he and indeed all landlords lost much of their social power through such extortions. By 1640–2, there was extensive protest in the countryside, and conflict in many towns also as craftsmen and small merchants tried to resist a trend towards oligarchic power.

In Manning's account the 'middling sort' are an essential element in the popular struggle, driven by a Puritanism portrayed as a form of class-consciousness. It 'inspired a concept of godliness that helped to create a self-conscious middle sort of people', distinct from both rich and poor, and taught them, 'to think for themselves and to assert their independence against king, lords and bishops'. Ultimately, the middling sort were an unstable and complex grouping, becoming fragmented by economic change, and unable to achieve a democratic revolution. Nonetheless, Manning's view is very different from the common current emphasis on the role of the middling sort in the institutions of government, and on their increasing identification with governing elites. Similarly, Manning sees Puritanism as an emancipatory rather than a repressive influence.

As the king was the landlords' champion, so Parliament became the best hope of the people. Thus in 1640–2 the peasantry, and most crucially the small merchants, craftsmen, and apprentices of London came to believe in Parliament's own propaganda that it was the 'Representative of the People'. The 'people' were to be sadly disillusioned by its representatives who proved staunch defenders of the interests of the wealthy, when faced by the radical criticism of the Levellers. But in the early 1640s popular pressure was still behind the parliamentary opponents of the king. It was such pressure which won the great victories of the first months of the Long Parliament, not parliamentary votes, or elite political manoeuvres. In a vivid narrative which deliberately hints at parallels between the London of the 1640s and the Paris of the 1790s, Manning argues that Charles's consent to Strafford's execution in May 1641, the exclusion of the bishops from the House of Lords in December 1641 and the king's own fatal flight from London after his botched attempt to arrest the five members in the following month were all produced by fear of the violence of the London crowd. The division of the political elite into royalists and parliamentarians is explained with reference to differing responses to the popular movement. Many were pushed into royalism. 'In reaction against these movements [in London] a party of order had come into existence in the ruling class'; it was 'very anxious for strong action to restore order and to put the people in their place'. On the other side there was a 'popular party' of parliamentarians who both used and feared the people. It expected a royalist coup and believed that:

the only defence against such a coup, and the only hope now of pushing through further moderate reforms, was popular support; but it was at the same time nervous of popular movements, and sought further moderate reforms as the means of diverting the people away from more radical demands, and would ally with the people with the aim of controlling and drawing the teeth of popular movements, so as to ensure the safety of the ruling class.

Manning's work was a pioneering and stimulating attempt to break away from sterile debates on gentry allegiance and formulate an alternative social explanation of the civil war. The attraction of royalism as the best defence of hierarchy and order in troubled times is a convincing explanation for much elite support for Charles; while the stress on the independent political actions of those outside the political elite, especially in London but also in many industrial areas, has broadened the terms of historical debate on the outbreak of war, even if it has provoked more disagreement than assent. Nonetheless there are several problems with Manning's account. As has been noted, the most convincing recent work on popular unrest suggests that it was declining in the years before 1642, not rising to a crescendo that provoked civil war. There was remarkably little popular upheaval in the 1640s, considering the degree of general political breakdown and military disruption. Few would agree that England was marked by such overt and conscious class hostility of the poor towards the rich as Manning suggests. The divergent characterisations of the 'middling sort' and of the nature of Puritanism discussed already suggest that a more complex understanding of the place of both in the coming of war is needed. Finally, Manning presents a mechanical and conspiratorial picture of elite parliamentarianism. It is never clear why parliamentarians were less afraid of social unrest than royalist gentry, or why they thought the best ploy was to put themselves at the head of a popular movement. Ideological conviction is not seen as playing an important part; there is little discussion of rival political principles amongst elites while, in Manning's framework, there is little room for genuinely Puritan peers or gentlemen.

The difficulties with Manning's interpretation are highlighted

if we examine the superficially similar discussion of William
Hunt, based on the coming of civil war in the county of Essex.
Hunt too stresses the middling sort, their support for Puritanism, and a widespread concern for social order but his concep-
tion of all three is in fact very different from Manning's.[19] Hunt
isolates fears of the increasing numbers of the poor and the
apparently subversive threat they posed as the most crucial
aspect of social change in the century before 1640. The 1590s
were a turning point as elites moved from mere panic to more
thoughtful measures. There was of course the systematic Elizabethan poor law, the 'great creative response of the Tudor upper
classes', and on the part of some a move to a Puritan inspired
'reformation of manners'. This programme of reformation was
carried out by an alliance of godly ministers, and local lay
notables who used zealous preaching and the agencies of local
government to attack sexual immorality, and drunkenness,
disorderly parish festivals and rituals. Hunt thus shares the view
of Keith Wrightson and David Levine, also based on research
into Essex society, that Calvinist Puritanism was particularly
attractive to the middling sort – parish elites who controlled the
offices of churchwarden, overseer of the poor and constable.
Calvinism gave a sense of mission and enabled the respectable to
distinguish themselves from the ungodly and disorderly poor; it
helped make sense of the anxious decades they lived through,
and offered a programme for reforming the manners and behaviour of the poor – in Hunt's words it offered a 'culture of
discipline'. Puritanism was attractive as well to many amongst
the Essex landed elite, notably the leader of Essex parliamentarianism, the Earl of Warwick; at this level godly reform was tied
in with a rousing Protestant international vision whereby domestic economic and social problems would be solved through an
anti-Spanish imperial foreign policy.

Hunt's Puritan coalition was thus made up of both modest
and wealthy property-holders, with a vision which integrated
local action against popery and ungodliness with a commitment
to a forward foreign policy. To this vision the Stuart kings were
seen as increasingly hostile, and royal initiatives were themselves
seen not as isolated actions but as part of an ominous whole. The

Book of Sports, first issued by James in 1618, was to Puritans a charter for disorderly, ungodly rituals and a threat to reform, with obvious and sinister connections with the proposed Spanish match for Prince Charles. The reissue of the Book by Charles in 1633 was similarly linked to the passive foreign policy of the 1630s. By 1642, in Essex, there was a broad social alliance of middling and upper groups who saw in Parliament the means to effect a godly crusade against popery at home and abroad, and who saw the king's religious and social attitudes as promoting disorder and idolatory. As with Manning's work, Hunt does seem to have identified one set of attitudes which underlay allegiance in 1642; many Puritans, especially amongst the clergy, referred to the issue of the 1633 Book of Sports as a horrible and ungodly move which fatally weakened their adherence to royal government, and justified their support for Parliament. As with Manning, again, however, Hunt's analysis is one-sided and raises the obvious problem of why Calvinist reform and anti-popery were not more uniformly attractive to middle and upper groups if they were so useful to the maintenance of social order. Local research on elite allegiance has emphasised in the first place the reluctance of many to get involved on either side, but of those peers and gentry who did play an active part it has been found that in counties such as Yorkshire, Lancashire, Cheshire, and Warwickshire about twice as many became royalists as supported Parliament.[20] Only in the counties close to London was the weight of gentry support on Parliament's side, and even in Essex, 'the first born of Parliament', there were significant Catholic, courtier and royalist elements.

Social Change and Cultural Conflict

Both Manning and Hunt focus on the ways in which social change had complicated the relationships between different social groups, and highlight concerns with the problems of order. Both are, however, too simple and neither incorporates in his analysis a full sense of the complexity of social change. Both also have too obvious a notion of 'social control': they straightforwardly assume that elites adopt particular ideas and practices to ensure that the lower orders accept and keep to their subordinate position in society. There are at least two problems here: elites might aim at 'social control' but this does not mean that their social inferiors received the message they were intended to, from Puritan preaching or a parish ritual. Secondly, a crucial aspect of the period before the civil war is that elites were divided over what the major threats to social order were and over the best ways of dealing with them. This division had very broad, disruptive implications. The recent important study by David Underdown does connect the problems of social change to the variety of responses by elites, and indeed by all social groups.[21] Underdown further links social change to cultural conflict, where 'culture' is very widely defined to include a whole way of life and the means through which it is portrayed and understood – religious beliefs and rituals, local festivities and games – rather than artistic and literary productions alone.

Underdown's basic argument can be summed up in his own words:

> The division in the English body politic which erupted in civil war in 1642 can be traced in part to the earlier emergence of two quite different constellations of social, political and cultural forces, involving diametrically opposite responses to the problems of the time. On the one side stood those who put their trust in the traditional conception of the harmonious, vertically-integrated society – a society in which the old bonds of paternalism, deference and good neighbourliness were expressed in familiar religious and communal rituals – and wished to strengthen and preserve it. On the other stood those – mostly among the gentry and middling sort of the new parish elites – who wished to emphasize the moral and cultural distinctions which marked them off from their poorer, less disciplined neighbours and to use their power to reform society according to their own principles of order and godliness.

The civil war was a conflict between cultures, which contemporaries expressed through the stereotypes they used to describe the combatants of the 1640s when frivolous, gaudy, drunken Cavaliers opposed hypocritical, sermon-addicted, repressive Roundheads. Parliamentarians, on the Hunt model, were pressing for godly reform and the rooting out of popery against royalists who found Puritan meddling more of a threat than popery and supported sports and parochial recreations as a means of embodying and defending a harmonious, deferential community.

Underdown extended his analysis by linking these cultural divisions to regional, social and economic differences. On the basis of the research he did on Somerset, Wiltshire and Dorset, Underdown argued that the 'royalist' response was more obvious in arable regions, the 'parliamentarian' in wood-pasture areas and where the cloth industry was important. In the arable, mixed farming areas found mostly in the downlands of the three counties, communities were usually 'nucleated' villages, grouped around the parish church and the manor house, whose inhabitants engaged in communal worship alongside their neighbours and lived by an agriculture whose practices were governed by a manorial court. In such communities Underdown suggested that hierarchy and deference survived best despite the economic changes already outlined; here parochial festivities like church ales and May games survived longest and royalism had most appeal. The wood-pasture and clothing areas of north Somerset and north Wiltshire had experienced more drastic economic change; economic opportunities and lack of manorial restrictions helped to produce large, unruly, socially polarised parishes with many poor people. Here in an argument again similar to Hunt's or Wrightson's it is argued that Puritanism appealed to some extent to small craftsmen, but especially to the middling sort who formed parish elites, and were at the forefront of economic enterprise. Puritanism encouraged the individual endeavour essential to prosperity but also provided the motivation for an attack on the disorderly recreations of the poor. Charles's clear anti-Puritanism and support for traditional sports and rituals made these areas naturally parliamentarian.

Underdown's argument is more complex than a brief summary can show. Alongside obvious contrasts between the gadders to sermons, and the habitués of the alehouse and the May game, are fascinating if speculative discussions of how football, a collective game, was especially attractive in the communal nucleated villages, while stoolball, a cricket-type game where individual clashes took place within a team framework, was better suited to the more fragmented wood-pasture communities. Attention is drawn to exceptions to the regional-cultural pattern such as the Blackmore Vale wood-pasture area on the Somerset–Dorset border which was culturally conservative and royalist in its civil war allegiance. Nevertheless Underdown does conclude that 'the overall patterns of regional contrast are clear enough'.

For the sake of clarity of analysis it is worth separating the two parts of Underdown's argument, the cultural and the regional-social. As the discussion of Puritanism, anti-Puritanism and Arminianism in chapter 2 suggested, religious divisions involved cultural divisions and inevitably incorporated different visions of how everyday life should be conducted. The issues stressed by Underdown are also crucial to the court 'high' culture looked at earlier, as the work by Marcus, Smuts and Norbrook has shown.[22] In Scotland, James had come to associate the defence of his royal authority with his capacity to resist the Kirk's opposition to traditional pastimes and in *Basilikon Doron* he advised that 'honest feasting and merriness' encouraged friendship and unity amongst neighbours. James gave enthusiastic backing to the creation of the Cotswold Games by the courtier Robert Dover, as did Ben Jonson, a crucial figure in the development of poetic interest in 'traditional' rituals. For Jonson, Dover's games advanced, 'true love and neighbourhood/And do both church and commonwealth the good'. As Smuts has commented, the Cavalier poets loved 'the traditional rituals of English life: May dances, weddings, church ales, Christmas feasts and the like'. Robert Herrick, a Devon clergyman by the 1630s but with important court and London connections, explored ideas and emotions in ritual and festive form in poems such as the 'Wake' or 'Corinna's going a-Maying'. Play and indulgence balanced and guaranteed social and religious order, as in Herrick's 'The Hock-Cart or Harvest Home':

> The harvest swains, and wenches bound
> For joy, to see the hock-cart crown'd. . .
> Drink, frolic, boys, till all be blithe

Feed, and grow fat; and as ye eat,
Be mindful, that the lab'ring neat
(As you) may have their fill of meat.
And know, besides, ye must revoke
The patient ox unto the plough
And harrow, (though they're hang'd up now).

In contrast Puritans saw May games as idolatrous, and poets such as Milton emphasised learning and rationality as counters to images and traditional culture. In his poem on Christ's nativity, Milton made no use of ideas of Christmas as a festival, but portrayed the birth of Christ as the beginning of humanity's deliverance from the thralls of pagan idolatory, when 'sullen Moloch fled' leaving in 'shadows dred,/His burning idol all of blackest hue'.

The preferences of poets are not necessarily evidence for general cultural divisions but there were widespread clashes between a festive, ritualistic culture and the reforming, rationalist tendencies of Protestantism in the reign of Charles I. Charles himself was less involved than James with the promotion of games and pastimes in their own right, and his personal habits did not mimic his father's lurches between excess and self-discipline. For Charles 'lawful recreations' were part of his ecclesiastical policy: the Book of Sports 'sacramentalised' games. The Laudians emphasised the sacred and distinctive nature of the church while the parish games and festivals sanctioned by that church provided both a contrast and a connection between the sacred and the pleasures of everyday life. 'Lawful recreations' were deliberately used against Puritan attempts to eliminate 'papist' and 'pagan' rituals and ceremonies. While the monarch himself, and the sophisticated court culture of the Cavalier poets, baroque painting and the masques was deliberately kept private and distant, the Book of Sports provoked culture conflict in many parishes.

Cultural conflict was found at many levels. We should be wary, however, of taking for granted terms like 'pagan', or 'traditional'. The conflict was not simply one of harmonious, communal 'tradition' versus Puritan innovation. Far from being a simple attempt to preserve tradition, the emphasis on 'traditional' recreations was deliberate and self-conscious; it often involved the 'invention' of traditions by those seeking to address the problems of social change. Robert Dover, who invented the Cotswold Games, was not a long-established paternalist local gentleman, but an attorney and a newcomer to Gloucestershire while most of his supporters had court links. Dover was trying to create an image of himself and his role in local society which would counteract the difficulties inherent in his actual situation. Herrick also was an outsider in practice – an intellectual from an urban background; for him ceremony, festivity and play were essential to make Christianity effective, and to create social solidarity. These approaches were as innovatory as any moves for Puritan reform.

The link between cultural differences and civil war allegiance in Underdown's analysis is convincing but the social and regional dimensions are more complex than he suggests. There is, for example, a tendency to identify parish recreations, May games and church festivals with a 'popular culture' under attack from Puritan elites. Yet we have seen that a festive culture was important also to many from an educated elite, although the meanings of similar practices very probably varied at different social levels. Likewise Puritanism could be attractive to men and women from many social groups, perhaps for different reasons, as has been emphasised at many points in this and the previous chapter.

The basic regional division used by Underdown between wood-pasture and arable sheep-corn areas has been pioneered by agricultural historians, notably Joan Thirsk.[23] They have shown how contrasts in geography and economic practices implied distinctive settlement patterns and social relationships, varying reactions to economic change, and often different religious preferences; their conclusions do not always match Underdown's suggestions. The characteristic settlement in sheep-corn areas was the nucleated village, centred around the parish church and very often a manor house with a resident lord. Frequently, the boundaries of the village, the manor and the parish coincided; structures of authority were visible and united. Social relationships were mostly close-knit and hierarchical. In some arable regions there had been significant enclosure, in others agriculture was organised communally through manorial courts. In the upland or forest wood-pasture areas the inhabitants lived by grazing, or dairying, often combined with industrial production. In these areas, parishes were larger and most people lived in scattered hamlets rather than villages. Each parish might include several manors, or no clear manorial system at all, and individual holdings rather than common fields were often the basis for agricultural production. The authority of church and lord was more distant and more divided than in the arable areas. These wood-pasture areas contained more poor and more independent small and middling landholders, but fewer greater gentry. They were often, as Thirsk has shown, 'open' communities where lack of manorial control and economic opportunities encouraged high immigration, which in turn encouraged further industrial development and agricultural innovation.

Frequently wood-pasture areas had experienced more rapid economic change in the sixteenth century than nearby arable areas – the West Country counties studied by Underdown and the Arden Forest region of north Warwickshire are good examples. But over England as a whole the regional patterns of economic change were more complex than this and Underdown's analysis is not necessarily applicable. One obvious problem is that many areas of the north or Wales, where royalism was strong, were upland pasture regions. Many years ago Hill dubbed these areas as 'backward' and many were at least places where great landlords still maintained much social power. Underdown's model of Puritanism as a doctrine attractive especially to the middling sort of parish notables in their drive to discipline the culture of the poor is associated especially with the account of Terling, Essex, by Wrightson and Levine. Yet this was a south-eastern arable, lowland village which had already experienced rapid economic change by the sixteenth century and was a socially polarised market-orientated community – such experiences were by no means confined to wood-pasture areas. On the other hand, many historians have portrayed wood-pasture and industrial areas rather differently from Underdown. Thirsk and Everitt have argued that these areas were relatively egalitarian, not more polarised and that it was their openness and independence from authority that encouraged the adherence to Puritanism and later to nonconformity. Here, of course, Puritanism is also differently conceived, as a radical and liberating doctrine, rather than as part of a 'culture of discipline'.

Thus it is impossible to draw straightforward conclusions about the nature of economic change and degrees of social polarisation or harmony simply from an examination of 'ecological' factors or farming practices. Religious and cultural characteristics, and civil war allegiances, are still more complicated. One set of social characteristics that seems to have encouraged the development of Puritanism and parliamentarian allegiance in 1642 was found in areas where small and middling property-owners or craftsmen were distant both from the dominance of great lords and from dependence on wage labour, but were used to cooperation in many aspects of their lives. Here concern for property rights, for laws and liberties and for representation seems to have been attractive. Often these were not simply wood-pasture regions but industrial areas. Popular allegiance in Lancashire has not yet been fully studied but there were clear regional patterns within the county: the south-eastern Salford hundred, around Manchester, was most solidly parliamentarian, the west and north more royalist. There was no distinction here between upland and lowland, or arable and wood-pasture, for much of Lancashire was an 'upland' region; the crucial economic difference was the presence of the textile industry in the south. Even within industrial areas there were significant variations. In Derbyshire, for example, the lead industry which involved large numbers of independent small masters was a fertile recruiting ground for Parliament. In the iron and coal industries of the same county, where most enterprises were on a larger scale and the workers were mostly dependent labourers, many landlords and masters were able to rally large numbers to the royalist side. Within the west Midlands 'Black Country' there were also sharp contrasts. The metal

workers and small iron masters of Birmingham were mostly parliamentarian, 'sectaries and schismatics' in Dugdale's phrase; in
nearby Dudley there was strong support for the king from
workers who were largely Catholic and apparently in a more
dependent industrial organisation.

Two more complications need to be raised in connection with
Underdown's arguments: the existence of social and cultural
contrasts *within* regions; and the varieties of ways in which
economic practices and cultural attitudes were combined. In
many industrial and wood-pasture areas where middling and
lesser men supported Parliament, elites seem to have become
most alarmed about social order and hierarchy, and more
inclined to an authoritarian politics than their more secure
neighbours. In Warwickshire, for example, the minority of the
county's greater gentry who lived in the northern, forest area of
the Arden were the most committed royalists. In areas like this
Manning's account of the royalists as the party of order seems
most convincing. In a long-term perspective, the gentry of north
Warwickshire had experienced the most significant social and
economic change from the sixteenth century, and lived in an
environment where their social inferiors had much independence; in the short term they were alarmed by the popular
support given to Parliament in an enthusiastic godly campaign
in 1642. Similarly in the west riding of Yorkshire, the people of
the clothing towns were often committed parliamentarians
whereas there were twice as many royalists as parliamentarians
amongst the gentry.

On the other hand, members of the elite who felt more socially
secure in their immediate communities were sometimes more
ready to risk defying the king, although the supposedly 'deferential' poorer inhabitants of nucleated villages were often loyal to
their king or their non-Puritan church rather than to their
immediate superiors. This pattern is found in the 1620s as well
as in the early 1640s. In the far north-eastern corner of Essex, a
deferential area dominated by great landlords but not a sheep-
corn area, the forced loan was enthusiastically supported by the
ordinary taxpayers but it was also the area where one of the
leading Puritan loan resisters, Sir Harbottle Grimston, lived.

Even in Grimston's own parish, most of those liable paid the loan without demur. In Warwickshire, most gentry resistance to the loan was in the arable south of the county; most middling-sort opposition was in the wood-pasture and industrial north. In the civil war the Warwickshire parliamentary leader Robert, Lord Brooke, obtained most support in the north of the county away from his own estates, while in his own town of Warwick there were signs of royalism amongst the common people in 1642.

Brooke's leadership in Warwickshire was thus not based on traditional landlord-tenant ties. Brooke was a newcomer to the county, the adopted heir of the first lord, and very concerned for the efficient and profitable management of his estates. In this he was very like the Earl of Warwick in Essex who was also 'go-ahead' in his economic attitudes and led a parliamentary-Puritan movement which was much broader than his personal connections. There were clearly tensions and contradictions in the local position of such peers and it seems that their rousing Protestant, 'country' leadership was partly a means of maintaining social and political pre-eminence in times when economic relationships as such were often tense. It cannot be argued that this is a complete explanation or that beliefs are determined by practical considerations alone; but it is equally partial to ignore the material influences and constraints on cultural and ideological attitudes. If a popular 'country' role was one common response by elites, another was the deliberate preservation or creation of institutions and practices that promoted hierarchy, deference and order. The courtiers and outsiders who developed the Cotswold Games, and the aggressive royalists of north Warwickshire are examples; another is the royalist Sir Thomas Aston of Cheshire who led the county's campaign to defend episcopacy, and was obsessed with the socially subversive implications of Presbyterian attacks on bishops. Aston and many of the Warwickshire men were improving landlords – their own actions were threatening the social harmony they were seeking in other fields to preserve. The 'country' and the 'reactionary' patterns are the most clear-cut, and it is possible that the more easy-going landlords were less 'ideological' in their religious or political outlooks, inclined to moderate Puritanism or conventional conformity.

The complexity of the connections between religious and cultural attitudes on the one hand, and the regional patterns of social and economic change on the other, might encourage a conclusion that there were no connections at all, and that patterns of belief and allegiance were entirely random. The regional characteristics of allegiance, and the recurrence of similar concerns about social order and cultural conflict in different circumstances, suggest that such a conclusion would be wrong. Furthermore the criticisms of Underdown's patterns, made here, and by other historians, should not lead to an underestimation of the importance of his contribution to a social interpretation of the civil war. Underdown has surely identified the crucial social and cultural elements in the broad conflict of 1642, although he has not explored all the ways in which these elements could fit together. The religious, cultural and political cleavages discussed in this and the previous chapter were intimately related to the anxieties and opportunities which emerged in a period of social change, to the reactions at all social levels to problems of order and readjustments in social relationships.[24] This is not as clear-cut an explanation as the notion of a rising, confident gentry seizing political power, but in its attention to the subtleties of both the economic changes of the sixteenth century and the ideological tensions of early Stuart England, it provides a more fruitful and satisfying framework.

In the Introduction the cleavage that has developed between the political and the social history of seventeenth century England was noted. It is often argued by 'revisionist' historians, that political conflict and breakdown can only be explained through a focus on the details of high politics – the day-to-day decisions and negotiations of monarchs, ministers and diplomats. One review of Underdown suggested that his approach could only explain why people took one side rather than another once civil war broke out; the origins of the war itself should be sought at court and in the actions of the king.[25] It has been suggested many times in this book that it is misleading to see high politics in isolation. The actions of leading politicians were profoundly influenced by the expectations and beliefs of the broader 'political nation', while similar habits of thought were found at many levels of society. A concern for the rule of law and a belief in the sanctions of history and tradition were found in 'popular culture' and in the ideas of Parliament-men and Councillors. Another link which has been demonstrated in this chapter is in cultural conflict, where similar divisions and concerns, albeit expressed in different forms, were demonstrated in the sophisticated work of poets and playwrights as well as in village tensions. A final vital connection between the anxieties brought by social change and the coming of political breakdown, is the 'crisis of the aristocracy', the readjustments in the nature of elite leadership before the civil war. This chapter will end with a discussion of this theme.

A Crisis of the Aristocracy?

Laurence Stone's thesis that there was a broad economic, social and cultural crisis of the aristocracy (by which he meant the peerage) in the sixteenth and early seventeenth centuries has been much criticised. Indeed, there seems little justification for treating the peers as an economic grouping distinct from the greater gentry; the economic fortunes of this broader group of great landlords were complex, and their position was if anything improving by 1640. Chapter 2 showed that the political influence of the peerage is now being stressed by historians, while J. H. Hexter has argued that only one element of Stone's general crisis could be substantiated – the peerage had suffered a decline in their independent military power. This view has been reiterated more recently by Pocock, who pointed out that for contemporaries, the 'crisis of the aristocracy' was not a matter of economics or politics, but to do with the decline in magnate military power. This was the view of Bacon, Raleigh, and especially of Harrington.

It was a cardinal point with Harrington that the Civil War came about, and took the course it did, because magnates with their armed tenants and retainers were no longer a serious military force;

the war was therefore a contest for control of the militia, and both sides were driven to rely on men who were neither tenants nor mercenaries, a new and revolutionary phenomenon.[26]

It is perhaps slightly strange that the independent political power of the peerage is being rehabilitated when social historians have decided that they should not be distinguished from the (greater) gentry, but nonetheless there is now much stress on peers' supposed dominance of the House of Commons through their allies and clients, and on the outbreak of the civil war in the counties as a series of conflicts between local rival peers. The peers have been credited with an ability to orchestrate the popular demonstrations in London in 1641–2, as well as being a crucial influence on the city authorities. For Paul Christianson, social distance is seen as the main determinant of the degree of political authority peers had over their subordinates so that John Pym was in a relationship of 'full clientage' to his employer the Earl of Bedford and operated in politics on the earl's instructions. On the other hand, the Earl of Warwick had a more equal political relationship with the leading Essex gentleman Sir Thomas Barrington, because their social rank was closer. In the more sophisticated work of John Adamson, Pym is still portrayed presenting to the Commons initiatives which had already been agreed on in private meetings dominated by peers: 'To the Commons, here was "King Pym"; but his king-makers were members of the House of Lords.' In Adamson's view, the politics of the 1640s were dominated by political rivalries amongst those peers who remained in London during the civil war; the Earl of Essex was the crucial figure of the early 1640s but his influence was increasingly resented and contested by a group centred on the Lord Saye and the Earl of Northumberland.[27]

Clearly members of the peerage played important roles in political life but the presence of similar names does not mean that the civil war was just like the baronial struggles against Edward II or in the Wars of the Roses. There were, to be brief, crucial differences in the nobles' relationships with other landowners and with the ranks below them; changes in the criteria by which nobility or aristocracy were defined or claimed; and a transformation in the nobility's relationship to central political power or to the 'state'. Two specific points need to be made about Stone's 'crisis'. His critics have done less damage to his argument than they suppose when they claim that the crisis was confined to military matters. A warlike role was essential to medieval definitions of nobility, and the erosion of this role was at the heart of a very broad change in the nature of political power. Secondly, a crisis is not the same as a decline but involves notions of difficulty, readjustment and change. Like the idea of a rise of the gentry, the crisis of the aristocracy is still a very useful concept in seeking to understand the outbreak of the civil war. Sometimes the crisis was one that mainly affected peers; most often it affected all great landowners who made up an aristocracy, including nobles and commoners.

As has already been argued in this chapter, one element of the crisis was economic, involving attempts to cope with or profit from inflation and population growth. This was a process that brought tensions within landed elites and created problems in their relationships with their social inferiors: obedience and respect could not be taken for granted. There was a general social and political readjustment within the landed classes whereby a broader county-based leadership in many regions replaced the noble dominance of vast areas characteristic of earlier times. In mid sixteenth century Suffolk the dominance of the great nobility, the dukes of Suffolk and Norfolk, was replaced by an 'oligarchy' of staunchly Protestant gentlemen. The changes in land ownership discussed above were one crucial aspect of this readjustment, another was the expansion of local, county government, with increasing responsibilities for the punishment of crime, the administration of the poor law, and the protection of the grain supply, the repairs of roads, and a multitude of other matters. The often tedious details of local government in fact involved the honour of acting in the royal or public service, and great influence over neighbours of all social ranks. It brought power and prestige to the greater gentry of the shires, who were therefore not dependent on peers for their local positions.

The holding of state office was thus increasingly the key to power at a local or a national level for gentry and for peers. Noblemen did dominate bodies like the lieutenancy, and offices at court and in council, but as royal nominees, not as independent magnates. The Tudor nobility have been compared to captains of industry after nationalisation; they still headed many bodies, but the basis of their authority was transformed. Furthermore, it was increasingly expected that peers would attend the monarch and the court in person to pursue power and wealth. This could be very profitable, especially under James, when Stone has calculated that 'perks' worth some £105,000 per annum were distributed to the peerage, compared to less than £8000 per annum under Elizabeth. Even under the more frugal regime of Charles, rewards were worth £25,000 per annum. The pursuit of profit at court had its price, however, in absenteeism from the peers' local bases of influence, leaving the senior gentry to wield effective control in the counties. The loss of peers' independent military power in particular had an important influence on the nature of the civil war. Stone has written that 'the outbreak of civil war in 1642 differed markedly from all previous uprisings'; noblemen were active in the early conflicts, as Adamson stresses, but they aimed to capture arms in the county magazines and take control of the trained bands. They were not merely stocking their own castles or raising private armies and from the later sixteenth century, 'the only hope of challenging the authority of the state was to lie in seizing some of its military stores and suborning part of its armed forces'. The decline in military independence was part of a broader change which Mervyn James has summed up as the nationalisation of honour. True nobility lay not in loyalty to some independent personal criteria of valour but in obedience and service to the monarch of the commonwealth. In the sixteenth century the roles of elites were being recast; Renaissance humanist and zealous Protestant or Puritan ideals of public service were turning warriors into politicians.[28]

These changes had very significant implications for the type of aristocratic power that was possible by 1642. In relation to the state, 'above' the aristocracy, it meant that dissatisfaction could not be expressed simply through independent personal rebellion, but had to be directed towards changing the general policies of royal government, or more broadly, the nature of central authority in accordance with some abstract criteria, such as those implied by the ideas of the 'country'. There was in turn an impact on how nobles, as individuals, were supposed to behave. Social, political and ideological changes together meant that nobility could not be defined or claimed simply through birth or wealth, but implied also some notions of godliness, or virtue, or service of the common good. In theory, at least, these attributes were not confined to one social group, and in practice below the aristocracy there was a large prospering group – the 'middling sort' of people – whose support or alliance had to be worked for. Political leadership was therefore more complex and more difficult than before. Some of the aristocracy, whether peers or greater gentry, earned a powerful political position by acting as godly leaders of the country; others sought to reinforce their position through a deliberate emphasis on the necessity for hierarchy, and opposed Puritanism and 'popularity' as subversive.

Many peers had to find new ways of justifying their role. The Sidneys, Riches, Russells or Devereux, who were so important in the later sixteenth and seventeenth centuries were not medieval barons, but newcomers who owed their position to service of the state, specifically in a Protestant interest. Social and political change had brought new men to the peerage, whose position was not in fact based on ancient lineage or the long possession of extensive landed estates. The frequent stress on medieval precedents for the general power of peers, or the invention of spurious ancient pedigrees for individual families were the more urgent because so many families were uncertain of the grounds for their authority. Robert Greville, the second Lord Brooke, is again a good example. His biographer emphasised his membership of a long-established gentry family, while Brooke's own writings stressed the independence of the peerage against the supine dependency of the bishops. Yet he was in fact the son of a very minor Lincolnshire gentleman and the adopted heir of the first Lord Brooke, the poet Fulke Greville, who in turn owed his peerage to government service as much as to his respectable gentry background. In his adopted county of Warwickshire many gentry regarded the second lord as a parvenu and Brooke associated not with the leading county gentry but mainly with a network of the godly comprising local clergy and lesser gentry who were thus put in touch with leading national figures like Bedford, Saye and Pym. As mentioned above, Brooke's leadership of par- liamentarians in Warwickshire was not based on his power as a landlord but on a rousing popular campaign which portrayed the war as an anti-popish crusade and rallied people to Parliament in defence of their laws, liberties and true religion. Parallels to Brooke's ideological role in Warwickshire can be found in the Earl of Lincoln's leadership of the resistance to the forced loan in Lincolnshire, and of course, in the Earl of Warwick's as the rallying point for the godly in Essex from the 1620s to the 1640s.[29]

The appeal of Warwick, Brooke and Lincoln was essentially an ideological one although it was also a response to political and social change. The latest work on the political importance of the peerage does emphasise that their relationship with their followers was not a simple one of dependency between patrons and clients. Members of the Commons, for example, were not 'tame lackeys' of the Lords; 'common ideological objectives' for the settlement of church and state bound politicians in both Houses together. There was, says Adamson, 'no antithesis between "faction" and "matters of principle"'. The relationship was, though, still more complex; principles and factions were not simply two distinct factors joined together; rather ideological criteria inevitably altered the whole nature of patronage and alliance. It is significant that the most important potential allies of peers in the Commons were rarely their closest dependents – their legal or financial 'men of business' – but were 'those members of the Commons who were figures of standing and repute within their own House'. In other words such members of the Commons were vital to the influence of peers, especially those who were critical of royal government or royal ministers; and peers had to act in a certain manner, adopt appropriate positions, in order to win support in the Commons. Dependency is not an appropriate way of describing such reciprocal relation- ships; they are better seen as a response to a crisis in the nature of aristocratic leadership.[30]

Similar points can be made about the relationship of the political elite, more widely conceived as gentry and peers, to the broader political nation discussed in chapter 2. For 'opposition' figures, the support of 'the country' in their localities was particularly crucial. The patronage and protection of men like Brooke, Warwick, Barrington and Lincoln was essential to Puritans in their areas, especially in the hard years of the 1630s; but equally the support of the godly was essential to the political standing and identity of their leaders. Courtier or royalist stresses on anti-Puritanism or on 'traditional' culture in its various guises also show how elites needed to make an effort to win broad support or to find ways of enforcing obedience. Elites could not rally the lower orders to any position they chose. The attitudes of people from below the landed elites themselves helped to structure the options that were available, and profoundly influenced the positions of their political leaders.

Social tensions and religious or political divisions reinforced each other in a sort of vicious circle. Worries about social change and social hierarchy exacerbated ideological divisions, and were an important influence on particular positions and styles of leadership. 'Court' fears of popularity were opposed by (and gave rise to) the 'country' or godly emphasis on socially broad ideological alliances in politics. A Puritan stress on reform or on self-development was countered by a communal, ceremonial, approach to the church and to social relationships. On the other hand religious divisions and political crisis increased anxieties about social order, as seen especially in the early 1640s, when demonstrations in London and unrest in fen and forest regions produced panic amongst many landowners.

The main body of this book has tried to show that many elements contributed to serious political difficulties in England and indeed in Britain as a whole. Practical or 'functional' problems, ideological cleavages and social tensions were all present and were often interconnected. But political difficulties do not inevitably lead to political breakdown, still less to civil war. The conclusion will seek to explain how conflict took the form it did in 1642.

4

KING AND PARLIAMENT
1625–1642

For most parliamentarians the civil war was a defensive war: in May 1642 the two Houses resolved that 'the king, seduced by wicked counsel, intends to make war against the Parliament'. Lord Saye, as shown in chapter 2, looked back on the 1640s as a struggle against moves to 'destroy the Parliament of England, that is the Government of England'.[1] This contemporary belief that Charles made the war, while the parliamentarians defended themselves, has found favour also with modern historians. Chapter 1 of this book explored arguments that Charles's particularly aggressive approach to the financial difficulties of the monarchy, and his stance on the problems of the multiple kingdoms of the British isles, were crucial to the collapse of his authority in England. Chapter 2 discussed the impact of Charles's adoption of 'new counsels' and his rejection of orthodox Calvinist divinity. The elaborate and remote culture of the Caroline court was a practical embodiment of Charles's kingship, as well as a symbol of it.

King Charles

Historians are virtually unanimous that Charles was, in the words of a recent study, 'woefully inadequate' as a reigning monarch. The victim, it appears, of an unhappy childhood and, as a younger son, unprepared for monarchy, Charles's personality was a fatal combination of superficially contradictory elements. He was an authoritarian meddler who could be obsessively concerned with the details of his policies while blithely unaware of the realities of the broader political context. The contradictions of Charles's naval and foreign policies in the 1630s illustrate these points only too well. Charles was at peace yet had to create a sense of emergency in order to justify the use of his prerogative powers to impose ship money regularly on England. The fleet was supposed to enforce what Charles believed to be self-evident – that he was sovereign of the seas around his kingdom; the king busied himself with all aspects of its construction and manning, yet it was irrelevant to the European dramas dominated by France, Spain, Sweden and the Netherlands. Charles's failure to join Gustavus Adolphus' 1631–2 campaign to recover the Palatinate as advocates of the 'Protestant Cause' urged, ensured he was in effect dependent on Habsburg condescension for the restoration of his exiled sister. The vagueness of his commitment to Spain nonetheless inclined the Spanish to favour Bavarian claims to the Palatinate. Perhaps a tenth of Scottish adult males were fighting in various European armies in the 1630s, not one of them fighting under Charles's own colours. The king's grandiose plans meant that his great ship, the technologically advanced and aptly named, *Sovereign of the Seas*, was sent out before she was ready while the fleet was manned by courtiers at a loose end, entertained by the fiddlers who were as essential as trained mariners. The ship money navy was most useful as an escort for the Spanish silver fleets; it was unwilling or unable to prevent the destruction of the Spanish fleet in English waters by the Dutch in October 1639, and was largely parliamentarian in the 1640s.[2]

Charles's personal sense of insecurity coupled with a very high notion of the nature of kingship too often prompted a relentless concern with loyalty, uniformity and hierarchy. Cust argues that during the forced loan, the king was approaching paranoia: he assumed there would be resistance, and so was continually testing the loyalty of the politically prominent. He was inflexible and curt with his Councillors, and contemptuous of those like Abbot who sought to moderate his policies. Charles's profound conviction that his powers and authority were God-given meant that any opposition to his will was illegitimate, the work of selfish, corrupt popular factions. The 'unwise assumption that his ends justified his means' meant Charles engaged without scruple in vindictive, shifty or dishonest behaviour if he believed it would defeat opponents. In 1628 the king agreed with the House of Commons that the Petition of Right should be printed with his second, less ambiguous and acceptable answer, but as soon as the session was over he ordered the destruction of all such copies and had a new version produced which added royal exceptions and qualifications. Personal threats to loan resisters in the 1620s, or leaving Sir John Eliot to die under close imprisonment in the Tower because he would not publicly submit to royal authority, are characteristic of his vindictiveness towards those he felt had wronged him. In 1628, as in the 1640s, Charles made concessions with an ill-grace and tried to reverse them as soon as possible. In 1628 he promoted Maynwaring and others punished by Parliament as soon as the Houses had been prorogued; in the first years of the Long Parliament, royal consent to reforming legislation was accompanied by complicity in elaborate plots and half-baked military coups.[3]

Charles's belief that kings should be obeyed without question made him scornful of everyday political skills. Secrecy, privacy and exclusiveness were the hallmarks of his political style, as described in the discussion of his court in chapter 2. Only under great pressure in 1642 did he accept the need to explain his policies to a broad audience; his Scottish plans in the later 1630s were kept secret from his English Privy Councillors. In 1627 Charles deliberately made it known that it was he, and not Buckingham, who was reluctant to call a parliament, almost deliberately forfeiting the possibility of blaming evil counsellors' for political conflicts. Similarly on several occasions in the early 1630s it was emphasised that it was the king himself who was opposed to calling a parliament. Charles would not play the 'games' that Elizabeth and James had used very successfully to preserve the credit of the monarchy.

There can be no doubt that the religious and political policies of Charles, as well as his whole manner of rule, exacerbated tensions in England. This concluding chapter will therefore draw together from earlier sections the key elements from the 1620s and 1630s which contributed to the breakdown of 1640, and provide more detail of events in England from 1640 to 1642 so as to show how the tensions of the first half of the seventeenth century erupted eventually in civil war. It is not intended to provide a full narrative of Charles's reign or even of events from the calling of the Long Parliament until the outbreak of war, and this is not simply out of considerations of space. The argument throughout this book has been that narratives of high politics or the doings of great men alone cannot explain the origins of the civil war, which need to be sought through analysis of long-term social, ideological and political developments. Charles's policies were not the random impulses of an unfortunate and unhappy personality, but explicable reactions or choices within rival interpretations of the way the English political system should be worked. His fear of popularity, for example, was clearly a response to real social developments and political stances; his policies did harm precisely because they dealt (in a ham-fisted way) with long-term structural problems which had been shelved or fudged in previous reigns.

This is not to argue that the civil war, in its precise form, was 'inevitable' but that the events which produced the form of breakdown which did occur have to be analysed within broader, long-term structures. These include ideological divisions over the nature of political authority and of true religion which are seen at their most obvious in the rival conspiracy theories which came to fruition in 1637–42. The royal fear of subversion of the monarchy through 'popularity' and Puritanism was fulfilled by the Scottish rebellion, while Puritan anxieties about an anti-Christian popish plot to subvert English liberties and godly Protestantism were confirmed by the Irish rebellion. Charles's political approaches have also, and more specifically, to be seen within a context of widespread belief in the institutional import-ance of Parliament. Finally there is a crucial social dimension involving sharp differences over the political implications of social change and contrasting reactions to the emergence of a broad, and frequently aroused political nation. The events of the 1620s and 1630s, and the reactions of the king and of his chief opponents in Parliament between 1640 and 1642 have thus to be understood within a pre-existing framework, while of course these same events helped to construct the ways in which succeeding developments were understood. The distinction between structures and separate events is an artificial one. Again the clearest illustration of this is in the way that both Charles's actions and those of his critics tended to reinforce and elaborate beliefs in widespread popish or Puritan conspiracies. It is in this light that the following account of crucial developments from the 1620s is offered.

Parliament and Politics in the 1620s

The 1620s was a crucial decade for both the monarchy and the broad political nation. There was a decisive shift, promoted by the king, to anti-Calvinist dominance of the church, while the imposition of the forced loan was in many ways the most revealing political event. It showed Charles's increasing preference for the 'new counsels' urging a reliance on prerogative taxation rather than parliamentary supply; and his growing suspicion of 'popular' Puritan subversion of monarchical authority. The loan was not simply of concern to elites: all subsidymen were liable to pay and therefore a broad cross-section of male property holders were brought to ponder the issues of prerogative power and property rights raised by the levy. In the end most of the loan was paid, but not without resentment, obstruction and a small, but important, group of resisters and martyrs; the judgement of the 'country' was seen with the return of 'patriot' MPs to the Parliament of 1628. The loan was intended for the European war but England's attempts to play a role in the Thirty Years War produced a series of fiascos and by the end of the decade Charles had in practice renounced any attempt to influence European events – an essential decision given his determination after 1628–9 to rule at home without recourse to a parliament.

To understand the impact of Charles's break with parliaments it is necessary to consider more directly than hitherto, the place of Parliament in political thinking and in practice. Chapter 1 demonstrated that Parliament may well have contributed to the financial weaknesses of the English monarchy, but that in the opinions of many of the political elite, financial problems could only be solved in cooperation with Parliament. Also stressed was the importance of Parliament in fostering a national integration that marked the English state as very different from continental monarchies like the French or the Spanish. Chapter 2 explored the place of Parliament in notions of English history, and conceptions of how political authority was acquired and political power should be exercised. The regular consultation of parliaments was crucial to definitions of monarchical authority as derived from consent or from the duty to defend fundamental laws; uncorrupted parliaments, chosen by free electors, were vital bulwarks against the attempts of papists or evil counsellors to undermine true religion and English liberties. The precise powers of parliaments were sometimes uncertain in the early seventeenth century and they have been much debated by historians, but more pertinent is the broadly defined and vitally important general place Parliament had, in both ideology and practice, for many, but not all, of the politically active.[4]

In examining the frequent parliaments of the 1620s it becomes clear that there were no unbridgeable cleavages between kings and members of the Lords and Commons. It is also clear that cooperation was only possible where there were broadly shared objectives and kings were prepared to bargain. Despite the recent historiographical emphasis on the Commons' unwillingness to use supply to put pressure on the government, it is worth noting that it was only in 1621 and 1625 that subsidies were voted without strings. The first session of the 1621 Parliament worked well because it focused on monopolies where James was prepared to make concessions; the 1624 Parliament was productive because deals had been made – 'undertakers' committed themselves to supporting a war against Spain after the failure of the Spanish match. This Parliament thus followed an Elizabethan pattern whereby the monarch was outmanoeuvred by leading Privy Councillors and their allies in the Commons, while in addition the 'reversionary interest' of Prince Charles was wielded against his father, notably in forcing him to sacrifice Lord Treasurer Cranfield, impeached for corruption but attacked mainly because he opposed the war.

These 'successful' sessions, however, were built on precarious alliances which frequently crumbled. The second session of 1621, embittered by divisions over foreign policy, left the parliament fearing for its own survival and King James incensed by the belief that Parliament was attacking the prerogative. After 1624, harmony between king and Parliament foundered on resentments caused by the dominance of Buckingham, the mismanagement of the war, the king's French marriage and especially on the anxieties produced by the increasing dominance of Arminians. Charles became increasingly impatient with a House of Commons he regarded as factious and troublesome, and increasingly willing to use the threat of dissolution if the duke was attacked or insufficient funds were voted. He threatened a snap dissolution in 1625 when no additional money was forthcoming, and after 1626 he collected as the 'forced loan' the subsidies which had been proposed but not voted in the parliament. In 1628, the more moderate members of the parliament proposed a strategy of limiting the king's powers by legislation rather than attacking Buckingham, which would provoke a dissolution. But 'fiery spirits' like Sir John Eliot were not satisfied with the Petition of Right and were determined to attack the duke, thus contributing to the king's decision to bring the session to an end. Peers were inevitably and enthusiastically prominent in the parliamentary attacks on Buckingham and on the cleric Richard Montagu, but many of the grievances raised in the 1620s parliaments were initated by the members of the Commons who were most closely exercised by their constituents' worries about the burdens of war. In turn Parliament's activities aroused much interest and had a significant influence. The passing of the Petition of Right was met with widespread rejoicing and when the policy of billeting soldiers on the population was challenged in Parliament reluctant cooperation in the country gave way to complete obstruction and breakdown.

The parliamentary conflicts of the 1620s, followed by the years without parliaments, had a major impact on the early 1640s. John Pym's famous speech of 17 April 1640, setting out the kingdom's grievances, began with 'the breaches of our liberty and privileges of parliament, and that divers ways'; the details of the abrupt dissolution of 1629 were still fresh in his mind, along with the evils resulting from the breaking of a parliament with 'petitions left not heard', debarring us from 'our last sighs and groans to his Majesty'. 'The intermission of Parliaments have been a true cause of all these evils to the Commonwealth'; and so the solution was to call annual parliaments. In the 1620s the king's unquestioned power to dissolve the parliament was the ultimate and effective weapon in defence of Buckingham. Parliamentary politics was, however, transformed in May 1641 when Charles gave his assent to the bill preventing the dissolution of the parliament without its own consent. Protected against dismissal in the turbulent months that followed, the Long Parliament acquired novel powers and responsibilities in the months before the outbreak of war. As we shall see, this expansion in Parliament's role was controversial and contested; by 1642 the euphoria and high expectations which greeted the parliament's convening in November 1640 had given way to suspicion and disillusion in many quarters. Nonetheless Parliament in the early 1640s commanded remarkable though of course incomplete obedience for its war effort against the person of the king. This degree of success was based on a long-term sense of Parliament's national legitimacy as a legislative body, and as a means of getting grievances heard as well as on the experiences of the 1620s and the fears of 1640–2.[5]

The Personal Rule

The assassination of Buckingham and the end of the European war removed some of the most obvious causes of political friction, but the 'comparative political calm' of the 1630s was deceptive. Without parliaments there was no obvious arena where a principled challenge to the king's policies could be mounted, which is not to say that principled opposition did not exist. Most public discussion of ship money, for example, focused on local struggles about rating and the amount of the levy, rather than on questions of the prerogative emergency powers under which it was levied. The attempts of Saye and Hampden to challenge the legality of the levy were untypical. Until the burdens of the Scottish war were added, most people paid ship money with little open dismay. In seeking to limit what they and their neighbours paid for ship money, men had to appeal to the Privy Council where constitutional attacks were clearly inappropriate, but alarm at the novelty of regular ship money levies is apparent in more private sources. Coventry drew up an elaborate narrative of the city's rating dispute with the county of Warwickshire, while records of discussions amongst the Kent gentry show clear worries about the constitutional implications. Local elites had little contact with the centre apart from accusations of Puritanism or the hectoring rebukes they received for their failure to live up to the king's expectations. Within the central government itself, it became increasingly harder to raise the possibility of a parliament or to oppose Arminianism, and the Calvinist Heath was sacked in 1634. On occasions men with contacts with the queen lobbied for an active, pro-French foreign policy which would require a parliament but for the most part, as Derek Hirst has stressed, important currents of political opinion remained cut off. The alienation of Puritans in the 1630s was more dangerous than in the 1580s, for example, when there were people at court who sympathised with Presbyterian campaigns. While the court became more exclusive, the 'enemies' of the king also drew closer together through involvement in bodies like the Providence Island Company, and vital informal networks. The regular meetings of leading politicians such as Bedford, Pym, Warwick, Saye, Brooke and Knightley, their clients and clergymen, served a defensive purpose in the 1630s; once the Long Parliament met they played a vital role in organising petitions and other positive measures for religious and political reform.[6]

Disquiet again affected broad social groups. Ship money sharply increased the numbers of those liable for national levies while religious and cultural divisions, as outlined in chapters 2 and 3, involved broad sections of society. Evidence is often lacking for those outside the political elite, but it is probably again significant that so many of those returned as MPs in 1640 had distinguished themselves by opposition to the king's religious and political policies. The thousands who emigrated to the 'howling wilderness' of New England, along with the many more who considered the step, are testimony to the fears for true religion in England. The contacts and attitudes of the obscure provincial professional men Thomas Dugard and Robert Woodford were discussed in chapter 2 while the diaries of Nehemiah Wallington provide a further insight into a humble Puritan's experience of the 1630s. These were dark days of popish conspiracy against the truth of the gospel and the proper observance of the Lord's Day; the Book of Sports, for Wallington, as for many others, was the worst measure of all. He was questioned with his brother in Star Chamber for spreading libels against the king's 'happy government' and like Dugard obtained subversive books such as Prynne's notorious *Newes from Ipswich*. Wallington had lost any trust in Charles I long before 1640 and saw 1639–41 as miraculous years. He completely supported the Scots who had delivered England from danger and eagerly read their propaganda.[7]

It is clear that Charles's personal rule was viable only as long as he avoided war; it was unfortunate but not accidental that the attack came from the Covenanters whom many of his English subjects did not regard as enemies at all. The prominence of George Con and Henrietta Maria's 1639 proposals for raising men and money from Catholics to oppose the Scots meant that the king's Scottish policy was widely seen as a Catholic policy. It matters little that rumour overestimated the prominence of 'popish' officers in the armies sent against the Scots, the fears created surfaced again and again to magnify the panics later plots aroused. An emotional anti-Celtic element was especially ominous: for the 1640 army a significant Welsh Catholic force was raised by the powerful Catholic Earl of Worcester, and their role was to become tangled up in 1640–1 with more profound fears of an Irish popish army to be used against the English and the Scots. The importance of religion to the unfolding of the 'British problem' has already been stressed and it was no less crucial in producing disaffection in England and the motivation to resist it. Arminianism blurred into Catholicism in the minds of many. The mood of the most determined was indicated in November 1638 when George Walker, a London Puritan clergyman, was imprisoned for a rousing Gunpowder Plot sermon which was said to have included 'things tending to faction and disobedience to authority' rather than 'preaching subjection to the higher powers'. It contained pointed references to the evil influence of Eve over Adam, and to a list of wicked princes from Saul to Jezebel, many of whom had come to sticky ends.[8]

The troubles in Scotland wrecked the personal rule in England because of the depth of alienation that existed anyway, amongst much of the political elite and elements of the broader populace. Anglo-Scottish relationships were covered in chapter 1, and only two crucial issues need be highlighted now. The first is that although cooperation between the Scots and the English opponents of Charles took something of the form of a religious crusade against Arminianism and popery, for the English politicians, religion was inextricably connected with constitutional matters. To quote again from Pym's speech of April 1640, 'Religion is in truth the greatest grievance to be looked into' but 'verity in religion receives an influence from the free debates in Parliament and consequently from the privileges in Parliament'. The second point to stress is that more than an aristocratic putsch was envisaged. Peers were the most prominent amongst opposition politicians who responded to the Scots quest for English support and the most notable English response was the petition of twelve peers for a parliament presented to Charles in early September 1640. However, peers worked closely with petitioners from the City of London who also urged a parliament and the ultimate aim was a free parliament which would confirm true religion and English liberties, punish evil counsellors and settle a lasting peace between the English and the Scots.[9] The parliament called for autumn 1640 was to give them their opportunity.

The Long Parliament and the Failure of Settlement

The renewal of war against the Scots after the failure of the Short Parliament and the provocative authoritarian, anti-Calvinist Canons issued by Convocation, had deepened the resolve of the English opposition. By November 1640 when the Long Parliament met, Charles's freedom of action was strictly limited by the Scottish occupation of the north of England and the need to raise money to pay off the armies of both sides. The meeting of Parliament was generally believed to herald a settlement of the kingdom's ills, yet within two years the hopes of November 1640 had given way to preparations for armed conflict. Well-justified scepticism about the king's trustworthiness was important to the failure of settlement, but behind personal matters was the uncomfortable fact that the ways in which settlement was sought were incompatible. Charles wanted the restoration of his authority and still seems to have expected help against the Scots. The 'opposition' leaders, with differences of emphasis, but with clear support from broader elements in the political nation, were determined to punish the evil counsellors who were held responsible for the personal rule with Strafford the chief target for politicians from all parts of the British Isles. They wanted to dismantle the measures and institutions, such as extra-parliamentary taxation or the Court of High Commission, that had characterised the personal rule, and establish safeguards that would prevent its recurrence. Their religious policies included the negative aims of eliminating Arminian doctrine and practices, and the more positive, but ill-defined desire to complete the staunchly Protestant reform of the church, worked for by Puritans since the 1560s. Finally, the most sophisticated opponents of Charles hoped to achieve a permanent settlement through themselves taking high office under the crown.

From November 1640 until the summer of 1642, periods of intense and hopeful activity when laws were passed or 'malignants' punished were punctuated by periods of crisis and deadlock. Contingent or personal events had their impact: the death of the Earl of Bedford in May 1641, it has been suggested, was an important factor in wrecking negotiations between

Charles and opposition leaders, many of whom had been added to the Privy Council in February. As Councillors, Bedford, Essex, Saye and Warwick were allowed little influence, however; like most of Charles' attempts at conciliation, this was mere window-dressing. This was not simply a result of defects in the king's personality, but a reflection of fundamental political divisions. Characteristic responses at moments of crisis reflect the different visions of politics and frameworks of authority discussed in chapter 2. The king's authoritarian approach inclined him to insincere concessions followed by attempts to retrieve his position by force or through plots. It was only in extremis in 1642 that Charles made a determined effort to explain his position and win public support. The parliamentarian leaders' beliefs, however qualified, in participation and consent, meant that their characteristic reaction was to appeal to the people, notably through the Protestation, or the Grand Remonstrance, although they too were increasingly willing to meet force with force.

Inevitably between 1640 and 1642 the broad opposition to Charles I became fragmented and more tenuous. Three issues seem especially to have created conflict. Firstly, there was significant suspicion of the influence of the Scots as well as enthusiastic alliance with them, and many resented the preferential treatment the Scots army received from Parliament compared with the niggardly treatment of the English soldiers stranded in the north. The slow progress of religious reform contributed to the emergence and spread of radical religious sects, especially in London. In the second place, then, many conservatives were alarmed and the radical upsurge helped to crystallise a previously unfocused adherence to an episcopal, ceremonial and comprehensive 'Anglican' church, not Laudian, but certainly not Puritan. Finally, many feared the novel extensions of Parliament's powers.[10]

The early measures of the Long Parliament were widely acclaimed, especially by Puritans. John Bampfield, whose son sat in the Commons, enthused at the start of 1641, 'the news of these times are so excellent that he deserves not to breath this British air who prayeth not god heartily for them . . . for ever be this Parliament renowned for so great achievements, for we dream of nothing more than a golden age'.[11] The impeachment of Strafford began almost immediately but problems in making their case led the opposition to switch to a Bill of Attainder – voting the earl a traitor, rather than proving him one through the judicial powers of the House of Lords. The bill passed the Commons on 19 April 1641, but the Lords agreed only on May 8, three days after the army plot had been revealed. Following demonstrations in London, Charles gave his consent two days later, on the same day as he agreed to the bill against the dissolution of the House. Archbishop Laud was consigned to the Tower and impeachment proceedings opened; others, like Secretary Windebanke and Lord Keeper Finch, avoided such fates by fleeing abroad. The execution of Strafford interrupted the dismantling of the personal rule. Ship money had been declared illegal in December 1640 and the Triennial Act passed in February 1641. Then from June onwards Acts were passed to abolish the prerogative courts, to collect tonnage and poundage only with the consent of Parliament, and to declare knighthood fines illegal.

Religious reform was more problematic. There seems to have been little opposition to episcopacy as such amongst English Puritans before 1640 but the identification of so many bishops with Laudianism, and the euphoria generated by the hopes of reform encouraged radicalisation once the Long Parliament met. On 11 December 1640, the City of London petitioned the Commons that the 'government of archbishops and lord bishops, deans and archdeacons' should be destroyed, 'with all its dependencies, roots and branches'. Further petitions against bishops came in from several counties, but a contentious bill to abolish episcopacy was kept in the background throughout 1641. Meanwhile, the Laudian 'innovations' in ceremonial and worship were the object of local attack, while in September 1641, a week before Parliament was to adjourn, the Commons, acting on their own and claiming a novel extension in executive authority, issued resolutions against ecclesiastical innovations. Churchwardens were ordered to take down communion rails and move the communion table from its 'altar-wise' position at the east end of the church. Crucifixes and images were to go; ritual bowing was condemned and strict observance of the Lord's Day was enjoined. These resolutions intensified local conflicts over religion and aroused much opposition in both the Lords and the Commons. County petitions were organised urging retention of episcopacy, and showing affection for the rituals of the Book of Common Prayer. In 1641–2, commitment to the 'established' church and opposition to religious radicalism became central to the emerging royalist 'party'.

The king's reactions to these developments were characteristic. In February 1641 Charles seems to have realised that it was not possible to save Strafford and defend episcopacy through negotiation.[12] He thus developed two strategies which, as so often with Charles, were mutually contradictory. The first was to build a moderate royalist party around men like the Earl of Bristol and Edward Hyde, capitalising on affection for episcopacy and resentment of the Scots. Secondly, he encouraged or at least acquiesced in a series of overlapping plots seeking to tap the discontent of the neglected English army still languishing unpaid in the north. Precise details are inevitably unclear but one plan was apparently to use the threat of force (as the Scots did) to put pressure on the parliament. A more dramatic plot hatched by men very close to the queen such as Henry Jermyn and Sir John Suckling, sought to bring the army south and rescue Strafford from the Tower. The army itself, displaying as Russell says, 'the instinctive constitutionalism of the English' did much to defeat these plots by refusing to cooperate and most of the conspirators fled in May 1641. Semi-public plans to seize the Tower remained in the air, and Charles never lost his habit of plotting. There were recurrent hopes that Irish forces could be used to recover his position in England and Scotland; renewed overtures to the English army in the summer of 1641 and the intrigues in Scotland in the early autumn. Finally, in the months before the outbreak of war there was the ill-judged attempt to coerce the parliament and arrest the 'five members' by force in January 1642.

Royal plotting both revealed and intensified the profound divisions between the king and the opposition politicians. Conrad

Russell has noted the startling contrast with Henry VIII's reign; where the Tudor monarch's threats of force intimidated opposition, Charles's encouraged intransigence. The plots had a fatal legacy in the king's lasting reputation for perfidy: his subjects' suspicions were sometimes exaggerated but they were rarely completely wrong, and they were always plausible. This thread runs through the rest of Charles's reign from the fears aroused by the king's trip north in August 1641 to the enraged exasperation which followed the second civil war of 1648 and provoked the regicide. The first Army Plot encouraged popular protest in London and emboldened Parliament into more determined measures. London citizens called for Strafford's blood, and it was in response to a City petition that the Lords sent one of their number to secure the Tower and pre-empt any royal coup. The plot hastened a process whereby both sides found it easier to contemplate carrying out their threats of force.

The plot's immediate effect was equally important. The details emerged at the height of the parliamentary conflict over Strafford's attainder and sealed his fate; in the aftermath of the plot Charles agreed to the Act against the dissolution of the Parliament. Perhaps the most significant outcome of the plot, however, was the 'Protestation' of 3 May 1641 which Russell has described as 'a declaration of readiness to resist a royal coup'. The Protestation described a popish rather than a royal plot, but it left little doubt that the king himself was implicated. It denounced, as already said in chapter 2, 'the designs of the priests and Jesuits' to undermine true religion and the fundamental laws. The grievances of the 1630s were rehearsed – the intermissions of Parliament, the religious innovations, the illegal taxation, the 'popish' army in Ireland – and the evil designs culminating in the attempt to 'bring the English Army into misunderstanding of this Parliament'. The Protestation thus shows once again and very clearly how specific events and policies of Charles's reign were put into a sinister and long-established framework. Above all the Protestation, like the Grand Remonstrance later, sought in practical terms to underline Parliament's role as the representative of the people. This was done by associating the people directly with its declarations.

The Protestation took the form of an oath of loyalty to defend 'with my life, power and estate', the true reformed religion against popery and 'popish innovations', according to 'my allegiance to his Majesty's royal person, honour and estate; as also the power and privilege of Parliament, the lawful rights and liberties of the subjects'. Significantly, there was no direct oath of loyalty to the king, instead all who took the Protestation engaged themselves to work for the punishment of those who plotted against Parliament, and for the preservation of the 'union and peace betwixt the three kingdoms of England, Scotland and Ireland'.

Notwithstanding the determination shown in the Protestation, by the summer of 1641 Parliament seemed to be losing its way, and fears of the consequences of Charles's trip to Scotland added to the unease. As described in chapter 1, these anxieties prompted the rapid settlement of long-term financial problems so that the armies could be paid off before the king could again exploit their discontent. There were suggestions for further extension of Parliament's powers: the 'ten propositions' of 24 June 1641 which suggested emergency measures to defend the country against papists and evil counsellors while the king was in Scotland was, in Fletcher's term, a 'working document' rather than a fixed policy, but it showed the direction in which some opposition figures were moving. The establishment of a 'committee of fifty' to manage business during the parliament's recess was also confirmation of the transformation of an occasional assembly into a permanent aspect of government.

The major response of Parliament's leadership to the sense of momentum lost was an explanation and appeal to the people, the 'Grand Remonstrance' which had been first discussed in April and May 1641, and was revived in August 1641 as the king left for Scotland. Within days of Parliament's reassembly, news of the Irish rising gave the Remonstrance a desperate urgency for many politicians. It was, writes Fletcher, 'a progress report, an agenda for action and a statement of common political aims'. A bleak account of the grievances of Charles I's reign reached a climax in the dangerous popish conspiracy of 1638–40. The Remonstrance justified the measures already enacted in

Parliament, and attributed the delays in completing necessary reforms to the continuing plots of malignants rather than to divisions or caution amongst Parliament-men. In part Pym and his allies wished to settle the doubts amongst Parliament's own membership, but more especially they wanted to re-establish the harmony between the people and their representative which had existed in the previous November. The Remonstrance was perhaps more successful in its second aim, for its stormy passage through the Commons revealed how divided the House now was. Clause 189, which blamed the bishops for the introduction of popish ceremonial to the church, passed by only 25 votes; the completed version succeeded by only 11 votes in a near-violent session on 22 November. Sir Edward Dering expressed the doubts of many:

> when I first heard of a Remonstrance, I presently imagined that like faithful councillors, we should hold up a glass unto his Majesty; I thought to represent unto the King the wicked counsels of pernicious councillors; the restless turbulency of practical Papists ... I did not dream that we should remonstrate downward, tell stories to the people and talk of the King as of a third person.[13]

As with Charles's plots, Parliament's appeals to the people were alarming precisely because of their plausibility. In London in particular, Parliament's activities were monitored and influenced by a vocal, well-informed and increasingly organised populace. Nehemiah Wallington described how he went to urge the Lords to condemn Strafford in May 1641, along with some 15,000 of his fellow citizens, all crying 'justice, justice'. Popular pressure from Londoners was crucial in forcing Charles to sacrifice Strafford; demonstrations against the bishops' sitting in the Lords forced their exclusion in December 1641 and fear of the city crowds was an important factor in the king's flight from London after the failure of his attempt against the five members in January 1642. These demonstrations were not completely spontaneous: religious networks and colonial interests gave many members of both Houses contacts with the city. It has been argued that London Puritan merchants were often second-rank figures in purely economic terms who were involved in the

North American colonial trades or in retailing which gave them close contacts with independent artisans and ordinary city consumers. Such men played a major part in channelling popular demonstrations, but this is not to say that they manipulated or distorted popular opinion. Support for Parliament, and fear of evil counsellors and popish conspiracy were clearly widespread in the City in 1640–2. The newly effervescent London press fed an insatiable demand for news and opinion: Wallington spent a fortune on tracts and petitions in the 1640s.[14]

Politicisation was not confined to the capital although it was perhaps here that it was most advanced. Wallington often witnessed the ritualised petitioning of men from the provinces, as in February 1642 when hundreds of Kentishmen rode into London with copies of the Protestation sticking in their hats. Out of 40 counties, 38 made some kind of response to the Grand Remonstrance between December 1641 and August 1642, calling for further measures against popery, or for religious reform. Some, like the Warwickshire petition, seem to have been rather hasty affairs, concocted in London rather than the county itself, others were clearly genuine canvasses or mobilisation of provincial opinion as in Derbyshire where a month was spent collecting signatures parish by parish. The county petitions were a practical realisation of the connections between local and national affairs. Local pressure was brought to bear on national divisions, while London-based politicians used the petitioning process as a means of involving and informing provincial opinion. Local people were of course divided, most obviously and increasingly over religion. Petitions against episcopacy were organised in 19 counties in 1641 but 22 counties, often the same ones, produced petitions in favour of bishops and the liturgy of the Book of Common Prayer from autumn 1641. Through these rival petitions religious and cultural preferences became more clearly focused, and the foundations were laid for royalist and parliamentarian allegiance on a local level.[15]

The rising of Irish Catholics was a nightmarish confirmation of the power of anti-Christ and it immediately intensified the political crisis in England. Of the tracts collected by the London bookseller George Thomason between November 1641 and June

1642, 23 per cent concerned Ireland; most of them outlined in vivid, gory detail the supposed atrocities committed on the Protestant settlers of Ulster. The dark suspicions that Charles was himself implicated in this dastardly Catholic plot meant many politicians would not contemplate trusting the king with the army necessary for its suppression. It was left to the settlers themselves and then to the Scots to mount holding operations in Ireland while in England Parliament moved to the ultimate challenge – against royal control over armed force. On 5 November 1641, a day resonant with anti-popish determination, Pym moved 'additional instructions' in the Commons, stating that if evil counsellors were not removed, the Commons itself would have to take measures to defend Ireland. His proposals passed by 151 to 110, a vote which again shows widespread unease at the enlargement of Parliament's claims, but also reveals how a sense of crisis and suspicion encouraged many to proceed. Parliament questioned suspected Catholics and urged vigilance on the western port towns against an Irish invasion, a clear exercise of executive powers.[16]

After Charles returned to London from Scotland on 25 November, events rapidly reached the point of no return. From 7 December the Commons discussed a bill giving Parliament power to nominate Lords Lieutenant of the county militias. In the City, staunch supporters of Parliament took control of the Common Council. Charles's response was to signal renewed plans for a coup by making the notorious Thomas Lunsford Lieutenant of the Tower. Demonstrations against Lunsford merged with a popular and parliamentary campaign to exclude the bishops from the Lords, where they formed the core of a 'royalist' group who could impeach the opposition leaders. After days of unrest it was the bishops themselves who were impeached on 29 December for protesting against their forcible exclusion from the House. Nevertheless on 3 January Charles attempted to impeach five members of the House of Commons: Denzil Holles, Sir Arthur Haselrig, Pym, Hampden and William Strode, along with Lord Kimbolton. They were all accused of treason: inviting a foreign army into England, subverting the fundamental laws and government of England, and levying war against the king. As shown above, the indictment is a good illustration of the conspiratorial view of the opposition developed by the king since the 1620s. When Charles came in person with a guard to the Commons to arrest them on the following day he found the members had taken refuge in the City where they remained until after the king left London for Hampton Court, and then the north.

Organising for War

Charles's failed coup and subsequent flight inaugurated some months of hesitant but nonetheless inexorable moves to war as propaganda campaigns went hand in hand with the raising of men and money. On 31 January 1642 the Commons completed its proceedings on the Militia Bill; although the Lords' consent was not forthcoming until 5 March, new nominations for Lieutenants had been discussed before this and indeed the reliable Philip Skippon had been entrusted with the London Trained Bands in early January. The Militia Bill was issued by Parliament as an ordinance intended to have the force of law despite lacking royal consent. The earliest jockeyings for practical military support occurred in Yorkshire where Charles was based from March until May. The king's personal involvement was no guarantee of success. In a crucial set-back, Charles was refused entry into Hull on 23 April by Sir John Hotham, and later meetings with the Yorkshire gentry to raise a personal guard met with limited support and some open opposition. Many in Yorkshire sought accommodation but it became clear that a determined royalist group blamed Parliament for political breakdown, while Puritan gentry, with significant support in the West Riding textile towns, argued that it was up to the king to make concessions.

On 20 May both Houses of Parliament resolved that the king, 'seduced by wicked counsel' was planning war against the parliament, and on 26 May they justified the defiance at Hull with a Remonstrance which made the potent distinction between the person of the king and the royal authority. Where Charles had claimed that the town of Hull was his property, in the same fashion as his subjects owned their houses or lands, Parliament described this as 'an erroneous maxim ... the root of all the subjects' misery, and of all the invading of their just rights and liberties' and argued that his kingdom was only 'entrusted unto him for the good and safety and best advantage thereof'. 'As this trust is for the use of the kingdom, so ought it to be managed by the advice of the Houses of Parliament, whom the kingdom hath trusted for that purpose.' The Houses denied that precedents 'can be limits to bound our proceedings, which may and must vary according to the different condition of times. . .'. In line with these arguments the 'Nineteen Propositions' presented to Charles on 1 June offered as 'humble desires and propositions' for the 'removing those jealousies and differences, which have unhappily fallen betwixt you and your people', what were in fact far-reaching claims. Parliament was to nominate the great officers of state, while the king was to accept the militia ordinance and the reformation of the church 'as both Houses of Parliament shall advise'. Public affairs were to 'be debated, resolved and transacted only in Parliament'.[17]

The Declarations and Propositions of spring and summer 1642 were as much propaganda efforts as genuine negotiation. As Fletcher has written, 'Declarations, orders, ordinances, speeches, letters from the Speaker to sheriffs, congratulatory petitions and fast sermons all poured from the London presses during the summer', and the king was, at last, equally systematic. Even the Lord Mayor of London received 38 copies of the king's proclamation about Hull. The king made a particular effort to set out his position through sympathetic judges and gentry at the summer Assizes of 1642, but both sides used the routine county meetings at Quarter Sessions and the Assizes as well as the pulpit, and extraordinary gatherings and musters in the prov-inces. Both sides tried to raise men and arms, partly by winning control of county militias, but also through attracting volunteers. Parliament's mechanism was the lieutenancy established under the militia ordinance, and MPs were usually prominent in its execution in some 14 counties between May and mid July, and 9 more from August until October. The king turned to the less familiar medieval practice of a commission of array which gave prominent named peers and gentry the power to raise forces in the county. The royalist local effort was less successful: the commission of array was executed in eleven counties between July and October 1642 while a further ten attempts failed or were abandoned. However, the royalists rallied forces in some counties where Parliament had earlier been dominant and the king won particularly strong support in the west of England, the Welsh borders, the north-west, and by late summer, Yorkshire.[18]

As local historians have emphasised, many were reluctant to become involved; however, their capacity for effective action was limited by the fact that there were no practical political avenues through which 'neutralism' could be expressed. There were petitions for accommodation from several counties, although these were fewer than the partisan petitions on the church, and some anyway blamed one side more than another for the conflict. In some areas peace was best preserved by joining the dominant side; in Gloucestershire in early summer Parliament won widespread adherence to its attempts to control the county forces although later military events showed that there was extensive royalist sympathy in many parts of the county. Similarly, the lukewarm or uncommitted swung behind the king in Yorkshire and Worcestershire. In most counties opinion was divided and in many areas there was a real choice between the sides in 1642–3, although in the far west, Wales and the north parliamentarianism was for the zealous and the foolhardy as royalism was in much of East Anglia or the south-east. Even a brief summary suggests that the civil war broke out in a very piecemeal fashion. There is no single date on which it started, although 15 July when the Earl of Essex was appointed Captain-General of Parliament's forces or 22 August when the king raised his standard at Nottingham are clearly significant landmarks.

Given the alienation from his rule in 1640, Charles obtained remarkable support from local elites; in those counties outside the south-east and East Anglia studied by historians, royalist gentry often outnumbered parliamentarians by two to one. Manning's argument that royalism was seen as support for the social order with the crown as both 'the pinnacle and the symbol' of hierarchy has much force. There was also much support, at many levels of society, for a corporate, episcopal church and conversely, widespread fear of the disorder that could be provoked by Puritan religious reformation as well as by sectarianism. Episcopacy, in the words of a Kent petition, was 'the most pious, most prudent, and most safe government' for the church, while there was deep affection for the liturgy of the Book of Common Prayer, 'celebrated by the piety of the bishops and martyrs who composed it . . . with a holy love embraced by the most and best of all the laity'.[19]

It is clear that royalist allegiance amongst the gentry was stimulated by profound unhappiness at the enlargement of Parliament's powers. Parliament's claims in the Nineteen Propositions were built on long-established beliefs in Parliament's involvement in government, but also on the immediate developments of 1640–2, when Parliament became a permanent institution. It raised the money to pay off the Scots and organised the disbanding of the two armies in the north; it gave orders for the transformation of worship in parish churches and took measures against papists. Finally, it was, of course, protected against dissolution without consent. Within Parliament itself, this permanence made necessary more sophisticated mobilisation of support, and organisation of factions; in the provinces Parliament's claims often met with incomprehension or resistance. In April 1642 leading Herefordshire gentry complained to one of the county's MPs, the Puritan Robert Harley: '[the king] summons you to parliament and had always the power to dismiss you. By virtue of his writ we send you, not with authority to govern us or others, but with our consent for making or altering laws as to his Majesty, the Lords and Commons shall seem good. This is our stronghold, let us stick to that and not with grasping more lose the hold we have.' In similar fashion, and indeed in a letter modelled on the Hereford Protest, Nottinghamshire royalists in July admonished their parliamentarian MP, Sir Thomas Hutchinson, that he was not to give them orders but to 'follow our sense, so far as you conceive it to be the sense of your county whose you are and for whom you serve'. He was merely their representative: 'We never conceived your only votes should be our law nor conceived that we had such a power to confer upon you.'[20]

From another point of view, however, this drastic expansion of Parliament's powers, established on its older claims to legitimacy, was extremely important in that it prepared Parliament to organise the war effort against the king and also familiarised potential supporters with the need to support Parliament's novel initiatives. It seems that the collective, representative character of Parliament blended more successfully with people's natural concern to defend their locality than did personal loyalty to the king. The links between the localities and their representatives were demonstrated concretely at many points in 1641 and 1642 – in the petitions sent up to Parliament, in the oaths of loyalty enjoined by Parliament, in the fasts kept at Westminster and in the provinces, and most obviously in the part played by parliamentarian peers and MPs in enforcing the militia ordinance. Parliament's corporate character and local links helped win it much greater support from towns – a conclusion supported by the most thorough local research, despite attempts to deny the affinity. Fletcher's account of the outbreak of war includes a map of 'towns that raised volunteers for parliament' in 1642 but there is nothing comparable for the king's side. Coventry, Taunton, Gloucester and Northampton are notable parliamentarian towns that were humiliated by royalist gentry at the Restoration.[21]

Parliamentarianism seems to have encouraged involvement in a cause, whereas royalism meant loyalty to a leader – a personal monarch. Along with the zealous godliness characteristic of parliamentarian campaigning, this involvement often meant that parliamentarians often did rather well in unpromising circumstances in 1642 – establishing vital bridgeheads in royalist areas in Yorkshire and the West Country, which were able to obstruct the royalists' war effort and form a basis for later parliamentarian resurgence. In contrast, royalists often failed to make the most of local dominance because so many of their supporters were sent away to follow the king. In Lancashire and Cheshire, for example, parliamentarians had much greater success than their initial strength justified because so many royalists had left the north-west for the king's southern head-quarters. Furthermore, the king offended local susceptibilities by seizing the arms of county militias, and by permitting Catholics to serve in his army. The royalist sympathisers who were clearly present in East Anglia and the south-east either left their localities for Oxford, the king's headquarters, or otherwise failed to establish the vital outposts which could harass local parliamentarians. In Norfolk and Kent, for example, royalists mounted only rearguard actions when it was too late to overcome Parliament's control.

In chapter 2, an attempt was made to stress the intertwined political and religious ideas which promoted opposition to Charles's rule. The civil war was not simply a war of religion. There were many reasons why people supported Parliament in 1642, but nevertheless it is clear that the major element encouraging determination and a willingness to fight was that parliamentarianism took the form of a religious crusade. This was a struggle against the popish menace but also for a general reformation, the building of a new Jerusalem. This crusade, which encompassed peers and humble men and women, and united Westminster and the provinces, emerged from the bleak experiences of the 1630s and matured during the months of glorious hopes and dreadful fears after 1640. Parliament's duty was put in sharp focus by the fast sermons preached before it in a regular series from February 1642. The first two were by Edmund Calamy and Stephen Marshall. Calamy outlined the purpose of this preaching: there would be

> twelve national, solemn, public Fasts every year which (if rightly kept) will be as the twelve gates of the New Jerusalem, spoken of, Revelations 21. Every fast will be a Gate to let us in, into a part of the New Jerusalem of Mercy, and happiness promised to the people of God, here upon the earth.

Marshall's sermon was the famous, bloodthirsty, *Meroz Cursed*, where the curse was against those who shrank from shredding blood, were reluctant to fight the Lord's battles. Fast sermons were preached on the same days in the localities – in the home parish of the Fairfaxes in Yorkshire they often concentrated on the fate of Saul – while people all over England could soon read the printed versions of the Westminster set-pieces. When Parliament's army marched to the Midlands in August 1642, some of the newly famous preachers – Obadiah Sedgewick, Simeon Ashe, Stephen Marshall – marched with it. Rousing sermons and speeches were given when Parliament rallied the militia or raised volunteers. In early 1643 Lord Brooke exhorted volunteers in Warwickshire:

> Lord we are but a handful in consideration of thine and our enemies, therefore O Lord fight thou our battles, go out as Thou didst in the time of King David before the hosts of the servants, and strengthen and give us hearts that we show ourselves men for the defence of Thy true religion and our own and the kingdom's safety.[22]

The initial political breakdown of 1642 had its immediate origins in the 'high' politics of the several British kingdoms. No one would argue that the 'sectaries and schismatics' of Birmingham, for example, would have raised an army against the king if Lord Brooke and other parliamentary leaders had not rallied them in a godly crusade. However, it was stressed in chapters 2 and 3 that the attitudes of the elites who participated in high politics were often influenced by their understanding of social change and by the opinions of their social inferiors. The nature of the civil war that broke out in England is explicable only within the context of a broad and aroused political nation with divided views and complex relationships to elites. As discussed in chapter 3, there were patterns to civil war allegiance which connected with different regional economies and social relationships, and varying cultural and religious attitudes. Sometimes the presence of a powerful garrison or a particularly energetic 'great man' was crucial in securing an area for king or Parliament but allegiance was rarely completely random. In particular, Parliament's attempts to involve the 'people' in its cause seem to have struck a particular chord in industrial areas and generally amongst independent small property owners.

The conservatism and hesitancy of parliamentarians in 1642 is often stressed and contrasted with the more radical developments of 1646 onwards.[23] Throughout, this book has avoided seeing the royalist-parliamentarian conflict in terms of any version of a conservative-innovative division. On the financial problems of the kingdom, the nature of political authority, or on religious divisions, the politically active were exploring solutions to unfamiliar problems. Of course many men who went to war against the king in 1642 had limited objectives, fought reluctantly and were horrified at the political and religious radicalism they had unleashed. But it is worth remembering that the parliamentarians of 1642 had indeed done much to unleash popular radicalism. They promoted the war against the king as a godly war in which all true Christians should join, and they had, as the representatives of the people, appealed to the people without defining too closely whom they meant. In 1647, in a now clichéd quotation, the New Model Army spoke nothing but the truth: 'We were not a mere mercenary army, hired to serve any arbitrary power of a state; but called forth and conjured, by the several declarations of Parliament, to the defence of our own and the people's just rights and liberties.'[24] One of the most distinctive features of the English civil war lies in its potential for radicalisation, a feature that links its causes and its consequences.

NOTES

INTRODUCTION

Place of publication is London unless otherwise cited.

1. J. C. D. Clark, *Revolution and Rebellion* (Cambridge, 1986), pp. 15, 37–8, 170.
2. Hansard, Proceedings in the House of Commons, 7 July 1988.
3. Laurence Stone, *The Causes of the English Revolution* (1972); Conrad Russell (ed.), *The Origins of the English Civil War* (1973); Christopher Hill, *The Century of Revolution* (first published Edinburgh, 1961) is a good example; Mark Kishlansky, *Parliamentary Selection: Social and Political Choice in Early Modern England* (Cambridge, 1986); Russell in a review in *London Review of Books*, 5 September 1985.
4. Stone, *Causes of the English Revolution*, p. 48; Russell is again the best example of the contrary trend.
5. R. C. Richardson, *The Debate on The English Revolution Revisited* (1988; first edition 1977); Howard Tomlinson (ed.), *Before the English Civil War* (1983); *Proceedings of the Short Parliament of 1640*, edited by Esther S. Cope and Willson H. Coates (Camden Society Fourth Series, 19, 1977).
6. Anthony Fletcher, *The Outbreak of the English Civil War* (1982), pp. xx, 38.
7. Richard Cust and Ann Hughes (eds), *Conflict in Early Stuart England* (1989), especially the editors' 'Introduction: After Revisionism', gives a fuller account of current debates. T. K. Rabb and D. Hirst, 'Revisionism Revised: Two Perspectives on early

Stuart Parliamentary History', and Christopher Hill, 'Parliament and People in Seventeenth Century England', all in *Past and Present*, 92 (1981) are earlier critiques of revisionist work. Those who have attacked older views do not necessarily agree amongst themselves and the term 'revisionist' is used as a convenient shorthand, rather than as a description of a coherent 'school' of historians.

8. G. R. Elton, 'A High Road to Civil War', in his *Studies in Tudor and Stuart Politics and Government*, 2 vols (1974).

9. David Underdown, *Revel, Riot and Rebellion* (Oxford, 1985); John Morrill, Brian Manning and David Underdown, 'What was the English Revolution?' *History Today* (March, 1984).

1 A BRITISH PROBLEM? A EUROPEAN CRISIS?

1. P. Zagorin, *The Court and the Country. The Beginning of the English Revolution* (1969), p. 5.

2. R. B. Merriman, *Six Contemporaneous Revolutions* (Oxford, 1938); Trevor Aston (ed.), *Crisis in Europe 1560–1660* (1965) for the articles by Hobsbawm and Trevor-Roper, and the subsequent debate, which first appeared in *Past and Present* in 1954 and 1959 respectively.

3. See especially the articles by Steensgaard and Elliott in Geoffrey Parker and Lesley M. Smith (eds), *The General Crisis of the Seventeenth Century* (1978); T. K. Rabb, *The Struggle for Stability in Early Modern Europe* (Oxford, 1975) is an excellent survey of the debate over the general crisis.

4. Michael Roberts, 'The Military Revolution' in his *Essays in Swedish History* (1967); Geoffrey Parker, 'The Military Revolution: A Myth?' in his *Spain and the Netherlands 1559–1659* (1979); J. R. Hale, *War and Society in Renaissance Europe* (1985).

5. Robert Forster and Jack P. Greene, *Preconditions of Revolution in Early Modern Europe* (1970); J. H. Elliott, *Richelieu and Olivares* (Cambridge, 1984); David Parker, *The Making of French Absolutism* (1983).

6. Conrad Russell, 'Parliament and the King's Finances' in Russell (ed.), *Origins of the English Civil War*; Russell, *Parliaments and English Politics 1621–1629* (Oxford, 1979), especially pp. 64–84.

7. The discussion of financial and administrative problems is based on David Thomas, 'Financial and Administrative Developments', in Tomlinson (ed.), *Before the English Civil War*; Russell as in n. 6 above; Menna Prestwich, *Lionel Cranfield: Politics and Profits*

under the Early Stuarts (Oxford, 1965); Prestwich, 'English Politics and Administration 1603–1625' in A. G. R. Smith (ed.), *The Reign of James VI and I* (1979); Smith, 'Crown, Parliament and Finance: The Great Contract of 1610' in Peter Clark, A. G. R. Smith and Nicholas Tyacke (eds), *The English Commonwealth 1547–1640* (Leicester, 1979); Robert Ashton, *The Crown and the Money Market 1603–1640* (Oxford, 1960).

8. For an up-to-date discussion of patronage see Linda Levy Peck, '"For a King not to be bountiful were a fault": Perspectives on Court Patronage in Early Stuart England,' *Journal of British Studies*, 25 (1986).

9. D. M. Hirst, 'The Privy Council and Problems of Enforcement in the 1620s', *Journal of British Studies*, 18 (1978).

10. Alan Everitt, *The Local Community and the Great Rebellion* (Historical Association Pamphlet, 1969); Everitt, *The Community of Kent and the Great Rebellion* (Leicester, 1966).

11. Russell, *Parliaments and English Politics*.

12. Additional information has been taken from Brian Quintrell, 'The Government of the County of Essex 1603–1642', London University PhD thesis (1965); the Lincolnshire letter is in *Seventeenth Century Economic Documents*, edited by Joan Thirsk and J. P. Cooper (Oxford, 1972).

13. Russell, *Parliaments and English Politics*, p. 76.

14. Russell, 'Parliament and the King's Finances'; Conrad Russell, 'Why did Charles I fight the Civil War?' *History Today* (June 1984).

15. For the general account see Prestwich, Thomas and Smith as in n. 7 above; Richard Cust, *The Forced Loan and English Politics* (Oxford, 1987).

16. Anthony Fletcher, *The Outbreak of the English Civil War* (1981), pp. 20–3, 29, 50–1, 408.

17. Derek Hirst, *Authority and Conflict* (1986), p. 58 especially.

18. Eric Lindquist, 'The Failure of the Great Contract', *Journal of Modern History*, 57 (1985); Pauline Croft (ed.), 'A Collection of Several Speeches and Treatises of the late Lord Treasurer Cecil', *Camden Miscellany*, 29 (Camden Society, 4th Series 34, 1987).

19. Simon Adams, 'Spain or the Netherlands? The Dilemmas of Early Stuart Foreign Policy,' in Tomlinson (ed.), *Before the English Civil War*.

20. Clive Holmes, 'The County Community in Stuart Historiography,' *Journal of British Studies*, 19 (1980); Ann Hughes, 'Local History and the Origins of the English Civil War', in Cust and Hughes (eds), *Conflict in Early Stuart England*; Kevin Sharpe,

'Crown, Parliament and Locality: Government and Communication in Early Stuart England', *English Historical Review*, 101 (1986).

21. David Parker, *La Rochelle and the French Monarchy* (Royal Historical Society, 1980); Richard Bonney, 'The English and French Civil Wars', *History*, 65 (1980); Kevin Sharpe, 'Crown, Parliament and Locality'.

22. David Stevenson, *The Scottish Revolution 1637–1644: The Triumph of the Covenanters* (Newton Abbot, 1973); Conrad Russell, 'Monarchies, Wars and Estates in England, France and Spain *c*.1580–*c*.1640', *Legislative Studies Quarterly*, VII (1982); Russell, 'The British Problem and the English Civil War', *History*, 72 (1987); Russell, 'The British Background to the Irish Rebellion of 1641', *Historical Research*, 61 (1988).

23. Russell, 'Parliamentary History in Perspective, 1604–1629', *History*, 61 (1976); Russell, 'The British Problem'; 'The British Background to the Irish Rebellion'.

24. The quotation is from Russell, 'The British Problem', while the general account is taken from the works cited in n. 22 above, plus David Stevenson, *Scottish Covenanters and Irish Confederates* (Belfast, Ulster Historical Foundation, 1981); T. W. Moody, F. X. Martin and F. J. Byrne (eds), *Early Modern Ireland 1534–1691* (*A New History of Ireland* vol. 3, Oxford, 1976).

25. Moody, Martin and Byrne (eds), *Early Modern Ireland 1534–1691*, p. 257; Russell, 'The British Problem'.

26. Stevenson, *Scottish Covenanters and Irish Confederates*; Russell, 'The British Background to the Irish Rebellion'.

27. Keith M. Brown, 'Aristocratic Finance and the Origins of the Scottish Revolution', *English Historical Review*, 104 (1989); David Stevenson, *The Scottish Revolution 1637–1644*; Maurice Lee, *The Road to Revolution: Scotland under Charles I, 1625–1637* (Urbana, Illinois, 1985).

28. This account is based mainly on Russell, 'The British Problem'; Moody, Martin and Byrne (eds), *Early Modern Ireland 1534–1691*; Keith Lindley, 'The Impact of the 1641 Rebellion upon England and Wales, 1641–1645', *Irish Historical Studies*, 18 (1972).

29. David Stevenson, *The Scottish Revolution 1637–1644*; Stevenson, *Scottish Covenanters and Irish Confederates*; Russell, 'The British Problem'; Russell, 'The British Background to the Irish Rebellion'.

30. Compare Russell, 'The British Problem' with David Stevenson, *The Scottish Revolution 1637–1644*. See also Russell, 'The First

Army Plot of 1641', *Transactions of the Royal Historical Society*, 5th Series, 38 (1988).

31. Russell and Stevenson, as in n. 30 above; see also Steven Ellis, '"Not mere English": The British Perspective 1400–1650', *History Today* (December 1988); Brown, 'Aristocratic Finance'.

32. Additional material is from Arthur H. Williamson, *Scottish National Consciousness in the Reign of James VI* (Edinburgh, 1979).

2 HIERARCHY, CONSENSUS OR CONFLICT: POLITICS AND RELIGION IN EARLY STUART ENGLAND

1. Stone, *The Causes of the English Revolution 1529–1642* (1972), pp. 91, 98, 112, 116.

2. Peter Laslett, *The World We Have Lost Further Explored* (1983); Mark Kishlansky, *Parliamentary Selection. Social and Political Choice in Early Modern England* (Cambridge, 1986); David Starkey *et al.*, *The English Court from the Wars of the Roses to the Civil War* (1987); J. C. D. Clark, *Revolution and Rebellion* (Cambridge, 1986).

3. Russell, 'Parliamentary History in Perspective 1604–1629', *History*, 61 (1976); Mark Kishlansky, 'The Emergence of Adversary Politics in the Long Parliament', *Journal of Modern History*, 49 (1977); Kevin Sharpe, 'Introduction: Parliamentary History 1603–29; in or out of perspective?' in Sharpe (ed.), *Faction and Parliament* (Oxford, 1979); Kevin Sharpe, 'Crown, Parliament and Locality'.

4. See Michael G. Finlayson, *Historians, Puritanism and the English Revolution* (Toronto, 1985); and Tyacke, Morrill and Haigh as in nn. 38–9 below.

5. Thomas Smith, *De Republica Anglorum: The maner of Governement or policie of the Realme of England*, edited by Mary Dewar (Cambridge, 1982; first published 1583), p. 76. See, for example, P. Zagorin, *The Court and the Country* (1969), p. 28.

6. G. J. Schochet, *Patriarchalism in Political Thought* (Oxford, 1975); J. A. Sharpe, *Early Modern England: A Social History 1550–1760* (1987), p. 107, for the *Homily*.

7. The stimulating work of Dr J. S. A. Adamson on the peerage is not yet fully in print but see, for example, 'The *Vindiciae Veritatis* and the Political Creed of Viscount Saye and Sele', *Historical Research*, 60 (1987); J. S. A. Adamson, 'Parliamentary Management, Men of Business and the House of Lords, 1640–49', in C.

Jones (ed.), *A Pillar of the Constitution: The House of Lords in British Politics 1640–1784* (1989); James E. Farnell, 'The Social and Intellectual Basis of London's Role in the English Civil Wars'; and Paul Christianson, 'The Peers, the People and Parliamentary Management in the First Six Months of the Long Parliament', both in *Journal of Modern History*, 49 (1977).

8. Compare Kishlansky, *Parliamentary Selection*, with J. H. Plumb, 'The Growth of the Electorate in England from 1600 to 1715', *Past and Present*, 45 (1969), and Derek Hirst, *The Representative of the People?* (Cambridge, 1975).

9. Laslett, *World We Have Lost*, pp. 216, 234; David Cressy, *Literacy and the Social Order: Reading and Writing in Tudor and Stuart England* (Cambridge, 1980), pp. 145, 148, 152.

10. A similar discussion can be found in Paul S. Seaver, *Wallington's World: A Puritan Artisan in Seventeenth Century London* (1985), p. 77; and now see the comments in an important article by David Wootton, 'From Rebellion to Revolution: the Crisis of the Winter of 1642–3 and the Origins of Civil War Radicalism', *English Historical Review*, 105 (1990).

11. Cynthia B. Herrup, *The Common Peace: Participation and the Criminal Law in Seventeenth Century England* (Cambridge, 1987); Herrup, 'Law and Morality in Seventeenth Century England', *Past and Present*, 106 (1985).

12. Tim Harris, *London Crowds* (Cambridge, 1987) especially chapter 1; Jill R. Dias, 'Politics and Administration in Nottinghamshire and Derbyshire 1590–1640', Oxford University DPhil thesis (1973); Richard Cust, *The Forced Loan and English Politics* (Oxford, 1987), p. 295.

13. Richard Cust, 'News and Politics in Early Seventeenth Century England', *Past and Present*, 112 (1986); Seaver, *Wallington's World*, p. 74.

14. Hirst, *The Representative of the People*; Richard Cust, 'Politics and the Electorate in the 1620s,' in Cust and Hughes (eds), *Conflict in Early Stuart England*; T. G. Barnes, *Somerset 1625–1640: A County's Government During the 'Personal Rule'* (Cambridge, Massachusetts, 1961), especially chapter 10.

15. Cust 'Politics and the Electorate'; Hughes, 'Local History and the Civil War'; Clive Holmes, 'Drainers and Fenmen: the problem of popular political consciousness in the seventeenth century', in Anthony Fletcher and John Stevenson (eds), *Order and Disorder in Early Modern England* (Cambridge, 1975).

16. See especially M. A. Kishlansky, *Parliamentary Selection*; Kishlansky, 'The Emergence of Adversary Politics'; also important are

Conrad Russell, 'Parliamentary History in Perspective', *Parliaments and English Politics*; and Kevin Sharpe (ed.), *Faction and Parliament*, introduction.

17. For the view that there were no serious cleavages between royalists and parliamentarians over fundamental political principle, see J. S. Morrill, 'The religious context of the English Civil War', *Transactions of the Royal Historical Society* 5th series, 34 (1984); Kevin Sharpe, 'Crown, Parliament and Locality', p. 232, says that there was 'no theoretical contention' about fundamentals of government.

18. Hirst, *Authority and Conflict*, pp. 84–6.

19. J. P. Sommerville, *Politics and Ideology in England 1603–1640* (1986), p. 4.

20. J. G. A. Pocock, *The Ancient Constitution and the Feudal Law. . . . A Reissue with a Retrospect* (Cambridge, 1987; first edition, 1957).

21. Pocock, *The Ancient Constitution*, pp. 293, 296; Russell, *Parliaments and English Politics*, chapter 6.

22. Perez Zagorin, *Rebels and Rulers 1500–1660* (Cambridge, 1982), vol. 1, p. 23; Michael Roberts, 'On Aristocratic Constitutionalism in Swedish History' in *Essays in Swedish History*; Holmes, 'Drainers and Fenmen', p. 195.

23. This and the following paragraph is closely based on Sommerville, *Politics and Ideology*.

24. Ann Hughes (ed.), *Seventeenth Century England: A Changing Culture*, vol. 1 (1980), pp. 51, 59.

25. Zagorin, *Court and Country*; the brief discussion in Stone, *Causes of the English Revolution*, pp. 105–8, has never been bettered.

26. Russell, *Parliaments and English Politics*, pp. 6, 424; Zagorin himself noted (*Court and Country*, p. 96) that some royal officials acted as part of the 'country'.

27. R. Malcolm Smuts, *Court Culture and the Origins of a Royalist Tradition in Early Stuart England* (Philadelphia, 1987); Martin Butler, *Theatre and Crisis 1632–1642* (Cambridge, 1984); Butler, 'Politics and the Masque: *The Triumph of Peace*', *The Seventeenth Century*, vol. II (1987); Kevin Sharpe, *Criticism and Complement* (Cambridge, 1987) and Sharpe, 'The image of virtue: the court and household of Charles I, 1625–1642' in Starkey *et al.*, *The English Court*.

28. Smuts, *Court Culture*; Sharpe, *Criticism and Compliment*; Judith Richards, '"His Nowe Majestie" and the English Monarchy: the kingship of Charles I before 1640', *Past and Present*, 113 (November 1986).

29. Patrick Collinson, 'Puritans, Men of Business and Elizabethan

Parliaments', *Parliamentary History*, 7 (1988); David Norbrook, *Poetry and Politics in the English Renaissance* (1984).

30. Cust and Hughes, 'Introduction: After Revisionism'.
31. S. R. Gardiner (ed.), *The Constitutional Documents of the Puritan Revolution* (1906 edition), pp. 206–7.
32. Patrick Collinson, 'The Monarchical Republic of Elizabeth I', *Bulletin of the John Rylands Library*; 69 (1987); Sommerville, *Politics and Ideology*, pp. 100–3, 124–6; Pauline Croft, 'Annual Parliaments and the Long Parliament', *Bulletin of the Institute of Historical Research*, 59 (1986).
33. Cust, *The Forced Loan and English Politics*, p. 219; Richard Cust, 'Charles I and a Draft Declaration for the 1628 Parliament', *Historical Research*, 63 (1990); Cust, 'Charles I, the Privy Council and the Forced Loan', *Journal of British Studies*, 24 (1985); Smuts, *Court Culture*, p. 273.
34. Kevin Sharpe, 'Crown, Parliament and Locality'; Ann Hughes, *Politics, Society and Civil War* (Cambridge, 1987), p. 115 for sheriffs; Christopher Hill, *Society and Puritanism in Pre-Revolutionary England* (first published 1964), pp. 102–3; James F. Larkin (ed.), *Stuart Royal Proclamations*, vol. II (Oxford, 1983), p. 662.
35. J. P. Kenyon, *The Stuart Constitution* (Cambridge, 1966 edition), pp. 241, 222–3.
36. Finlayson, *Historians, Puritanism and the English Revolution*; Patrick Collinson, *The Religion of Protestants* (Oxford, 1982).
37. Peter White, 'The Rise of Arminianism Reconsidered', *Past and Present*, 101 (1983); Kevin Sharpe, 'Archbishop Laud', *History Today*, 33 (August, 1983); Sharpe, 'Archbishop Laud and the University of Oxford' in H. Lloyd-Jones *et al., History and Imagination* (1981).
38. Nicholas Tyacke, *Anti-Calvinists: The Rise of English Arminianism c. 1590–1640* (Oxford, 1987), especially pp. 106, 253–63; see also J. T. Cliffe, *The Puritan Gentry: The Great Puritan Families of Early Stuart England* (1984), p. 149.
39. Morrill, 'The Religious Context'; C. Haigh, 'The Church of England, the Catholics and the People', in C. Haigh (ed.), *The Reign of Elizabeth I* (1984).
40. See especially, Keith Wrightson, *English Society 1580–1680* (1982) and William Hunt, *The Puritan Moment: The Coming of Revolution in an English County* (Cambridge, Massachusetts, 1983); Morrill himself does not see Puritanism as specifically attractive to the 'middling sort'.
41. Christopher Hill, *Society and Puritanism in Pre-Revolutionary*

England (first published 1964); Hill's recent work on John Bunyan, *A Turbulent, Seditious and Factious People* (Oxford 1988) shows how Calvinism could appeal to the socially humble; Collinson, 'Men of Business'; Fletcher, *Outbreak of the English Civil War*, chapter 6.

42. R. T. Kendall, *Calvin and English Calvinism to 1649* (Oxford, 1979); Peter Lake, 'Calvinism and the English Church 1570–1635', *Past and Present*, 114 (1987); Lake, *Anglicans and Puritans? Presbyterianism and English Conformist Thought from Whitgift to Hooker* (1988).

43. Peter Lake, 'Anti-Popery: the Structure of a Prejudice', in Cust and Hughes (eds), *Conflict in Early Stuart England*; Lake, 'Constitutional Consensus and Puritan Opposition in the 1620s: Thomas Scott and the Spanish Match', *Historical Journal*, 25 (1982); Michael Walzer, *The Revolution of the Saints* (1966 edn).

44. Clark, *Revolution and Rebellion*, pp. 88–9.

45. K. Fincham, 'Prelacy and Politics: Archbishop Abbot's defence of Protestant orthodoxy', *Historical Research*, 61 (1988); Lake, 'Calvinism and the English Church'; L. J. Reeve, 'Sir Robert Heath's Advice for Charles I in 1629', *Bulletin of the Institute of Historical Research*, LIX (1986).

46. Kenneth Fincham and Peter Lake, 'The Ecclesiastical Policy of King James I', *Journal of British Studies*, 24 (1985).

47. For this and the following paragraphs see Thomas Cogswell, 'England and the Spanish Match', in Cust and Hughes (eds), *Conflict in Early Stuart England*; Lake, 'Calvinism and the English Church'; Fincham and Lake, 'The Ecclesiastical Policy of King James I'; Tyacke, *Anti-Calvinists*, pp. 113–14, 166–72.

48. Larkin (ed.), *Stuart Royal Proclamations*, vol. II, p. 91; Tyacke, *Anti-Calvinists*, p. 188.

49. Tyacke, *Anti-Calvinists*, pp. 106, 113, 118–126, 170–2, 181, 200–1, 246; see also Lake, 'Calvinism and the English Church'; Andrew Foster, 'Church Policies of the 1630s', in Cust and Hughes (eds), *Conflict in Early Stuart England*.

50. Lake, 'Calvinism and the English Church'; Tyacke, *Anti-Calvinists*, pp. 186–8, 224–5; Cust and Hughes, 'After Revisionism', pp. 32–3.

51. Morrill, 'Religious Context'; Adamson, 'The *Vindiciae Veritatis*'; E. S. Cope and W. H. Coates (eds), *Proceedings of the Short Parliament of 1640* (Camden Society, 4th Series, 19 (1977), p. 149.

52. Caroline Hibbard, *Charles I and the Popish Plot* (Chapel Hill, North Carolina, 1983), pp. 50, 56, 100; David Hoyle, 'A Commons

Investigation of Arminianism and Popery in Cambridge on the Eve of the Civil War', *Historical Journal*, 29 (1986).

3 A SOCIAL AND CULTURAL CONFLICT?

1. Cf. R. C. Richardson, *Debate on the English Revolution Revisited*, p. 129, on the lack of discussion of the nature or origins of the 'English Revolution' in recent social history textbooks.
2. Christopher Hill, 'A Bourgeois Revolution?' in *The Collected Essays of Christopher Hill*, vol. 3 (Brighton, 1986), p. 95.
3. Russell, 'Introduction', in *Origins of the English Civil War*, p. 7.
4. A. Macfarlane, *The Origins of English Individualism* (Oxford, 1978); R. Brenner, 'Agrarian Class Structure and Economic Development in Pre-industrial Europe', *Past and Present*, 97 (1982); Laslett, *The World We Have Lost*; J. C. D. Clark, *English Society 1688–1832* (Cambridge, 1985).
5. Russell, 'Introduction', pp. 6–8; Robert Brenner, 'Dobb on the Transition from Feudalism to Capitalism', *Cambridge Journal of Economics*, 2 (1978); cf. Hill, 'A Bourgeois Revolution'.
6. C. Hill, *The English Revolution 1640* (first published, 1940; these quotations are from the 1976 edition); R. H. Tawney, *Religion and the Rise of Capitalism* (1926); *The Agrarian Problem in the Sixteenth Century* (1912); 'Harrington's Interpretation of his Age', *Proceedings of the British Academy*, XXVII (1941); 'The Rise of the Gentry 1558–1640', *Economic History Review*, XI (1941); both articles are now also available in J. M. Winter (ed.), *History and Society: Essays by R. H. Tawney* (1978). A survey of the whole 'gentry controversy' is found in Stone, *Social Change and Revolution*.
7. H. R. Trevor-Roper, *The Gentry, 1540–1640*, *Economic History Review Supplement*, 1 (1953); C. Hill, 'Recent Interpretations of the Civil War', in his *Puritanism and Revolution* (first published 1958, 1986 edition is quoted here; Michael Bush, *The English Aristocracy. A Comparative Synthesis* (Manchester, 1984).
8. Laurence Stone, *The Crisis of the Aristocracy* (Oxford, 1965); J. H. Hexter, 'Storm over the Gentry' in his *Reappraisals in History* (1961).
9. Hill, 'Recent Interpretations'; Hughes (ed.), *Seventeenth-century England*, pp. 87, 89.
10. Alan Simpson, *The Wealth of the Gentry 1540–1660. East Anglian Studies* (Chicago and Cambridge, 1961); J. T. Cliffe, *The Yorkshire Gentry From the Reformation to the Civil War* (1969); B. G.

Blackwood, *The Lancashire Gentry and the Great Rebellion* (Chetham Society, 3rd Series, XXV, 1978); D. Brunton and D. H. Pennington, *Members of the Long Parliament* (1954).

11. This discussion of social change is based mainly on C. Clay, *Economic Expansion and Social Change*, 2 vols (Cambridge, 1984), and Sharpe, *Early Modern England*. Coward, *Social Change and Continuity* is the most recent survey.

12. Joan Thirsk, *England's Agricultural Regions and Agrarian History 1500–1750* (1987).

13. Clay, *Economic Expansion and Social Change*, p. 143; Bush, *The English Aristocracy*.

14. Seaver, *Wallington's World*, chapter 5.

15. V. H. T. Skipp, *Crisis and Development: an Ecological Case Study of the Forest of Arden* (Cambridge, 1978); K. Wrightson and D. Levine, *Poverty and Piety in an English Village: Terling 1525–1700* (1978); Paul Slack, *Poverty and Policy in Tudor and Stuart England* (1987).

16. Sharpe, *Early Modern England*; John Morrill and John Walter, 'Order and Disorder in the English Revolution', in Fletcher and Stevenson (eds), *Order and Disorder*.

17. Stone, *Causes of the English Revolution*, pp. 14–16.

18. Brian Manning, *The English People and the English Revolution* (first published 1976; Penguin edition of 1978 is quoted), pp. 9, 83, 133–41, 178–80.

19. Hunt, *The Puritan Moment*.

20. John Morrill, 'The Northern Gentry and the Great Rebellion', *Northern History*, 15 (1979).

21. David Underdown, *Revel, Riot and Rebellion* (Oxford, 1985), especially p. 40.

22. Smuts, *Court Culture*, p. 201; Norbrook, *Poetry and politics*; Leah S. Marcus, *The Politics of Mirth: Jonson, Herrick, Milton, Marvell, and the Defense of Old Holiday Pastimes* (Chicago and London, 1986).

23. Thirsk (ed.), *The Agrarian History of England and Wales*, vols 4 and 5 (Cambridge, 1967, 1984); *England's Agricultural Regions*.

24. See J. S. Morill's review of Underdown, *Journal of British Studies*, 26 (1987); Hughes, 'Local History and the Origins of the Civil War', and Laurence Stone, 'The Century of Revolution', *New York Review of Books*, 26 February 1987, for this discussion of Underdown.

25. Conrad Russell in *London Review of Books*, 7 August 1986.

26. Stone, *Crisis of the Aristocracy*; J. H. Hexter, 'Storm over the Gentry'; Pocock, *The Ancient Constitution . . . A Reissue*, p. 331.

27. Farnell, 'The Social and Intellectual Basis of London's Role'; Christianson, 'The Peers, the People and Parliamentary Management'; Adamson, 'Parliamentary Management, Men of Business and the House of Lords'.

28. Diarmaid Macculloch, *Suffolk and the Tudors* (Oxford, 1986), pp. 73, 95; Penry Williams, *The Tudor Regime* (Oxford, 1981 paperback edition), p. 436; Stone, *Crisis of the Aristocracy*, pp. 269–70, Appendix II; M. James, *English Politics and the Concept of Honour* (*Past and Present* Supplement 3, 1978) now reprinted in Mervyn James, *Society, Politics and Culture* (Cambridge, 1986).

29. Hughes, 'Local History and the Origins of the Civil War'.

30. Adamson, 'Parliamentary Management'.

4 KING AND PARLIAMENT 1625–1642

1. Kenyon, *The Stuart Constitution*, p. 196; Adamson, 'Saye'.

2. L. J. Reeve, *Charles I and the Road to Personal Rule* (Cambridge, 1989), p. 3; Hirst, *Authority and Conflict*, p. 162 are quoted. See also C. Carlton, *The Personal Monarch* (1983) and for foreign and naval policy, Brian Quintrell, 'Charles I and his Navy in the 1630s', *The Seventeenth Century*, vol. III (1988).

3. Cust, *The Forced Loan*; E. R. Foster, 'Printing the Petition of Right', *Huntington Library Quarterly*, 38 (1974–5).

4. Russell, *Parliaments and English Politics* is at present the most important discussion.

5. Cope, *Proceedings of the Short Parliament*, pp. 149–50, 155; Adamson, 'Parliamentary Management'; Bonney, 'The English and French Civil Wars'.

6. Esther Cope, *Politics without Parliament* (1987); Kevin Sharpe, 'Crown, Parliament and Locality'; Hirst, *Authority and Conflict*; Cust and Hughes, 'Introduction'.

7. Seaver, *Wallington's World*, pp. 158–63.

8. Hibbard, *Charles I and the Popish Plot*, pp. 108–9, 153–5.

9. Cope, *Proceedings in the Short Parliament*, p. 149; P. H. Donald, 'New Light on the Anglo-Scottish Contacts of 1640', *Historical Research*, 62 (1989).

10. The account of the period from November 1640 until the outbreak of war is based mainly on Anthony Fletcher, *The Outbreak of the English Civil War* (1981). Quotations from Parliament's declarations etc. are from Kenyon, *The Stuart Constitution*, and Gardiner, *Constitutional Documents*.

11. Cliffe, *The Puritan Gentry* (1984), p. 223.

12. Russell, 'The First Army Plot of 1641' is vital for this account.

13. The account of the Remonstrance is from Fletcher, *The Outbreak of the English Civil War*, pp. 81–90, 145–57; Dering is quoted from Hughes (ed.), *Seventeenth Century Culture*, p. 73.

14. Manning, *English People and the English Revolution*; Seaver, *Wallington's World*, p. 151; Hirst, *Authority and Conflict*.

15. Fletcher, *The Outbreak of the English Civil War*, chapter 6, pp. 93, 285.

16. Lindley, 'The Impact of the 1641 Rebellion'.

17. Kenyon, *Stuart Constitution*, pp. 242–7.

18. Fletcher, *The Outbreak of the English Civil War*, pp. 344, 349, 357.

19. Hirst, *Authority and Conflict*; Everitt, *The Community of Kent and the Great Rebellion* (paperback, 1973), p. 97.

20. Adamson, 'Men of Business'; Fletcher, *The Outbreak of the English Civil War*, pp. 304, 307; Kevin Sharpe, 'Crown, Parliament and Locality'.

21. Fletcher, *The Outbreak of the English Civil War*, map, p. 354; for this and the following paragraph see Ann Hughes, 'The King, the Parliament and the Localities during the English Civil War', *Journal of British Studies*, 24 (1985).

22. Fletcher, *The Outbreak of the English Civil War*, pp. 344–5; Hughes, 'Local History and the Civil War', p. 346. The information about the Fairfax sermons is from Bill Sheils.

23. John Morrill (ed.), *Reactions to the English Civil War* (1982), Introduction, especially p. 5.

24. *A Declaration or Representation*, quoted in William Haller and Godfrey Davies (eds), *The Leveller Tracts* (reprint, Gloucester, Massachusetts, 1964), p. 55; David Wootton, 'From Rebellion to Revolution'.

FURTHER READING

It is impossible to give a comprehensive bibliography for this, one of the most studied periods of British history, so the following concentrates on books and articles which are representative of recent work, or are themselves useful guides to further reading and to debates. Additional material will be found in the notes to each chapter.

A brief account of some recent divergent interpretations of the civil war is John Morrill, Brian Manning and David Underdown, 'What was the English Revolution?' *History Today* (March, 1984). More wide-ranging guides to the historiography include: Howard Tomlinson, 'The causes of the war: a historiographical survey' in Tomlinson (ed.), *Before the English Civil War* (1983); Richard Cust and Ann Hughes, 'Introduction: After Revisionism' in Cust and Hughes (eds), *Conflict in Early Stuart England: Studies in Religion and Politics 1603–1642* (1989) and the most comprehensive, R. C. Richardson, *The Debate on the English Revolution Revisited* (1989).

Contrasting examples of general interpretations are Laurence Stone, *The Causes of the English Revolution 1529–1642* (1972); Conrad Russell (ed.), *The Origins of the English Civil War* (1973); and John Morrill, *The Revolt of the Provinces* (first published 1976, 2nd edition 1980); Gerald Aylmer, *Rebellion or Revolution: England from Civil War to Restoration* (Oxford, 1987); J. C. D. Clark, *Revolution and Rebellion* (Cambridge, 1986). Despite their similar titles, Aylmer's and Clark's views are very different. Aylmer is a very balanced survey of recent controversies while Clark is an impassioned critique of what he regards as Liberal and Marxist distortions of the seventeenth and eighteenth centuries. Its view contrasts sharply with that expressed here. Kevin Sharpe (ed.), *Faction and Parliament* (Oxford, 1978, reissued in

196

paperback, 1985) is an important collection of essays, by no means all 'revisionist' in their approach, although the editor's introduction takes a revisionist position. Useful criticisms of revisionist scholarship are found in T. K. Rabb and D. Hirst, 'Revisionism Revised: Two Perspectives on early Stuart Parliamentary History', and Christopher Hill, 'Parliament and People in Seventeenth Century England', all in *Past and Present*, 92 (1981).

Up-to-date textbooks combining analysis and narrative with useful guides to reading are Barry Coward, *The Stuart Age 1603–1714* (1980); Derek Hirst, *Authority and Conflict 1603–1658* (1986); Roger Lockyer, *The Early Stuarts: A Political History of England 1603–1642* (1989). Coward is the best straightforward introduction, Lockyer the most detailed work and Hirst has the most sophisticated analysis.

1   A BRITISH PROBLEM? A EUROPEAN CRISIS?

A selection of studies of the general European crisis can be found in Trevor Aston (ed.), *Crisis in Europe 1560–1660* (1965) and Geoffrey Parker and Lesley M. Smith (eds), *The General Crisis of the Seventeenth Century* (1978); T. K. Rabb, *The Struggle for Stability in Early Modern Europe* (Oxford, 1975) is a useful survey of the debate while Richard Bonney, 'The English and French Civil Wars', *History*, 65 (1980) is a pioneering attempt at comparative history.

Our understanding of the 'British problem' will be transformed when Conrad Russell's major work on the fall of the British monarchies is published. In the meantime his articles are invaluable: 'The British Problem and the English Civil War', *History*, 72 (1987); 'The British Background to the Irish Rebellion of 1641', *Historical Research*, 61 (1988); 'The First Army Plot of 1641', *Transactions of the Royal Historical Society*, 5th Series, 38 (1988); 'Why did Charles I fight the Civil War?' *History Today* (June 1984). David Stevenson, *Scottish Covenanters and Irish Confederates* (Belfast, Ulster Historical Foundation, 1981) presents fascinating material in a refreshingly new perspective.

The best introduction to developments in Ireland is still T. W. Moody, F. X. Martin and F. J. Byrne (eds), *Early Modern Ireland 1534–1691* (*A New History of Ireland* vol. 3, Oxford, 1976); English policy is covered in H. F. Kearney, *Strafford in Ireland: A Study in Absolutism* (Cambridge, 1989).

For Scotland see David Stevenson, *The Scottish Revolution 1637–1644: The Triumph of the Covenanters* (Newton Abbot, 1973); Maurice Lee, *The Road to Revolution: Scotland under Charles I, 1625–1637*

(Urbana, Illinois, 1985); Walter Makey, *The Church of the Covenant* (Edinburgh, 1979).

For the 'functional breakdown' in England, Conrad Russell, 'Parliament and the King's Finances' in Russell (ed.), *Origins of the English Civil War* and Russell, *Parliaments and English Politics 1621–1629* (Oxford, 1979), are vital. For contrasting emphases on both Parliament and finance in the 1620s and the early 1640s see Richard Cust, *The Forced Loan and English Politics* (Oxford, 1987); Christopher Thompson, 'Court Politics and Parliamentary Conflict in 1625', in Cust and Hughes (eds), *Conflict in Early Stuart England*; Anthony Fletcher, *The Outbreak of the English Civil War* (1981).

A thorough and clear survey of financial and administrative problems can be found in David Thomas, 'Financial and Administrative Developments', in Tomlinson (ed.), *Before the English Civil War.* Menna Prestwich, *Lionel Cranfield: Politics and Profits under the Early Stuarts* (Oxford, 1965) is a classic study; while Pauline Croft (ed.), 'A Collection of Several Speeches and Treatises of the late Lord Treasurer Cecil', *Camden Miscellany*, 29 (Camden Society, 4th Series, 34, 1987) gives an insider's vivid perceptions of financial problems.

Contrasting views of the relationships between the centre and the localities are presented in Alan Everitt, *The Local Community and the Great Rebellion* (Historical Association Pamphlet, 1969) and Everitt, *The Community of Kent and the Great Rebellion* (Leicester, 1966) on the one hand; and Clive Holmes, 'The County Community in Stuart Historiography', *Journal of British Studies*, 19 (1980); Ann Hughes, 'Local History and the Origins of the English Civil War', in Cust and Hughes (eds), *Conflict in Early Stuart England*; and Hughes, *Politics, Society and Civil War: Warwickshire 1620–1660* (Cambridge, 1987) on the other.

Simon Adams, 'Spain or the Netherlands? The Dilemmas of Early Stuart Foreign Policy,' in Tomlinson (ed.), *Before the English Civil War*, is the best brief introduction to conflicts over foreign policy; Thomas Cogswell, *The Blessed Revolution* (Cambridge, 1989) is a detailed study of the crucial period of the aftermath of the failure of the Spanish match.

2 HIERARCHY, CONSENSUS OR CONFLICT: POLITICS AND RELIGION IN
EARLY STUART ENGLAND

The best short introduction to politics in a social context is J. A. Sharpe, *Early Modern England: A Social History 1550–1760* (1987). P. Zagorin, *The Court and the Country. The Beginning of the English*

Revolution (1969) is still worth consulting. Peter Laslett, *The World We Have Lost Further Explored* (1983) presents a picture of hierarchical politics in a traditional society while Mark Kishlansky, *Parliamentary Selection. Social and Political Choice in Early Modern England* (Cambridge, 1986) has an illuminating if controversial account of political transition in the mid seventeenth century. David Starkey *et al.*, *The English Court from the Wars of the Roses to the Civil War* (1987) is an important summation of recent research on the importance of the court. The first part of Russell, *Parliament and English Politics* is very useful, while the general interpretations listed above have much to offer.

Political participation and the political awareness of those below gentry ranks is covered in Derek Hirst, *The Representative of the People?* (Cambridge, 1975); Richard Cust, 'News and Politics in Early Seventeenth Century England', *Past and Present*, 112 (1986); Richard Cust, 'Politics and the Electorate in the 1620s', in Cust and Hughes (eds), *Conflict in Early Stuart England*; Clive Holmes, 'Drainers and fenmen: the problem of popular political consciousness in the seventeenth century', in Anthony Fletcher and John Stevenson (eds), *Order and Disorder in Early Modern England* (Cambridge, 1975). Studies of well-documented individuals often provide a stimulating route to understanding broader issues: John Fielding, 'Opposition to the Personal Rule of Charles I: the Diary of Robert Woodford, 1637–1641', *Historical Journal*, 31 (1988) deals with a provincial lawyer; Paul S. Seaver, *Wallington's World: A Puritan Artisan in Seventeenth Century London* (1985) with a London artisan.

The ideological foundations for political action and division are covered in J. P. Sommerville, *Politics and Ideology in England 1603–1640* (1986); and J. G. A. Pocock, *The Ancient Constitution and the Feudal Law . . . A Reissue with a Retrospect* (Cambridge, 1987; first edition, 1957). The documents and commentary in J. P. Kenyon, *The Stuart Constitution* (Cambridge, 1966, 2nd edition 1986) are extremely useful.

One of the most fruitful means of understanding early Stuart politics has been through the examination of culture, broadly conceived. Pioneers in the study of court culture are Roy Strong and Stephen Orgel. Strong, *Van Dyck. Charles I on Horseback* (1972); and Orgel, *The Illusion of Power* (Berkeley, California, 1975) are representative. R. Malcolm Smuts, *Court Culture and the Origins of a Royalist Tradition in Early Stuart England* (Philadelphia, 1987); Martin Butler, *Theatre and Crisis 1632–1642* (Cambridge, 1984); Kevin Sharpe, *Criticism and Complement* (Cambridge, 1987); and David Norbrook, *Poetry and Politics in the English Renaissance* (1984) are the best of the recent exciting work.

J. S. Morrill, 'The Religious Context of the English Civil War', *Transactions of the Royal Historical Society* 5th series, 34 (1984) makes a vigorous but disputed case for the English civil war as a war of religion. Michael G. Finlayson, *Historians, Puritanism and the English Revolution* (Toronto, 1985) is the latest but doubtless not the last exercise in definitions. Patrick Collinson, *The Religion of Protestants* (Oxford, 1982) is a wide-ranging study of the pre-Laudian church.

For those who still believe there was something called Puritanism Christopher Hill, *Society and Puritanism in Pre-Revolutionary England* (first published 1964) is the classic exploration of its potential social functions. Keith Wrightson, *English Society 1580–1680* (1982) and William Hunt, *The Puritan Moment: The Coming of Revolution in an English County* (Cambridge, Massachusetts, 1983) use a version of Hill's analysis in their particular studies. Martin Ingram, 'Religion, communities and moral discipline in late sixteenth and early seventeenth century England: case studies' in Kaspar von Greyerz (ed.), *Religion and Society in Early Modern Europe* (1984) provides a different perspective, while Christopher Haigh emphasises the unpopularity of zealous Protestantism: see for example, 'The Church of England, the Catholics and the People', in C. Haigh (ed.), *The Reign of Elizabeth I* (1984).

Peter White, 'The Rise of Arminianism reconsidered', *Past and Present*, 101 (1983) denies that there was a distinctive change in the English church in the 1630s, but here Nicholas Tyacke, *Anti-Calvinists: The Rise of English Arminianism c. 1590–1640* (Oxford, 1987), and Peter Lake, 'Calvinism and the English Church 1570–1635', *Past and Present*, 114 (1987) have been preferred. The ambiguities of religious policy under James are explored in Kenneth Fincham and Peter Lake, 'The Ecclesiastical Policy of King James I', *Journal of British Studies*, 24 (1985), while Andrew Foster, 'Church Policies of the 1630s', in Cust and Hughes (eds), *Conflict in Early Stuart England* is useful for the impact of Laudianism.

Some of the connections between religion and politics are covered in Peter Lake, 'Constitutional Consensus and Puritan Opposition in the 1620s: Thomas Scott and the Spanish Match', *Historical Journal*, 25 (1982) and Michael Walzer, *The Revolution of the Saints* (1966). Anti-popery was a crucial mechanism for integrating religion and politics: Peter Lake, 'Anti-Popery: the Structure of a Prejudice', in Cust and Hughes (eds), *Conflict in Early Stuart England*; and Caroline Hibbard, *Charles I and the Popish Plot* (Chapel Hill, North Carolina, 1983) are the most important recent studies.

3 A SOCIAL AND CULTURAL CONFLICT?

The 'gentry controversy' and social interpretations of the civil war in general are surveyed in Laurence Stone, *Social Change and Revolution in England 1540–1640* (1965); Christopher Hill, 'A Bourgeois Revolution?' in *The Collected Essays of Christopher Hill* vol. 3 (Brighton, 1986) is the most significant recent addition to the literature, while Laurence Stone, *The Crisis of the Aristocracy* (Oxford, 1965) is the most important single work to have been produced as part of the debate on the fortunes of landed elites. It is still extremely useful for the social, political and cultural history of England before the civil war.

The most comprehensive textbook on economic change is C. Clay, *Economic Expansion and Social Change*, 2 vols (Cambridge, 1984), while Jim Sharpe, *Early Modern England*, provides a briefer but broader treatment. Wrightson, *English Society* is also important and Barry Coward, *Social Change and Continuity in Early Modern England 1550–1750* (1988) is a useful general introduction to the recent concerns of social historians. Joan Thirsk, *England's Agricultural Regions and Agrarian History 1500–1750* (1987) covers a particularly important aspect of recent work.

Brian Manning, *The English People and the English Revolution* (first published 1976; Penguin edition 1978) took 'social interpretations' into new directions; it now needs to be read in conjunction with John Morrill and John Walter, 'Order and Disorder in the English Revolution', in Fletcher and Stevenson (eds), *Order and Disorder*. Like Manning, William Hunt, *The Puritan Moment*, emphasises the importance of social relationships in determining allegiance in 1642 and David Underdown's ambitious *Revel, Riot and Rebellion* (Oxford, 1985) attempts an integration of social, cultural and regional factors in explaining the civil war. Hughes, 'Local History and the Origins of the Civil War', is in part, a discussion of Underdown.

The works on culture listed for chapter 2 are also relevant here, and Leah S. Marcus, *The Politics of Mirth: Jonson, Herrick, Milton, Marvell, and the Defense of Old Holiday Pastimes* (Chicago and London, 1986) is particularly important.

Stone, *Crisis of the Aristocracy*, is, of course, the crucial work on the readjustments amongst political elites; Mervyn James, *English Politics and the Concept of Honour* (*Past and Present* Supplement 3, 1978) now reprinted in Mervyn James, *Society, Politics and Culture* (Cambridge, 1986) is a subtle and wide-ranging discussion of one aspect of the crisis.

INDEX